THE DOWNFALL OF ABBA HILLEL SILVER AND THE FOUNDATION OF ISRAEL

Modern Jewish History
Henry Feingold, *Series Editor*

Other titles in Modern Jewish History

American Jewish Political Culture and the Liberal Persuasion
Henry L. Feingold

The "Bergson Boys" and the Origins of Contemporary Zionist Militancy
Judith Tydor Baumel

Bundist Counterculture in Interwar Poland
Jack Jacobs

Contemporary Sephardic Identity in the America: An Interdisciplinary Approach
Margalit Bejarano and Edna Aizenberg, eds.

Judah L. Magnes: An American Jewish Nonconformist
Daniel P. Kotzin

Louis Marshall and the Rise of Jewish Ethnicity in America: A Biography
M. M. Silver

The Seven Lives of Colonel Patterson: How an Irish Lion Hunter Led the Jewish Legion to Victory
Denis Brian

"Silent No More": Saving the Jews of Russia, the American Jewish Effort, 1967–1989
Henry L. Feingold

Will to Freedom: A Perilous Journey through Fascism and Communism
Egon Balas

THE DOWNFALL OF Abba Hillel Silver AND THE Foundation of Israel

OFER SHIFF

SYRACUSE UNIVERSITY PRESS

First Edition 2014
14 15 16 17 18 19 6 5 4 3 2 1

∞ The paper used in this publication meets the minimum requirements of the American National Standard for Information Sciences—Permanence of Paper for Printed Library Materials, ANSI Z39.48-1992.

For a listing of books published and distributed by Syracuse University Press, visit our website at www.SyracuseUniversityPress.syr.edu.

ISBN: 978-0-8156-1035-9 (cloth) 978-0-8156-5280-9 (e-book)

Library of Congress Cataloging-in-Publication Data

Shiff, Ofer.

The downfall of Abba Hillel Silver and the foundation of Israel / Ofer Shiff. — First edition.

pages cm. — (Modern Jewish history)

Includes bibliographical references and index.

ISBN 978-0-8156-1035-9 (cloth : alk. paper) — ISBN 978-0-8156-5280-9 (ebook) 1. Silver, Abba Hillel, 1893–1963. 2. Rabbis—Ohio—Cleveland—Biography. 3. Zionists—United States—Biography. I. Title.

BM755.S544S55 2014

320.54095694092—dc23

[B] 2014003015

Manufactured in the United States of America

Dedication: To my wife and best friend, Ofra

Ofer Shiff is Associate Professor at the Ben-Gurion Research Institute (at Ben-Gurion University), where he served as director from 2001 to 2004. He also served as head of the "Israel Studies Program," Department of History, Ben-Gurion University. Among his topics, the most prominent are comparative studies on patterns of Israeli and American Jewish coping with the Holocaust and the post-1948 reality of Jewish sovereignty. In his many articles and edited volumes he examines the writings of the leading American Zionist thinkers of the immediate years after Israel's foundation and their efforts to reframe the post-1948 mission of the Zionist movement. His manuscript *American Reform Jewish Universalism and the Holocaust* was published by Brill in 2005.

Contents

THE DOWNFALL OF ABBA HILLEL SILVER AND THE FOUNDATION OF ISRAEL

Introduction

IN EARLY FEBRUARY 1949, Clark Clifford, special counsel to President Harry S. Truman, telephoned the New York office of American Jewry's most popular and powerful leader, Abba Hillel Silver, to personally inform him that the first American loan to Israel—$100 million in economic aid—had been approved. To his astonishment, he was told that Silver had summarily resigned from all his official positions within the Zionist movement and had left New York for Cleveland, returning to his post as rabbi of one of the largest and most venerable Reform synagogues in the United States. Thus ended, with startling abruptness, the promising career of a figure that, just a few years earlier, many regarded as a potential successor to Chaim Weizmann at the helm of the Zionist movement and a leader who offered an alternative approach to David Ben-Gurion's Israel-centric Zionism.

Although Silver gradually came to terms with his political defeat, he never saw it as a rout on the ideological plane. Now that the State of Israel had come into being, he felt that it was time for the Zionist movement to embrace a new Diaspora-Zionist perspective—a goal to which he devoted the last decade and a half of his life until his passing in November 1963. The uniqueness of Silver's brand of Diaspora Zionism lies in its conception of Jewish statehood as merely a scaffold—albeit a supremely important one—for the construction of a religious-national identity capable of integrating without assimilating into the non-Jewish environment of the Diaspora.[1] This diasporic approach to Zionism led to an ongoing conflict

1. On the Diaspora-oriented approach to American Zionism, see Gal (1999); Halpern (1979).

with the leading Israeli approaches of the period. Diaspora leaders, like Silver, who felt that the statist-Israeli agenda should be subordinated to a broader Jewish one, were positioned at odds with those who sought to subordinate the pan-Jewish agenda to the endeavor for Israeli statehood.[2]

The power struggle between these two approaches erupted in full force immediately after the founding of the State of Israel. During the early years of the state, reactions to Silver's political and ideological advocacy spanned the linguistic and political spectrum. The sheer number of news items and full-length articles devoted to Silver would have led the impartial observer to regard him as a major contender in the Zionist political arena, one equal in stature to members of the Israeli leadership. On closer scrutiny, however, it quickly became clear that Silver's political struggle vis-à-vis the dominant Israeli Zionist agenda had no chance of succeeding, even within the American-Zionist arena. In retrospect one also discerns a significant discrepancy between Silver's key role in pre-state Zionist politics and his marginality in Zionist historiography.[3] In this respect, this book deals with a version of Zionism that suffered a nearly unconditional defeat—an ideological and political alternative that has been long forgotten and, to all appearances, decisively rejected.

One reason for Silver's relegation to the margins of Zionist politics was the internal tension that characterized his approach to Israel—the tension between a commitment to exalt Israel and affirm its centrality and a countervailing obligation to impose conditions, in accordance with Silver's universalistic vision, on this centrality. A salient characteristic of

2. For an example of the scholarly debate generated by the conflict between the Diaspora-Zionist and the Israel-sovereign approaches, see Gorni (2004). For a discussion of the political dispute between the American Zionists and the Yishuv/Israeli leadership, see Feldstein (2003); Segev (1999); Shimoni (1999). On the tension between the Ben-Gurionist sovereign approach and the social Zionist vision, see Kedar (2009, 80–83).

3. Despite Silver's centrality to American-Zionist and Jewish history, just one biographical study has been published (see Raphael 1989). A number of scholars have emphasized the unusual discrepancy between Silver's central role in the Zionist arena during the 1940s and early 1950s and his marginal status within Zionist historiography as a whole (see Frank 1966; Schindler 1997; Shapira 1997).

this internal tension was Silver's great difficulty in challenging Israel-centric Zionism, especially in the context of the continuing need to mobilize on behalf of Israel's survivalist struggles. In view of this difficulty, one may characterize Silver's internal Zionist struggle during the early 1950s as the reflection of a much broader struggle, still relevant today, against those, whether ultra-Zionists or anti-Zionists, who believe that there is an unbridgeable contradiction between an adamant struggle for Jewish survival and the struggle for universal Jewish values. From this perspective, the present study does not deal with a forgotten version of Zionism, but rather with a Zionist option that is, at least below the surface, still relevant, and that continues to address the same dilemmas faced by Silver when he formulated his Zionist vision. More concretely, this investigation of Silver's career attempts to explore the impact of Israel's establishment on the viability and long-term self-reliance of the largest Jewish Diaspora community, especially in light of that community's attempts to turn the identification with the Jewish homeland into a major component of a distinct and independent diasporic Jewish identity.

In order to address these issues, this book incorporates two types of discussions: first, in Parts 1 and 2, I discuss Silver's religious and philosophical views and their cultural and social backgrounds, especially in light of the challenge posed by the establishment of the State of Israel; and, second, in Part 3, I engage in a historical discussion of Silver's political activism aimed at reinforcing his diasporic Jewish and Zionist outlook as a viable option despite his personal political defeat to the Israeli Zionist leadership. The combination of these two modalities in the concluding section reveals a new and more nuanced perspective, which transcends the zero-sum "winners and losers" approach to the intra-Zionist struggle that took place during Israel's early years and, thus, provides a reassessment of what Silver's brand of Zionism might mean for us today.

PART ONE

The Early 1950s

1

The "Bridges and Walls" Approach

When asked to describe Silver's brand of Zionism, I often refer to it as the "bridges and walls" approach, relying on his mid-1950s construal of the aphorism, "Good fences make good neighbors," in the context of the well-known poem by Robert Frost, "Mending Wall." Silver's understanding of the saying underscored the importance of "walls" to demarcate the boundary that separates Diaspora Jews from their non-Jewish surroundings, thereby ensuring the Jewish individual a sense of safety and belonging. At the same time, Silver was highly critical of those who sanctified the walls in and of themselves. Similar to Frost, he viewed the national-religious sanctification of particularistic walls as a kind of benighted neo-paganism—a negative isolationist approach based on hatred and prejudice.

In this context Silver regarded Zionism's main ideological contribution as the rediscovery of an original Jewish model that, while erecting walls to provide the Jewish individual with a sense of belonging in relation to one's non-Jewish surroundings, also entrusts Jews with a social responsibility of building bridges to connect with different religious and cultural groups.[1] It is my contention that this approach, including its development and the problems encountered in its implementation, is key to understanding Silver's life story. In employing this motif, one must embrace a view of Silver's life story that deviates from the conventional

1. Although the basic features of this approach existed throughout Silver's career, it nevertheless underwent a process of consolidation and refinement during the 1950s. *Where Judaism Differed* (Silver 1956) is the main publication in which he elucidated his approach (see also American Public Welfare Association 1956; Silver 1955c).

focus on his Zionist leadership during the 1940s and focuses instead on his activity and leadership during the 1950s.

In order to elucidate these arguments, one should first note that Silver's leadership became paramount during the 1930s and 1940s. He first attained the status of a national leader during the 1930s when he headed the movement to boycott Nazi Germany. His status was subsequently elevated in 1938 when he was chosen to head the main philanthropic Zionist organization, the United Palestine Appeal (UPA). In his struggle against what was coming to be viewed as apathy on the part of the American government regarding efforts to rescue European Jewry, Silver reached the height of his political power during the 1940s.[2] His most striking achievement was his successful transformation of American Jewry into a leading force in the political struggle for Israel's establishment. His period of leadership ended with the founding of the Jewish state—a new chapter that heralded a different role for American Zionism and a distinct set of dilemmas for American Jewry.

Scholarly examinations of Silver's life story cannot ignore his status as the preeminent leader of American Jewry during the 1940s. This is particularly true of the period following Silver's groundbreaking speech in August 1943 at the first meeting of the American Jewish Conference, an organization created to unite the then fragmented American-Jewish population. With this speech, Silver succeeded in garnering the near-unanimous endorsement of the hundreds of delegates to the conference for the main points of the Biltmore Program, which called for an end to the British White Paper's restrictions on Jewish immigration to Palestine and for the establishment of a Jewish national home.[3]

2. One must distinguish between the opposition mounted by Silver to the Zionist establishment under Stephen Wise and various non-establishment opposition figures, such as the revisionist leader Hillel Kook, who were much more aggressive in their criticism of the inactivity of the American government and the Jewish leadership. For examples of scholars who have called attention to Silver's combative leadership style, see Gal (1991); Ganin (1984); Shpiro (1994); Urofsky (1978). On the Bergson Group, see Wyman and Medoff (2002).

3. Even prior to the Biltmore Program, in January 1941, Silver had played a major role in the UPA's call for the Jewish community in Palestine to function as a sovereign Jewish

From that point onward, Silver occupied a preeminent leadership position within American Jewry, to a large extent due to his role as head of the American Zionist Emergency Council (AZEC), the organization that represented and coordinated all Zionist political activity in the United States. Silver's influence and clout grew during the critical three and a half years (from mid-1945 to early 1949) in which he served as AZEC's sole chairman.[4] During this period he was virtually the undisputed leader of American Jewry in its campaign to enlist American support and votes in the United Nations General Assembly in favor of the establishment of a Jewish state. Moreover, after having been one of the major forces, together with Ben-Gurion, behind Weizmann's resignation from the presidency of the World Zionist Organization during the twenty-second Zionist Congress in Basel in late 1946 (Tevet 2004, 852–903), Silver was appointed head of the American section of the Jewish Agency—a move that consolidated his status within the world Zionist hierarchy. During the three months that preceded the UN partition plan resolution, which was put to a vote on November 29, 1947, Silver reached even greater heights as the foremost representative of the Jewish collective before the nations of the world. During this intensive three-month period, he was regarded in both the United States and internationally as embodying—via his public persona and his oratory—the Jewish collective's unwavering demand for a sovereign national home.

This activity on the political-diplomatic plane was the pinnacle of Silver's public career. It is rightly considered to be an achievement of historic

entity. His collaboration with Ben-Gurion in this area had already been established at the 1938 UPA conference (Gal 1991, 19, 127–30). The Biltmore Conference was held on May 9–11, 1942, in New York; in November of that year, the Zionist General Council, convening in Jerusalem, approved the Biltmore Program, which thereby became the Zionist movement's official political platform. On the clashes that ensued between Ben-Gurion and Chaim Weizmann, see Gorni (1976, 112–35). For an analysis of the speeches at the Biltmore Conference, see Feldstein (2003, 18–20).

4. In September 1943, Silver was appointed co-chairman, together with Stephen Wise, of AZEC. It was only in June 1945, after having stepped down for a period of six months, that he became AZEC's sole chair.

magnitude in Jewish and Zionist history, and a milestone in American ethnic-religious politics. This is undoubtedly the reason why those scholarly studies that have deviated from the conventional format and focused on earlier or later periods of Silver's life, or on the non-Zionist aspects of his public activity,[5] have generally done so as a means of examining the Zionist struggle of the 1940s from a broader perspective. Silver himself essentially took the same tack while writing his unfinished autobiography. Rather than starting chronologically with childhood memories, Silver devoted the beginning paragraphs to a ceremony held on January 24, 1943, honoring him on his fiftieth birthday and marking a quarter-century of service as rabbi of Cleveland's Reform Tifereth Israel congregation ("The Temple"). He particularly focused on the speech in which Weizmann predicted that the day was not far off when Silver would be invited to join the uppermost echelon of the Zionist leadership. Only after noting how, in retrospect, Weizmann's speech had heralded his ascension as American Zionism's foremost leader did Silver undertake to chronicle his childhood narrative as the son of immigrant parents in New York City's Lower East Side (Silver 1963a).

Even when he described his youth (1902–1911) in the immigrant ghetto, Silver's presentation proved selective, emphasizing three events that, in his words, shaped his Zionist worldview. Rather than mentioning the first nine years of his life in Europe, or his family's experience in the Lower East Side, he began with his father's tearful announcement to the family that Theodor Herzl, the founder of the Zionist movement, had died. Continuing with a description of how soon after, along with his older brother, he founded the first Zionist youth club in the United States,[6] he concluded with a recollection of the celebrated Zionist orator Zvi Hirsch Masliansky, who mentored the young Silver and permitted him to sit in the wings of the stage while he delivered his sermons. By focusing on the "Zionist" events of his childhood, Silver essentially communicated that his early

5. Two major works have dealt with the non-Zionist and non-Jewish facets of Silver's career (see Diner 1997; Segev 2007).

6. For a discussion of the Zionist youth club under Silver, see Neumann (1976, 33–34).

years were worth including mainly as evidence that his future illustrious career as an American Zionist in the 1940s had its roots during this early formative period.

Moreover, Silver affirmed the conventional interpretation of his life story, one which viewed all of the chapters of his life as merely serving to illuminate the glory he enjoyed in the 1940s, when he led the American-Zionist struggle for the establishment of the State of Israel. Silver thus marginalized other life experiences, including his early years in Europe, in the Lithuanian town of Naumiestis (Neustadt);[7] his youth in New York's Lower East Side; his years of rabbinical studies at Cincinnati's Hebrew Union College (HUC) and graduate work at the University of Cincinnati (UC), culminating in a doctoral degree; his forty-five-year career as the rabbi of one of the largest Reform congregations in the United States; his years (1945–1947) as president of the Central Conference of American Rabbis (CCAR); his lifelong efforts on behalf of workers' rights; his close association, from the 1940s on, with the Republican Party's leadership; his long and consistent stance against anti-Communist hysteria and the Cold War; his role as one of the first to champion the struggle of Soviet Jewry; and his intellectual career, which fully flourished during the 1950s. He thus even marginalized the exceptional degree of honor and esteem bestowed on him during the last years of his life in both the American and Zionist spheres, exemplified by becoming the first Jew to be invited in an official capacity to offer a prayer at a presidential inauguration—that of President Dwight D. Eisenhower on January 20, 1953—and, during his last visit to Israel in 1963, the attendance of Ben-Gurion at an event marking Silver's seventieth birthday, where he delivered a lengthy speech in which he extolled Silver's career as a Zionist and as a Jewish leader (Gal and Shiff 1999).

In contrast to the above view, my basic argument is that the 1940s struggle for the establishment of a Jewish state was indeed important, even critical in Silver's eyes, but merely as a first stage in a larger objective—as a vehicle to remove an insular and insecure Jewish mentality rife

7. The town of Neustadt was part of Russia, bordering East Prussia, near the German town of Schirwindt.

with distrust that had developed over centuries of persecution in exile. In Silver's view, the Holocaust threatened to reinforce this negative Jewish mentality—a dangerous process to which the Jewish state was necessary to serve as a counterforce. This view thus informs the focus of this book, which lies not on the heroic Zionist struggle of the 1940s, but rather on the less eventful decade following Israel's establishment, the period when the main tenets of Silver's Diaspora Zionism were supposed to be fulfilled.

On the face of it, the 1950s and early 1960s seem less important, whether from a Zionist perspective, or, indeed, from the perspective of Silver's own status as one no longer part of the Zionist movement's elite policymaking cadre.[8] It is therefore not surprising that a significant portion of the literature on Silver actually belittles, or altogether ignores, the importance of the period spanning the 1950s and early 1960s. The impression is that, after the struggle for statehood was realized and Silver resigned from the Jewish Agency administration and the leadership of AZEC in early 1949, the meaningful part of his Zionist career also came to an end, rendering the fifteen remaining years of his life until his death on November 28, 1963 a mere "gray footnote" to an illustrious career. Indeed, while various scholars have noted some of Silver's activities during the 1950s and early 1960s, they have done so in the same manner that sports commentators talk about "garbage time": the players are still on the field, they may even be performing impressive athletic feats, but since everyone knows which team has won the game, these feats are of no real significance.

In contrast to this approach, I argue in this study that from Silver's perspective the importance of the campaign for Israel's establishment in the 1940s was quite different from its conventional interpretations. In Silver's view, a sovereign Jewish entity should have been regarded as a basic necessity, like oxygen: when absent it becomes the sole object of interest, but when available, critical though it may be, it is still just a means, not an end in itself. Silver had expressed this idea as early as 1929, against the background of the Nazis' ascension to power and the rise of European

8. On the relative marginality of American Zionist activity after the achievement of Israeli statehood, see Segev (1991, 493–94).

and American anti-Semitism; he repeated this theme during the Holocaust years and during the thick of the battle for the United Nations' approval of the partition plan and the founding of the Jewish state. Time and again, whenever the dream of Jewish statehood appeared to be on the verge of realization, Silver affirmed that statehood could not be mankind's ultimate objective:

> Certainly, it is not the substance of our own ancestral tradition, whose motif is not nationalism but prophetism. . . . After its national life is secured, Israel must push on to the frontiers of the new world—the world of internationalism, of economic freedom, of brotherhood and of peace. (Silver 1940)[9]

The stance manifested in the above quote may well explain the difficulties that scholarship on Silver has faced up to now. Many scholars, trained to view Zionism's ultimate goal as that of Jewish national self-determination, have found it difficult to comprehend a Zionist approach that regarded statehood simply as the means of realizing a universalistic religious-prophetic agenda. It is, therefore, not surprising that a large portion of Silver's Zionist approach—and in particular the complex statements in which he expressed his reservations about nationalism—were forgotten and remained unaddressed.[10] Moreover, the centrality of the "bridges and walls" approach to Silver's Zionism has made it difficult for scholars to identify him with a particular trend within Zionism. Thus, when Silver, in the 1940s, emphasized the Herzlian political goals of Jewish statehood, he did not define Jewish sovereignty as Zionism's ultimate objective. After

9. This speech appeared in different versions over the course of Silver's career; the earliest among them may be found in Weisgal (1929). All works dealt with the theory of "prophecy" that Silver had developed in his doctoral thesis of 1924, which was published in 1927 (see Silver 1927).

10. Some of the more sophisticated Silver scholarship has focused on one of the many internal tensions that characterized his activity and thought. Outstanding examples include Michael Meyer's (1997) article on the tension between Silver the Zionist and Silver the classic Reform Jew, and studies by Arthur Aryeh Goren (1997) and Allon Gal (2000) on the tension between Silver's right-wing conservative political identity and his progressive views.

Israel's establishment, when Silver appeared to identify with Ahad Ha'am, he still differed from the latter in that his subjective negation of the exile referred only to the Jewish pre-statehood mentality and not to Diaspora life per se (see Ahad Ha'am 1950).[11] Silver also differed from non-Zionist circles such as the Bund. Like him, these groups objected to the exilic way of life rather than to exile as a social phenomenon; however, in contrast to Silver, they refused to view the Zionist center in Palestine as a force capable of changing the meaning of exile as a negative political and moral phenomenon (Gorni 1999, 356–58; 2006).

Thus, if we are to understand Silver's Diaspora-Zionist approach, we have to analyze it using Silver's own criteria and indices. Silver saw the pre-state Zionist endeavor primarily as a struggle to transcend a situation that, in his view, had made the universalistic Jewish mission untenable, inasmuch as "a defeated people inspires no confidence in its mission." In contrast, he regarded the post-independence period as one destined to liberate Jewry from the defensive mentality of a people forced incessantly to fight for its very existence:

> The restoration of the State of Israel with its tremendous psychological implications has freed our people from the spirit of depression and forlornness, the fears and the confusions of the long weary and homeless centuries. It is now possible, if so we will, to move forward on our appointed task as a covenanted people with a new heart and a new song. (Silver 1950a)

In the context of this passage, it is hardly surprising to note that, after an initial period of euphoria, Silver was disappointed to discover that statehood had not abated existential Jewish anxieties. On the contrary,

11. For a discussion of the topic by Silver, see Silver (1940). For an analysis of Silver's shifting emphasis from spiritual Zionism during the 1920s and 1930s, to political Zionism in the 1940s, and back to spiritual Zionism in the 1950s, see Meyer (1997, 29). On the distinction that Silver himself made between the Herzlian Zionism necessary prior to statehood and the Ahad Ha'am Zionism that, in his opinion, suited the post-statehood period, see Silver (1950a).

he ultimately found that Israel became an object of collective existential worry for world Jewry and, indeed, an entity whose struggles intensified these anxieties. How Silver coped with this realization is a central issue addressed in this book.

Those studying Silver's response to this latter challenge may divide his post-statehood activity into two sub-periods. During the first five years of statehood (1948–1952), Silver still believed that it was possible to generate an internal revolution within Zionist ideology, enabling his Zionist approach to replace the defensive attitudes that had characterized the pre-state period. At this stage, Silver believed that his Diaspora outlook must determine the Israeli public agenda and not merely those of American and world Jewry. In the second period (1953–1963), Silver made a complete about-face and abandoned any direct attempt to challenge the Israeli-dominated Zionist agenda. In this context, this book seeks to evaluate the degree to which Silver's cessation of efforts to challenge Israel-centered Zionism should be interpreted as an abandonment of his "bridges and walls" Zionist vision, or whether this concession testifies to the development of an alternate American-Zionist approach of which Israel's centrality is a mere component.

In the context of the latter option, assuming that Silver's change of attitude toward Israel represents an attempt to develop a distinct pattern of post-1948 Diaspora Zionism, one must examine the impact of Silver's American surroundings, especially the discourse characteristic of post-war American society, on his brand of Zionism. Silver drew an analogy between Judaism's universalistic mission and the American global mission. In his view, the latter mission stemmed from the lofty social-moral standard of American democracy, which he identified with the Jewish heritage in its universalistic-Reform manifestation.[12] This was a solution

12. One major address in which Silver linked the founding of the State of Israel with a commitment to realizing Reform Judaism's religious vision was delivered in the early 1950s at an event honoring the HUC's seventy-fifth anniversary (Silver 1950b). For a systematic discussion of the idea of "mission" in American Zionism, see Gal (1986, 1989).

that enabled Silver to affirm classical Reform precepts dating from the nineteenth century, which regarded Judaism's raison d'être as expressing the most definitive model of progressive thinking. This analogy also made Silver a participant in a general American discourse, characteristic of the postwar period, which will be elaborated on in the next chapter.

2

The "American Century" in the Wake of the Holocaust

EVERY FEW YEARS, Silver would formulate a kind of template for repeated use in his lectures and sermons. The last of these templates would ultimately serve him through nearly the entire final decade of his life. In this book I will refer to it as Silver's "hope lecture"—a lecture that was primarily an affirmation of his optimistic faith in the inner strength of an enlightened American democratic way of life and a golden future for the American-Jewish community.

On April 21, 1953, at the biannual conference of the Union of American Hebrew Congregations, a Reform organization, held in New York, Silver delivered one of the earliest versions of his "hope lecture" (Silver 1953b). This version, titled "On the Threshold of the Fourth Century," appears, at first glance, fairly typical of the period in which it was composed. It was one of many speeches in which American Jews noted the upcoming tercentenary of the arrival of the first Jews in North America in 1654,[1] and Silver himself was ultimately to deliver a number of speeches on this very topic. The tone taken by many of the authors of these tercentenary speeches was cogently characterized by the historian Ben Halpern as an attempt by American Jews to declare that "America is different,"

1. During Silver's lifetime the arrival of individual Jews prior to that year had already been established. However, because it was in 1654 that local authorities first addressed the issue of Jews' rights and obligations as a group, it had become customary to view the arrival of thirteen Jewish refugees from Brazil as marking the beginnings of American-Jewish communal life.

European-style anti-Semitism was foreign to the democratic American spirit, and catastrophes on the order of the Holocaust were neither likely nor even possible on American soil (Halpern 1956). Although Silver's version differed from many of these anniversary speeches in that it did not adopt an apologetic tone, it resembled them in the way it linked a fervent belief in the greatness of American democracy with expectations of a glorious future for American Jewry. In this regard, Silver was continuing an established American discourse that dated back to the eighteenth and nineteenth centuries (Silver 1919b; see also Meyer 1997, 17, 30). Moreover, an optimistic attitude toward American democracy's greatness and global destiny was not limited to the Jewish public. It was typical of broad segments of the American populace, especially during the postwar period. Thus, from this perspective, the messages that Silver was imparting were hardly unique.

However, this lecture also had a special meaning of its own, one that touched on Silver's belief that the founding of the Jewish state would trigger a revolution in the isolationist Jewish mentality. Silver hoped that Israel's foundation would bring about a liberation from the Jewish people's long-standing preoccupation with existential anxieties and, thereby, from its fundamental suspicion of the non-Jewish world. Silver saw a Jewish community inextricably fused with American democracy as the quintessential answer to the grave existential concerns that had arisen during the Holocaust. In this context he referred to a *midrash* on the biblical Jacob, when he sought to reveal the future to his sons:

> No one can foretell a people's future . . . no one could have foreseen the practical disappearance of European Jewry. One hundred sixty years ago no one could have foretold that in the U.S. there would arise the largest Jewish community in history . . . the question to which I would like to address myself is, can we think hopefully of the next century as Jews, as Americans, as members of the human family? (Silver 1953b)

In answering his own question, Silver enthusiastically proclaimed that if American Jews managed to shake off the welter of exilic anxieties in which they had been mired until Israel's founding, they would discover that "this age in which we live is truly a great age, one of the greatest in human history." In effect, Silver chose to address fears regarding post-Holocaust Jewish survival by highlighting the robust state of American society and humanity at large. In Silver's view, human society, under American leadership, had done more in the present generation than in any other to improve conditions for the average man, including improving his health and educational status and protecting him from the ravages of disease, unemployment, and old age. This advancement was also translated into liberty for national groups around the world. Silver pointed out that over the seven years since the end of World War II, a quarter of the world's population had escaped political subjugation. With great confidence, he declared the death of colonialism; the "backward peoples," as he called them, were pressing toward the light of a new day, and the exploitation of the world's "dark races" was coming to an end. Those who learned to see the inner essence of current developments, not just their outer shell, would ultimately realize that, despite what the profound crises of the last generation might imply, human society was not about to collapse; rather, the opposite was the case—humanity was in the midst of a radical reorganization, a fundamental change with positive implications for human social development.

As we read Silver's words, it is hard not to feel that by preaching the adoption of a new perspective, he was expressing an almost excessive optimism. He downplayed the issue of dictatorial or racist regimes—which had only recently plunged humanity as a whole, and the Jewish people in particular, into horrific catastrophe—and made almost no mention of the fear, prevalent during the 1950s, of a third, nonconventional world war. Even when he did refer to these issues, he described them as the flotsam and jetsam of yesteryear, churned up from the depths by the winds of the present era and left scattered along the path of progress. But in no way were these obstacles capable of halting mankind's progress:

> The on-moving tides of man's spirit, fathoms deep and irresistible, have now swept over the shuttered ruins of some of these sinister aberrations and dark conspiracies of the rebels against light—though they have not as yet entirely been obliterated . . . they will surely succumb.

> They cannot, in the long run, win the contest for man's heart. . . . Man has struggled through the long weary centuries to free himself from the bondage of nature. He will not voluntarily and for long submit to the bondage of man. Neither dictatorship, nor racialism, nor statism . . . can or will command the fortune of the human race. They represent the sunken wreckage of the past which the storms of our days have dredged up again from the bottom of their buried depths and have set them afloat again dangerously along the ship lanes of the world. (Silver 1953b)

Silver contended that the main trends of the era were ones oriented toward bringing humanity closer to the lofty goal of the "good society"—a term he had borrowed from the progressive Christian American discourse and that, during the postwar period, he used frequently to denote a divinely ordained mission of promulgating enlightened values. He identified three main trends whose status could shed light on the degree to which the objective of a "good society" was being reached—the struggles against war, poverty, and racism—and insisted that in all three areas humanity was moving in the right direction and had already achieved significant gains.

Silver described this positive development as a global process that was also reaching the Communist bloc, a process that, on the face of it, was neither culture dependent nor colored by any particular political leaning. However, a close analysis shows that when Silver spoke of the victory of human progress, he was referring to its American democratic manifestations. Silver proclaimed that the new era that was dawning would be a glorious one for the United States, and that the coming hundred years would be the "American century." In ardent terms, he declared American democracy to have been fated to lead humanity and save it from the social and political crises of recent generations. As the world's preeminent force for progress, it was America's responsibility to mark out a path of mutual coexistence for communism and capitalism, and of dialogue with the third world. America must not be allowed to head in the direction of a global arms race; rather, it should chart a course for courageous diplomacy, while strengthening the United Nations and assisting "disadvantaged" peoples. Silver believed that leadership of this kind, which was not motivated by selfish imperialistic interests, would necessarily inspire hope and gratitude worldwide—particularly among the "backward" peoples who, in Silver's view, yearned for an infusion of American democratic values—and thereby bring about the global triumph of progress.

This attitude should be seen in the context of an American discourse of pride and confidence in the superiority of the American way of life. Although this discourse was already under fire in some quarters,[2] it was not unusual even for proponents of global cultural pluralism to regard the United States as an unselfish actor on the world stage, and the American way as one that had demonstrated its superiority to other cultures and worldviews. This approach, which conceived the American way as a universalistic, quasi-religious calling, harked back to the Calvinist ethos of the early colonial period. During the postwar period, its sense of mission was prevalent among liberals and conservatives alike, as evidenced by Senator Robert Taft, Silver's political ally who headed the Republican Party's conservative wing. Taft and Silver ascribed to the United States a mission of "generosity," free of self-aggrandizing or colonialist interests, and entirely devoted to making the American vision of the "good society" an international reality. Silver, like Taft, advocated an international

2. Early articulations of a view of the United States as protector of enlightened values had appeared in reaction to World War I and the inefficacy of the League of Nations. For example, the British philosopher Bertrand Russell believed, in the years following World War I, that the United States had proven itself to be motivated not by imperialist interests, but rather by moral-humanistic concerns, and that it ought, therefore, to take on the role of a superpower that—like Alexander the Great and Rome in ancient times—would advance the progressive values of democracy, peace, and social justice throughout the world. During the post–World War II period, this view was widely opposed; many questioned not only America's role as a fair-minded proponent of progress, but also the very ideological basis of progress. One outstanding early example of this is Claude Lévi-Strauss's *Race and History*, published in 1952. In contrast to Silver, Lévi-Strauss put forward his cultural-relativism approach as the basis of a thoroughgoing critique of the concept of progress, which, in his view, entailed a Western ethnocentric perspective (Feuer 1987, 39–40; Lévi-Strauss 1952; Russell 1922, 70; 1941, 18–19).

constitution that would, in conformity with the worldview and values inherent in the American Constitution, define the rights and obligations of the various nations of the world. He accordingly called for the creation of an international military force capable of enforcing the provisions of this constitution.[3]

In retrospect, Silver's stance on this matter seems jarringly inconsistent with his multicultural "bridges and walls" approach. His self-proclaimed principles of multicultural dialogue notwithstanding, Silver actually partook in an internal American discourse that saw it as America's task to impose on the world—if only peacefully—its own mindset and way of life. Silver, who courageously criticized American policy on sensitive patriotism issues, such as the battle against communism, did not, in this respect, measure up to the standards that he himself had set. He failed to adopt any kind of critical perspective that rose above a patronizing American judgmentalism vis-à-vis the rest of the world and, in particular, non-Western cultures.

Was this optimistic American attitude a means of quelling particularistic anxieties regarding Jewish continuity after the Holocaust? There is doubtlessly a measure of truth to this explanation, and as may be seen in many of the speeches marking American Jewry's tercentenary, faith in the "American century" and belief in the ultimate victory of American democracy were widely seen among the American-Jewish leadership of the era as fitting reassurances to the fears of a reoccurrence of the Holocaust. Still, when we look at the second part of Silver's "hope lecture" we find that faith in America's global mission was not the only way in which he sought to respond to post-Holocaust concerns over Jewish survival. While the first part of the lecture dealt with faith in the universal democratic ideals that Silver viewed as incumbent on his listeners as American citizens, the second part focused on their responsibilities as Jews.

3. These shared views may indicate that the Silver-Taft alliance was not restricted to the arena of the Zionist struggle, but actually had a deeper moral-ideological basis. For a discussion of Taft and the divinely ordained mission that he attached to the American democratic way of life, see Pfaff (2007).

Silver proclaimed his belief that the coming century of American greatness would usher in a golden age for American Jewry. As a minority, he explained, the Jews were powerless to fight the kind of hatred and demagoguery sparked by war and economic collapse. However, in a state of peace and economic stability, American Jewry would be able to flourish and enjoy an almost limitless enrichment of its religious and cultural life. This flowering of Jewish life should by no means be taken for granted. It would be up to the Jews to cultivate their heritage and prevent total assimilation into American society. Silver's main concern was not active assimilation, but rather the indifference caused by the unchallenging routine of American Jewish religious life. In his opinion, many of his Jewish and non-Jewish contemporaries sought a religion of convenience, one that entailed no active social responsibility. No faith, he declared, had value if it demanded nothing of its adherents. A meaningful religious life was therefore key to Jewish survival—particularly in the open and accepting environment of American democracy. Silver called on American Jews to take responsibility for cultivating a distinctively Jewish way of life, and to make their community a flourishing hub of Jewish culture, one serving as the dynamic heart of the Jewish Diaspora. He presented this responsibility as a lesson for Diaspora Jewry in the wake of the Holocaust, calling it a fitting response to the destruction of the Jewish religious and cultural hubs of Europe.

The question, then, is how these two parts of the lecture fit together, and whether there is a contradiction between the universalistic thrust of the first part and the Jewish particularistic message of the second. My contention is that Silver did not see the call for a distinctively Jewish way as contradicting the idea of a lofty universalistic mission for American democracy. Rather, he perceived the two concepts as mutually dependent. This stance clearly echoed the "cultural pluralism" approach that Horace Kallen, a prominent and original thinker in both American and Zionist discourses, had articulated at the beginning of the twentieth century.[4]

4. Kallen developed his cultural-pluralism theory in a series of essays that first appeared in *The Nation* in 1915 and were collected later, in 1924, in *Culture and Democracy*

Kallen saw the ideal of a fully realized existence within two parallel circles of identity—Jewish and American—as a supreme embodiment of the American value of individualism; he regarded the "melting pot" approach as a reactionary stance that distorted what he saw as Jewish and American civilizations' authentic pluralist ideals.[5] In Kallen's view, the authentic American approach was not one in which the distinctive ethno-cultural features of minority groups needed to be eradicated in favor of the dominant Anglo-Saxon culture; to the contrary, the Americanization process should provide for the cultivation of each ethnic group's unique characteristics. The metaphor of an "orchestra," in which each instrumental group stands for one of the cultural groups that make up the American populace, was his answer to the melting pot and entailed an active convergence of the American concept of patriotism and the Jewish concept of solidarity.

This convergence was a recurring motif in Silver's work, appearing in his oratory as early as 1917. In a lecture entitled "Assimilation," he addressed the issue of whether, in the context of a democratic American society, the Jew should insist on his religious-cultural uniqueness or assimilate into that society. His answer was that assimilation actually endangered the democratic American way of life. That is, the act of assimilating was essentially antipatriotic, not only from a Jewish standpoint, but also, first and foremost, from an American standpoint. Silver's metaphor of the ideal American democracy was a garden in which flowers of many different kinds could grow; uniformity was inimical to a healthy society that benefited, rather, from the contribution of each and every one of its component religious and ethnic cultures. The greatest contribution that Judaism could make to American society was the cultivation of its

---

in the United States (Kallen 1998). On Silver's opposition to the "melting pot" idea, and his call for a more nuanced understanding of cultural pluralism in the United States, see Gal (2000, 11–12).

5. Kallen used the term "Hebraism" in order to define the core ideas of both Judaism and Americanism. He described Hebraism as the authentic embodiment of the pluralistic and democratic characteristics of both Jewish and American civilizations.

distinct "character." "The Jew," Silver proclaimed, "can give nothing to the world culturally by destroying himself, but he will give much to the world by retaining his unique identity."[6]

It was against this background that Silver's "hope lecture" of 1953 identified a tendency toward indifference and monotonous routine in Jewish religious life as the main danger facing Judaism. Silver exhorted the Reform leaders who made up his audience to view the cultivation of an active Jewish religious life as an inseparable part of their commitment to the American way. Kallen, in a speech of his own in honor of American Jewry's tercentenary, made a similar point. He roundly condemned the theme chosen by the committee responsible for organizing the tercentenary events, "Opportunities and Responsibilities under Freedom" (Kallen 1954, 9–11),[7] for its failure to call for an internal Jewish awakening. He saw in this theme an exclusive preoccupation with the civil rights struggle and warned against shirking the duty to cultivate Jewish identity. Without such a commitment, he warned, the Jews could make no tangible contribution to the development of American democracy and America would become an assimilationist and repressive force rather than a liberating one.

According to Silver, a major obstacle in fulfilling this particularistic Jewish obligation was a lack of self-confidence in the powerful contribution of Judaism's universalistic mission. Silver believed that, just as democratic America was committed to respond to external and internal threats by exemplifying adherence to a democratic worldview, American Jewry was obligated to respond to its inner anxieties and external threats by exemplifying faith in the "bridges and walls" vision—one that cultivates Jewish identity, and at the same time transforms the particularistic concerns into a universalistic responsibility. One of the major challenges facing Judaism in this context was its mode of addressing the existential anxiety brought forth by the Holocaust. Silver felt that after Israel's

6. To further illustrate his point, Silver employed the image of a drop of perfume losing its distinctive scent once mingled with the water of the ocean (Silver 1917).

7. Kallen himself was a member of the committee, which, according to him, had chosen the theme before he had joined it.

foundation it was time for a new religious-social perspective preoccupied not with threats to Jewish survival, but with Judaism's universalistic contribution to America and humanity in general. In this context, efforts to grapple with the memory of the Holocaust needed to avoid the danger of perpetuating a victim mentality that would strengthen Jewish tendencies toward suspicion and self-segregation. Instead, a Jewish view of the Holocaust needed to become a manifestation of the metamorphosis that Jewish particularism should undergo as it overcame its basic existential exilic anxieties and replaced them with the "bridges and walls" approach.

In retrospect, this approach should be seen as the realization of a vision that Silver had formulated during the dark years of the Holocaust. In the 1940s, Silver explained the unpopularity within the Zionist current discourse of what he viewed as Judaism's authentic prophetic vision by noting that in times of danger the Jewish community's immediate concern was to isolate itself from the threatening non-Jewish surrounding. In Silver's eyes this tendency, though understandable, ought not to have been confounded with Judaism's aspiration to a universalistic perspective. He therefore expressed his hope that once statehood was achieved and Jewish survival assured, the Jewish people would mobilize for their universalistic mission (Silver 1940). It took more than a decade before Silver would feel that the time was ripe to fulfill his vision. Silver believed that the foundation of the State of Israel ought to generate a mentality transformation and that, rather than calling attention to the insecurity inherent in a state of homelessness, American Jews must now use the Holocaust to emphasize the enormous importance of cultivating Jewish life.

Silver was cognizant that the "negation of exile" philosophy represented in the eyes of many in Israel the main incontrovertible lesson of the Holocaust, and it was precisely against this background that he sought to advance a Diaspora-Zionist message that, while identifying with Israel, challenged the pessimistic lesson it drew from the Holocaust regarding the long-term prospect of Jewish life in the Diaspora. Thus, in a sermon given on May 20, 1951, in which Silver reported on a three-week trip to Israel that he had made in late April through early May (Silver 1951), he gave an emotional account of his visit to the Chamber of the Holocaust on

Mount Zion on May 10, Israeli Independence Day.[8] He spoke of burned Torah parchments and thirty-one urns containing human ashes collected from the concentration camps of Europe. Elaborating on the importance of these remnants, he explained that Israeli statehood ought to produce a mentality transformation, making it possible for Jews in Israel and abroad to see the history of Diaspora Judaism in a new light—not via the image of the passive, victimized Diaspora Jew, but rather through the lofty moral heritage associated with what Silver now defined as the heroic spiritual struggle of exile. Only by identifying with the heritage of Diaspora spiritual heroism, and making it the core of the modern Jewish faith, could one hope to fill the void in which young Jews, both in Israel and the Diaspora, found themselves, now that the battle for political Jewish independence had been won.

> The people of Israel do not wish to forget . . . they want their children to know what their forefathers had experienced in lands of exile. . . . Nationalism is not enough for them or for us or for any other people, and the ideal of Israel was never merely the establishment of a State, although that was always an integral part of the vision of Judaism. The State, too, was not an end in itself . . . Israel, by having finally a normal, healthy, independent life of its own may then continue to attempt to realize the exalted spiritual and ethical ideal of the prophets of Israel. (Silver 1951)

Another indication of this new approach toward the lessons that should be drawn from the Holocaust may be found in an introduction that Silver wrote to a new edition of Paul Goodman's *History of the Jews*.[9] Although he did not state it explicitly, it is clear that his introduction to the book constituted a reaction to the "*galuyot ve-hurbanan*" ("Diasporas and their destruction") theory promulgated by the Israeli historian Ben-Zion

8. In the context of Silver's visit to the Chamber of the Holocaust, it is worth noting that 1950s Israeli society was conflicted about how the Holocaust should be commemorated (see Stauber 2001).

9. Eight editions of this work have appeared since 1911. Silver completed his work on the introduction in March 1952 (see Goodman 1953; Silver 1952b).

Dinur. During this period, Dinur served as Israel's minister of education; he was later to become the first chairman of Yad Vashem, the Israeli "Holocaust Martyrs' and Heroes' Remembrance Authority." His historiographical approach, one strongly aligned with the "negation of exile" line of thought, had been set forth in a famous 1943 essay, which viewed the rise and fall of Jewish centers in the Diaspora not as natural demographic phenomena, but rather as recurring instances of the destruction to which all Jewish communities were doomed by virtue of their exilic status. In Dinur's view, "this affair, the Holocaust, is not new in our history," and "destruction is merely the shadow of the exile, any exile"; nothing but Jewish sovereignty in Eretz Israel had the potential to disrupt the vicious cycle of "*galuyot ve'hurbanan*" (Dinur 1978, 175, 190).[10]

Silver used similar terminology and began by characterizing Jewish history as a series of dislocations, in which centers of Jewish life moved from one place to another. He placed special emphasis on the fact that an exceptionally important hub, that of European Jewry, had been eradicated by the Nazis. However, unlike Dinur, Silver did not take a deterministic view of Diaspora existence; he did not regard it as a foregone conclusion that Jews would encounter hostility from their non-Jewish environments or that all exilic centers would eventually be destroyed. On the contrary, he viewed the multiplicity of centers as testimony to the vitality of Jewish existence in the aftermath of the Holocaust. In his eyes, the main lesson to be learned from the Holocaust was recognition of the responsibility borne by American Jewry to develop its communal vitality and replace the Old World centers that had been destroyed. Rather than directly challenging Dinur's Israel-centric view, Silver chose to broaden it, to encompass not only the State of Israel's emergence but also the impressive vitality of American-Jewish life as a counterbalance to the Holocaust.

In a 1956 sermon, Silver expanded this interpretation of the Zionist perception of the Holocaust even further. He described the American-Zionist lesson of the Holocaust as a countervailing force vis-à-vis the Old World heritage of repression and intolerance:

10. For a discussion of the Holocaust in Dinur's thought, see Stauber (2000, 74–78).

> Judaism is mankind's religion of hope and renewal; those who were the most persecuted and hurt by life were the most hopeful and confident of life . . . Israel saw itself as having been assigned a role in the shaping of humanity, in the development of human conscience. Hence its indomitable clinging to life, its capacity, time and time again, to rise from ruin, and slaughter, and tragedy. (Silver 1972b, 25)

The latter assertion hints at a new development in Silver's conception of the post-Holocaust Jewish mission. Rather than merely calling on Jews to rid themselves of their suspicious attitudes toward their non-Jewish surroundings, Silver put forward a new model in which the existential anxieties occasioned by the Holocaust had to be translated into a global universalistic message. The major area in which Silver expressed this approach was not in the inner Zionist discourse, but rather in the area of Jewish–Christian dialogue, where he employed the Holocaust to posit Judaism's ability to mobilize for a multifaith struggle.

One example of this was an address that he delivered at a World Brotherhood meeting in Belgium in July 1955 (Silver 1955b, 1955i). In composing this address, he once again used his America-centric "hope speech" template of 1953. Undeterred by the European surroundings, Silver exhorted his listeners to see not the "minor details" of murder, discrimination, and social injustice, but rather the larger picture of progress, including progress in the area of racial equality. Most interesting in this context is that Silver had prepared a different speech with polemical characteristics for the event, but he decided not to use it.[11] An indication of this speech's polemical character was the way in which it addressed the "racial imperialism" practiced by the Nazis. In a passage exhibiting a tone reminiscent of Benjamin Disraeli's address a century earlier to the British Parliament, Silver noted that the Germans, like all of the northern European peoples, were barbarians at a time when the Jewish people had already founded glorious civilizations of their own:

11. This additional speech, entitled "The One and the Many," was found in the same file with Silver's official speech in English at the World Brotherhood Meeting and its French translation (Silver 1955j).

> The vaunted superiority of the peoples of Northwestern Europe is of very recent date. . . . If these races had possessed superior natural endowments, they would have evolved the first civilization of mankind instead of the last. . . . Up to the fourteenth century the Prussians were heathens and barbarians. . . . These "superior" peoples were utterly unknown when . . . a little Asiatic people, the Jews, was evolving a God-idea, which is today the cherished faith of two-thirds of mankind. . . . All that northern Europe has today of art, literature and religion—of the essential values of social life—have come to it from Asiatic and Mediterranean peoples. (Silver 1955j)

What, then, was the reason for Silver's decision to repress a proud Jewish retort to those who had annihilated a third of the Jewish people? The fact that a decade earlier he had undertaken a thorough combative patriotic Jewish struggle makes an explanation of that decision even more necessary. Perhaps the title of the suppressed speech, "The One and the Many," hints at a possible explanation.[12] The main question raised by the speech was whether Judaism's monotheistic approach to an absolute truth reflected a pluralistic ethos or whether this approach merely concealed an all-too-human inclination to exclude competing ideologies, making it a force detrimental to peace and dialogue. In the suppressed speech, Silver deployed all of his rhetorical capabilities in order to delineate a complex religious worldview, which while emphasizing Judaism's superior pluralistic message, nevertheless viewed itself as merely one of many possible interpretations of a divine universal truth. However, Silver was well aware, even as he advocated this complex religious worldview, of the existence of opposing approaches characterized by dogmatism and intolerance. In the suppressed speech he decried these approaches as manifestations of ideological imperialism responsible for sowing hatred and injustice. Ultimately he decided to refrain from directly challenging these approaches. Had he adopted the more polemical stance of the suppressed speech, he would have been "fighting fire with fire"—countering Nazism with claims for Jewish cultural supremacy vis-à-vis German and

12. For an earlier version of this lecture, see Silver (1930).

European culture. In place of this, Silver preferred to engage his audience at the interfaith conference in Belgium with his American "hope speech"—a speech whose positive tone raised it above the welter of Jewish anti-German sentiment and promoted dialogue between all religious and political worldviews.

Silver's inclination to avoid polemical interreligious conflict disappeared entirely when faced with approaches that undermined the legitimacy of any form of religious belief. He was aware of the atrocities that Nazism and fascism had perpetrated in the name of absolute truth, and he repeatedly denounced the inherent tendency of various doctrines to declare their commitment to peace and social progress as a means of advancing their own selfish interests. The loftier the stated goals, he pointed out, the greater the danger that they would be used to further inappropriate objectives (Silver 1953a). Nevertheless, he felt that the main danger that he, as a religious leader, should be cautioning against was that of the relativism that had gained popularity in the wake of the two world wars. For Silver, the main challenge was to ensure that the struggle against distortion of the true religious message did not result in a complete delegitimization of the religious aspiration to a single universal truth. In his eyes, an outcome of this kind would be far more dangerous than the intolerant aggression that any religious or ideological pretensions to absolute truth might seek to justify. This being the case, Silver felt that a more constructive path had to be found—one that resisted "improper" uses of religion, but in a way that strengthened, rather than undermined, the foundations of monotheistic faith. He believed that this path would emerge through an internal reform of all religions modeled after Judaism's "bridges and walls" prophetic approach.

Evidence of the latter approach can be found in an eight-page passage, under the heading "bridges and walls," that Silver added to his address before the interfaith gathering in Belgium (American Public Welfare Association 1956; Silver 1955c). In this addition (which, from then on, became an inseparable part of the "hope speech" template), Silver sought to underscore both the beneficial character of the "walls" that distinguish between different faiths and the danger posed by such walls in the absence of connecting "bridges." Marshaling for this purpose the well-known line from Robert Frost that "Good fences make good neighbors," Silver strove, simultaneously, to condemn the isolationism and intolerance perpetrated in the name of religious-ideological pretension to absolute truth and to elucidate the way in which religious and national "walls" contribute to humanity's moral development. As Silver saw it, the Jewish perspective was a particularly important antidote to the skepticism that had emerged in reaction to the ideological imperialism that had drawn the world into World War II, and which a decade later posed an even greater threat in the form of a nuclear holocaust.

This approach is exemplified in yet another version of the "hope speech," one that Silver delivered on Passover Eve (April 11, 1953) addressing the issue of nonconventional warfare (Silver 1953a). The sermon opened with a question-and-answer passage that, while ostensibly addressing the threat of physical annihilation posed by the atomic age, actually focused on the qualities needed in order to survive this era of anxiety without abandoning monotheistic faith. Silver set forth his view that the great danger at hand was not that the American populace, or humanity altogether, might be physically annihilated, but rather that nihilism and skepticism might gain ascendancy.

Although intending his speech to elucidate the danger posed by relativism's spread, Silver nevertheless began it by affirming some of that outlook's premises. He noted a growing recognition of the limitations and inadequacy of scientific inquiry. Silver did not take a negative view of this "awakening," nor did he feel that it necessarily undermined any faith in the human benefit of science. To the contrary, he explained that it was precisely the awareness of science's inability to shed light on the true nature of the forces at work in the universe that made it possible to focus on the more modest goal of harnessing nature to improve the conditions of human life. This disillusionment with naïve positivism need not undermine basic progressive assumptions regarding the human value of scientific innovation; rather, a more informed approach should make it possible to take fuller advantage of these innovations for the good of humanity—without the "side effect" of arrogance that Nazism and fascism had exemplified.

According to Silver, man's relinquishing of pretensions to fully control nature and reveal its secrets was a positive development and one that ought to be extended into the sphere of religious faith. Monotheistic Jewish belief in one abstract God had taught man that the tools at his disposal were insufficient to enable him to grasp the ultimate, divine, universal truth. However, religion, like modern science, also taught man that he was not completely in the dark; the recognition that he could hope to achieve only a partial understanding of the universe actually constituted a step forward in the sphere of religious faith. Silver described this partial and nuanced understanding as "faith through a dark glass." "A clear knowledge of God is possible to no one, but a true worship of God is possible to everyone." Monotheism intended to cure man from the notion that religion could help him to grasp the full essence of the divine; what religion could do, however, was to shed light on the divine code of laws—justice and humility—and how it worked. Man could then strive to live by these laws and build a better and more progressive society. Furthermore, Silver felt, this disillusioned "through a dark glass" perspective could potentially produce a religious faith that was stronger and more determined—yet also more modest and tolerant of other faiths.

Silver was aware of the impossibility of supporting a declaration of religious faith through logical arguments or scientific proof; but it was precisely this difficulty that, in his eyes, underscored the importance of religious faith in holding at bay the chaos that would otherwise inevitably ensue. According to Silver, if life was nothing more than a conjunction of coincidences, then man was destined to lose all hope, be overcome with fear, become alienated, and fall victim to moral nihilism. This conclusion was, in his view, inconceivable; it ran contrary to the basic religious instincts that had existed in every human community. In this context he quoted Albert Einstein, who, when asked about the meaning of life, replied that those who insist on scientific answers to this question are guilty of pulling the rug of human civilization out from under their feet (Silver 1955f). Silver added that man's inability to grasp the truth about the meaning of life in its entirety, notwithstanding the very effort to do so, provided a moral basis for human life and imbued it with meaning.

Silver's thinking on this score is clearly reflected in his repeated criticisms of the British philosopher Bertrand Russell, particularly his *Unpopular Essays,* which were published during this period (Russell 1950). On the face of it, Silver might have seen himself as having considerable common ground with the 1950 Nobel Laureate in literature. He certainly could have identified with Russell's struggle against the Cold War and advocacy of nuclear disarmament. At first glance, it also appears that he would have agreed with the main thrust of Russell's argument in *Unpopular Essays,* namely, that "science is what you know; philosophy is what you don't know." Russell identified philosophy as the sphere of hypotheses that science had yet to prove; like Silver, he attached an immanent importance to man's recognition of his own lack of knowledge. He decried the tendency to applaud the wonders of science while forgetting what science "doesn't know" and, like Silver, also criticized the opposite tendency to despair of science and to focus solely on those areas where rational inquiry falls short. However, it was precisely this common ground that brought the differences between Silver and Russell into the forefront.

Russell felt that philosophy's main task was to define the limits of scientific knowledge; thus, in his view, philosophy by definition could not pretend to offer its own answers to questions regarding the nature of human existence. The mission of philosophy was to teach people to identify areas of uncertainty, thereby helping them to reject the tempting, but baseless, answers offered by various religions or ideologies. Answers of this kind, Russell warned, divide humanity into groups of fanatics; each group adheres to its own baseless beliefs, which it is convinced constitute the one and only sacred truth, while all other faiths are heresies that must be combated. "Dogmatism is an enemy to peace, and an insuperable barrier to democracy," Russell proclaimed. "In the present age . . . it is the greatest of the mental obstacles to human happiness."

On his part, Silver opposed the view that fighting dogmatism necessarily entails skepticism concerning all religious or ideological insights. Unlike Russell, he felt that there were certain basic religious premises that must not be questioned. In particular, he pointed to three premises, which in his view were rooted in man's instinctive response to questions regarding the nature of life. The first of these premises was embodied in the general declaration that "there is a purpose to the universe"; from this followed two additional assumptions: "the importance of man" and "man's commitment to a moral society." Silver felt that the diverse forms that these premises took on within the world's religions were subjective cultural interpretations that could not be equated with absolute truth; nevertheless, the assumptions themselves were common to all religions. Thus, although different faiths might explain the meaning of the universe and of human life in different ways, they all were in consensus that the universe does have meaning and, from this meaning, the more specific purpose of human existence could be derived.

Like Russell, Silver believed that the key to saving human society was to internalize recognition of the limits of human knowledge; however, he proposed a means of acting on this approach that was contrary to Russell's. Russell saw in the recognition of limits to human knowledge the basis for a worldview in which people chose their actions according to their potential benefit or harm. What Silver desired, by contrast, was that this recognition would inspire faith in the existence of a higher purpose for the universe. This dialectical approach was the only one capable of offering man a sense of greatness within the huge universe. Silver cautioned that man could not have a sense of meaning in a world where divine truth is known in advance, or in a world without God. In both cases, the inescapable conclusion would be that of man's utter unimportance and lack of moral accountability—a pessimistic conclusion that would erode any possible basis for human civilization.[13]

Silver titled this dialectic use of the recognition of limits of human knowledge as the "faith through a dark glass," and offered it as the foundation for a comprehensive perspective on the modern age with all of its calamities and positive potential. He saw the spread of relativism on the one hand, and of dogmatism on the other, as the great dangers facing the modern era, inasmuch as both views treated the individual as an object devoid of any value in and of itself. He believed that the main challenge facing humanity was embodied in a fruitful tension between the spheres

13. For similar ideas during the same years, see Berlin (1969).

of religious faith and skepticism—the former striving for collective unity, and the latter seeking to throw off all forms of tradition or collectivism. As Silver saw it, continuous dialectical tension between the individual and the cultural traditions against which he rebels became paramount during the modern era and was what gave that era its unique dangers as well as its tremendous potential for human betterment.[14] The affirmation of this tension also formed the basis for Silver's conception of progress and its associated dangers. The victories for individual freedom that had heralded the modern era, he cautioned, were by no means secure. If man wished to be liberated from the fear of subjugation to collectivist ideologies, one had to ensure that the modern era's liberationist trends did not undermine the religious, suprarational basis of the traditional collective frameworks and that they did not regard these frameworks as obstacles on the path to progress. Humanity's continued liberation was not a matter of eradicating religions, but rather of redefining and transforming them. Only those religions that adopted the dialectical stance of "faith through a dark glass" would be able to ensure the existence of the desired individual/collective tension, and thereby enable the individual to actualize his freedom.

Silver was convinced that the "dark glass" approach to faith precisely defined Judaism. Judaism's urgent mission was essentially that of inspiring the American polity—and, by extension, mankind as a whole—to adopt this approach. In contrast to his aversion to making Jewish polemical "use" of the lessons that should be drawn from the Holocaust, in this instance he advocated an uncompromising "Jewish" religious struggle.

14. Silver enumerated three great movements that had emerged during the past five hundred years of Western civilization in which this tension had figured prominently: the Renaissance, the Protestant Reformation, and the French and American revolutions. In each of these movements, he identified a victory for the individual human spirit: the Renaissance had demanded intellectual autonomy, the Reformation had called for religious and spiritual autonomy, and the American and French revolutions had called for freedom and political autonomy. The long-term significance of all of these victories lay in the fact that they had refrained from destroying the relevant collective frameworks of identity; to the contrary, they had strengthened these frameworks and imbued them with new meaning.

Thus, in a speech marking Hebrew Union College's seventy-fifth anniversary, he called movingly for Judaism to realize the vision of the Reform educational institution's founder, Isaac Mayer Wise—the vision of a liberal, courageous, and combative Judaism that did not hesitate to declare itself as mankind's global religion (Silver 1950b).

An important question that remains to be considered in this latter context is whether Silver's representation of Judaism as the quintessential expression of authentic religiosity itself constituted a kind of "religious imperialism" or pretension to moral supremacy, as though only the Jewish religion offered an effective means of countering the double danger of dogmatism and relativism that characterized the modern era. Was the sense of mission, entailed by the "bridges and walls" struggle, not in itself a form of camouflage for Jewish ethnocentric aspirations of monopolizing the ideals of tolerance and pluralism, as though only the "dark glass" mode of Jewish religiosity was capable of upholding these ideals? Was Silver's mission-oriented approach not indicative of an overarching pretension to "convert" American society, and did this not constitute a distortion of the ideals of interreligious dialogue on which his "bridges and walls" advocacy was supposedly based? In the coming chapter, I will attempt to answer this question by evaluating how Silver positioned the universalistic-prophetic mode of faith that he considered unique to Judaism vis-à-vis Christianity and American society as a whole.

3

Where Judaism Differed

A Call for External and Internal Reform

SILVER IDENTIFIED the "dark glass" approach with the heritage of the Hebrew prophets. In his view, it was precisely man's cognitive limitations that provided the foundation on which the Hebrew prophets had built their edifice of religious faith (Silver 1954c). Recognition of the prophetic heritage as Judaism's core message could offer a means of resolving what, in the modern era, was widely regarded as a contradiction between free will and suprarational religious faith. Silver contended that Judaism had turned this apparent contradiction into a major feature of religious-social commitment. It was this idea that he explored in his books *Where Judaism Differed* (Silver 1956) and *Moses and the Original Torah* (Silver 1961b).

As Silver understood the prophetic ethos, it was the concept of "faith through a dark glass"—recognizing man's limited ability to grasp divine truth while nevertheless cleaving to a belief in the existence of such truth—that obliged the religious believer to behave as though he had full responsibility for his social-moral choices. Silver believed that the great danger to humanity lay in the attractiveness of the opposite conclusion, namely, that man's cognitive limitations deprived him of free will and of any ability to change his social environment. Silver associated this pessimistic outlook with social determinism and regarded it as conducive to the rise of totalitarian regimes. It was Judaism's task to counter this pessimism, especially when it emerged in religious garb:

> Pessimism is a form of atheism, for it omits God from man's calculations, and ignored the spirit of God that is in man . . . Judaism admonished

> man not to despair of the future . . . nor of mankind's inexhaustible spiritual resources. (Silver 1957d)

Judaism's call to transform human limitations into a source of moral responsibility was, in Silver's view, part of a venerable tradition, one that was most evident during its clash with Hellenistic culture, which viewed ethics as a system of abstract values. In contrast, the Jewish prophetic ethos held that the sole means of approaching divine knowledge was through human commitment to moral behavior:

> Plato speculated long about the nature of the Good, and having found a satisfactory definition in terms of the four cardinal virtues, whose prototype was a heavenly form, he did nothing about this Good. It remained an aristocratic intellectual truth. . . . He did not rush out into the Agora and, lifting his voice like a trumpet, declare unto the Athenians their transgressions and to the House of the Achaeans, their sins, surmounting them to repentance and reformation. Nor can one conceive of Plato, or Aristotle, or Epictetus passionately pleading with the Almighty, in the name of Justice to save the wicked city of Sodom, for the sake of the few righteous men in it. Judaism did not speculate much on the nature of the Good, but it told man what . . . the Lord required of him "to do justly, to love mercy and to walk with God." (Silver, 1957d)

Silver did not set forth this conception of the Judaism–Hellenism conflict for purposes of historical-theoretical scrutiny. He employed it in order to draw a complex comparison between American Jewry and the Christian majority. He began this comparison by underscoring the shared Jewish-Christian insight; he explained that monotheism had diverged from paganism precisely when the recognition dawned that human material terms were inadequate to express the divine. Both monotheistic religions acknowledged man's inability to fully comprehend the world of which he is a part. Moreover, in all likelihood Silver had found an inspiration for his Jewish "dark glass" approach in the New Testament and St. Paul's First Epistle to the Corinthians (13:12): "For now we see through a glass, darkly; but then face to face: now I know in part; but then shall I know even as also I am known." This emphasis on commonality between

Christianity and Judaism was not coincidental; it indicated the degree to which Silver partook in the contemporary discourse celebrating America's Judeo-Christian heritage.[1]

However, according to Silver, it was precisely this shared Judeo-Christian monotheistic approach that obliged him, as a Jewish cleric, to underscore the differences between the two faiths—particularly the divergent conclusions that they drew from their awareness of human limitations. Silver underscored this divergence by focusing on the ways the two faiths approached "sin." He explained that, unlike Christianity, Judaism countered "sin" not with "redemption" but with "repentance" (*teshuva*). While Christianity concludes that man should humble himself and accept his powerlessness,[2] Judaism takes a contrary view, namely, that man's very ability to sin proves that he is endowed with free will; thus, the awareness of his limitations, rather than absolving him of responsibility, imposes it on him. Silver noted that Judaism requires of its adherents no mystical redemption in order to obtain forgiveness; rather, the active process of "repentance" was the quintessential expression of free will. It is repentance that forms the basis of man's self-respect and sense of freedom.

It is important to note that by emphasizing these differences Silver chose to ignore the existence of liberal-humanistic Christian worldviews, of which he was well aware. He actively participated in Jewish–Christian dialogue groups,[3] and in many respects he was intellectually aligned with the nineteenth-century philosopher Ralph Waldo Emerson and his Transcendentalist movement, in particular its rejection of Christian preoccupations with sin and its pessimistic attitude toward man and life in this world. Silver's outlook also accorded with Emerson's individualistic

1. For an example of Christian religious "dark glass" discourse during this period of the 1950s, see Brunner (1954). The discourse that emphasizes commonality between Christianity and Judaism is quintessentially manifested in Herberg (1955).

2. Silver saw a direct connection between Christianity's emphasis on human powerlessness and modern-day existentialism.

3. For some examples of Silver's activity in the sphere of interfaith dialogue, see Silver (1952d, 1955a, 1955e, 1955i).

optimism and his interest in enhancing man's self-confidence and positive attitude toward earthly life.

Indeed, although Silver had frequently elucidated his ideas about the connection between faith and individual moral responsibility in his earlier sermons, the effort to portray it as a feature that distinguished Judaism from Christianity was something new. Thus, in a Yom Kippur sermon during World War II (Silver 1972d, 46–51), Silver explained that the purpose of Yom Kippur was to teach people the concept of moral responsibility as the only way to rid themselves of the burden of guilt connected with sin. He presented this view as part of a Judeo-Christian American message—that of opposition to the Nazis. He linked this message with the biblical verse that the American founding fathers had inscribed on the Liberty Bell: "Proclaim liberty throughout all the land unto all the inhabitants thereof" (Leviticus 25:10), noting that America's Judeo-Christian ethos entailed interdependence between freedom and active struggle against exploitative authority, in contrast to the Nazis, who understood freedom as permission to enslave and dominate those weaker than them.

In contrast, Silver's approach appears to assign Christianity an inferior status to that of Judaism. However, this should be positioned within the context of the Reform movement's concept of mission. In many respects Silver was a quintessential product of classical Reform ideology, which, as far back as the nineteenth century, had posited Judaism as the purest model of universal monotheism and therefore as uniquely destined to bear its message to humanity at large. However, while in the 1930s and 1940s he often criticized the naïve attitude of the early Reform leaders toward Judaism's universalistic mission, during the 1950s he often praised Reform Judaism's early leaders; in particular, he noted the intrepidity that these leaders had displayed in proclaiming Judaism as the one true universal religion of mankind.[4]

4. Thus, when called on to honor the memory of Rabbi Isaac Mayer Wise, he noted Wise's vision of a liberal, courageous Judaism, and lauded him for seeking no theological ceasefire but rather affirming Judaism's mission as a light unto the nations (Silver 1957g).

Indeed, the mission concept was, for Silver, a mechanism capable of expressing the mentality transformation that was supposed to have occurred within the Jewish people in the wake of Israel's establishment: enabling American Jews to imbue American society with prophetic meaning, legitimizing America's role as standard-bearer of democracy, and urging it toward radical reform of its Christian attitudes. This new approach also provides the context in which one should understand Silver's attempt to compose a new historical account of the complex relationship between Judaism and ancient Christianity. In his books and articles of this period, he claimed that the historical conflict between the two religions hinted at a recurrence of a conflict between the Jewish worldview and the pagan attitudes that Christianity had absorbed from Hellenism. In order to ensure the durability of the modern democratic value system, Silver averred that Judaism would now have to triumph, while Christianity would have to undergo a thorough reform, divest itself of its Hellenistic influences, and adopt the authentic monotheism represented by Judaism. This approach is evident in a lecture that Silver delivered at a symposium on the differences between Judaism and Christianity, held in 1957 at the Jewish-affiliated Dropsie College in Philadelphia (Silver 1957e).

In explaining the rift between the two religions, Silver focused on Jesus' declaration of himself as the Messiah. This self-proclamation proceeded from an assumption that the end of the world and its established social order was approaching and that there was no longer any point in striving to mend existing social conditions. This worldview had engendered an ethical system that looked with disdain on earthly life and required its adherents to conduct themselves in this world in the manner of prisoners awaiting redemption—"in it, but not of it." This constituted a fundamental divergence from Jewish doctrine, which held that man's only means of attaining "redemption" was to take active social-moral responsibility for bettering himself and his environment. When Jesus declared that the Kingdom of Heaven was not of this world, he set off a process destined to end in an irrevocable schism between a pessimistic view of man as incapable of personal responsibility and a Jewish view in which the Kingdom of Heaven could be brought about through striving for justice and peace in this world.

This decisive parting of the ways was, according to Silver, a result of the pagan attitudes that Christianity had absorbed from Hellenism. Paul established Christianity during a period of crisis in the Hellenistic world in which the old pagan beliefs were being discredited—thereby casting Judaism and Christianity as competing solutions to the prevailing turmoil. Silver noted that Judaism stood no chance against Pauline Christianity, inasmuch as the concept of "redemption" that Paul added to Judaism's core monotheistic doctrine actually accorded with the mind-set of Greek paganism. This mind-set viewed man as a being powerless in the face of cosmic powers greater than himself. Silver's conclusion was that Christian theology's historical victory had essentially constituted the triumph of Hellenistic paganism; Hellenism, however, should not be allowed to emerge victorious from the current crisis of faith that threatened modern civilization. The challenge facing Judaism during this present period of crisis was to keep mankind from being seduced by promises of mystical "redemption." Now, in contrast to the Hellenistic-pagan era, and subsequent to the cultural and political revolutions that had characterized the modern age, mankind was ripe for Judaism's prophetic message. Moreover, Judaism, in the era of Israeli statehood, could now finally take up the challenge of promoting its prophetic message to Christian America and, by extension, to all mankind. This latter conclusion was stated explicitly in an address from 1957:

> My friends, the future belongs to Judaism! Judaism is the faith of tomorrow! Not its forms and rituals—these are intended and important only for us so as to discipline and alert ourselves for our covenanted tasks and our appointed destiny—but its spiritual message and program. . . . It offers mankind a gospel of social progress and it summons men to social action, to the building of the good society . . . it has confidence in man's inexhaustible spiritual resources. It teaches a boundless reverence for life and for all that contributes to the noble fulfillment and enjoyment. All these are original ideas of Judaism. (Silver 1957g)

Even when not addressing Jewish audiences, many of Silver's speeches during the 1950s were based on his pretension to proclaim this Jewish mission. This may be seen in a written testimony that he sent in 1954 to the Senate Sub-Committee on Labor and Public Welfare, which was then deliberating on legislation against employment discrimination (Silver 1954e, 1963a).[5] Silver was known as a tireless advocate of social and labor legislation: during the 1920s and 1930s he had spearheaded the struggle for unemployment insurance in Ohio. After numerous setbacks over the course of seven years, the struggle had ended in 1936 with the passage of the Ohio Plan, a package that ultimately served as a model for local and federal labor legislation. Two decades later, in 1950, he was involved in legislation against employment discrimination in Cleveland.[6] It was thus reasonable to expect that in 1954 Silver would be invited to testify before a Senate subcommittee, not specifically as a Jewish leader, but rather as an expert on labor legislation. Being aware of this possibility, Silver opened his remarks by asking the subcommittee not to see him in this light, noting that he was speaking in his capacity as a Jewish cleric and that his aim would be to discuss the religious basis for antidiscriminatory legislation. He deplored the atmosphere of fear and the lack of moral commitment that were threatening the integrity of the American way. He contrasted this atmosphere with the empowering view that man bears personal responsibility for his actions. This prophetic Jewish message, Silver felt, should also be the message communicated by American global leadership; America, he declared, could not enjoy the trust of peoples struggling against inequality when it was itself unable to commit to that very struggle.

Silver's aspiration to educate the American public in the spirit of prophetic Judaism was also evident in a May 1957 speech before the Medical Society of the State of New York (Silver 1957a). In this speech he elucidated the importance of religious faith as part of a Jewish holistic approach to medical science. Prayer, he explained, was no replacement for a doctor's prescription; rather, it expressed the yearning for God felt by people when they are in pain. Thus, the physician who looks at the totality of the patient's needs will understand the healing power of prayer. From this

5. Letter from Mrs. Ruth M. Sparrow (Silver's secretary) to Mr. Roy E. James (staff director, Senate Committee on Labor and Public Welfare), February 22, 1953, AHSP V 616.

6. On Silver's involvement in social and labor legislation, see Silver (1963a).

Silver extrapolated to the crisis of religious faith as a major factor behind the current rise in mental illness and quoted Carl Jung on the utility of faith in the psychological healing process. He noted that the scientific achievements of modernity were unable to give man the sense of spiritual meaning so necessary to him. In this context, Judaism's attitude toward medicine was most important. In contrast to Christianity, Judaism did not view the body as a prison, but rather as the temple of the soul. Judaism had never found it necessary to mortify the body in order to exalt the soul; on the contrary, it had striven to confer spiritual meaning to earthly life.

Yet another instance in which Silver expressed his belief in Judaism as an antidote to the erroneous Christian worldview was an address that he delivered in Wheeling, West Virginia. Silver was the guest of honor at an event marking the twenty-fifth anniversary of the Oglebay Institute, a recreational facility that had been founded in 1930 for the public benefit on the wealthy Oglebay family's country estate. Wheeling was the first locality in which Silver had served as rabbi (1915–1917), and it was there that he had met his wife, who belonged to a prominent family in the local Jewish community (Silver 1955b).[7] Silver devoted his speech to an affirmation of the value of leisure in modern life.

He began by deploring Christianity's negative attitude toward activities related to the enjoyment of earthly life. He rejected this tradition, explaining that precisely at the present time, in the "age of machines," such a negative attitude toward leisure was particularly dangerous. For most people, leisure time is their only opportunity to nurture their untapped creative faculties. Only a religious approach that sanctified life in this world could ensure a positive attitude to leisure. In the absence of such an approach, the "American dream" risked becoming what Karl Marx had referred to as the "opiate of the masses," that is, a vehicle for consumerism and for the sale of illusions, rather than a noble commitment to individualism and social responsibility. Although Silver did not state this explicitly, those who heard his speech could hardly fail to catch his allusions to Senator Joseph McCarthy's famous "enemies from

7. On Silver's stay in Wheeling, see AJA MS 210-4/4, November 29, 1963.

within" speech—delivered five years earlier in 1950 in honor of Abraham Lincoln's birthday on February 9, also in Wheeling. In that speech, McCarthy had described the war on communism as a conflict between Western Christian culture and Asian Communist culture; in particular, he had contrasted Western Christian culture with Marx's condemnation of religion as a fraud. Silver, in his address, touched on similar concepts, but rather than using them in order to attack communism, he adopted a critical tone toward Christianity, warning that without a fundamental internal reform, in the spirit of the Hebrew prophets, one that was capable of empowering the individual and bolstering his sense of moral responsibility, the American democratic idea risked losing all real meaning and becoming an "opiate of the masses."

This approach, it should be noted, also influenced Silver's position regarding intra-Jewish discourse. Silver essentially assigned Judaism the same function within the American nation that he attributed to the United States within the international arena. Just as the United States was expected to exemplify the democratic way of life, so Judaism had to epitomize the ideals of egalitarian interfaith dialogue in order to fulfill its mission of disseminating humanistic values throughout the world. Thus, just as Silver saw it as his duty within a national American context to advocate widespread religious reform in the spirit of prophetic Judaism, he also saw himself as obligated to urge a similar, internal reform within the various Jewish denominations.

The desire for intra-Jewish reform was particularly evident in Silver's attitude toward the religious intolerance exhibited by ultra-Orthodox Judaism. In a 1958 speech marking a decade of Israeli statehood (Silver 1958b), Silver strongly disapproved of the fact that the United States, with its tradition of religious tolerance, was now home to a growing ultra-Orthodox sector whose rabbinate prided itself on its avoidance of any cooperation with those streams of Judaism not subject to its jurisdiction. Silver associated this ultra-Orthodox stance with Nebuchadnezzar's dream of the tree in the Book of Daniel. In Daniel 3:31–4:34, Nebuchadnezzar sees himself in his dream as a tree reaching to the heavens, whose fruit nourishes human civilization as a whole. Daniel interpreted the dream to mean that Nebuchadnezzar would be punished for failing to accept heavenly dominion.

Silver took up where the biblical story left off, casting himself in the role of Daniel and warning ultra-Orthodox Jewry that "there is no one single tree which could give food—the food of faith—to all people, not even the tree that grows in Brooklyn."[8]

Despite his continuous criticism of secular Zionism (Shiff 2006), in this context Silver felt it necessary to denounce the ultra-Orthodox for not seeing the idealism of young secular Jews who, without ever attending synagogue, nevertheless adhered to a humanistic outlook with clear roots in Hebrew prophecy. He saw this idealism as the cornerstone of the desired Jewish inner reform and blamed the ultra-Orthodox establishment for the aversion displayed by so many young Israelis toward the Jewish religion. Still, American ultra-Orthodoxy did not represent in Silver's eyes the most urgent focus of the required intra-Jewish reform. At this stage, the growing power of the American ultra-Orthodox community was a relatively marginal one, particularly compared with the Reform and Conservative movements then at the height of their popularity.

Thus, Silver did not see the ultra-Orthodox trends of religious exclusionism as the main danger facing American Jewry; the real danger and the most urgent focus of the required intra-Jewish reform, he felt, came from the impoverishment of religious faith that characterized, in his view, many adherents of Reform and Conservative Judaism. Silver maintained that it was time to reconsider the excessive stress placed on changing Jewish ritual by nineteenth-century Reform leaders. In his view, the major problem of his era was not that of adapting Jewish ritual to the spirit of the age, but rather that of reviving religious faith:

> What is needed today is not the innovation or renovation or reformation or reconstruction of Judaism, but the conversion of the Jew to his faith. It is no longer a question of less or of more: [but of] the godlessness, secularism, and materialism which have blighted our people, along with all other peoples, but to which we, because of our unique position in the world, can least of all submit. (Silver 1963a)

8. For similar criticism that Silver expressed toward ultra-Orthodox Judaism, see Silver (1957c).

Silver felt that the various denominations should join forces against this common danger of waning religious faith. He underscored the three denominations' shared spiritual basis, one that shied away from any pretension to overcome human cognitive limitations, but strove, rather, to make these very limitations the basis for Jewish aspirations to build the good society. A specifically American aspect of this call for a new religious-social Jewish commitment was reflected in two addresses that Silver delivered in May and November 1957 (Silver 1957c, 1957g). In both speeches, he cautioned against a distorted American "messianic" view of the flourishing state of American Jewry during the 1950s. Silver affirmed that the American-Jewish community had made impressive gains: the number of synagogues had increased greatly, their memberships had soared, and demand had grown for more intensive Jewish Sunday and day school education. Even the situation of Orthodox Judaism, whose demise had been predicted by many, had improved: by the late 1950s, its communities were expanding, including the number of its synagogues and yeshivas. All of these factors formed a positive basis for Jewish life. However, Silver cautioned, these achievements were still in the nature of a many-branched tree whose roots—the roots of Jewish vitality—had not struck deep. The great threat to American Judaism during this period was that of an unfounded belief that the good society had already been achieved, or nearly so.

Silver felt that the lack of Jewish religious fervor might be rooted not merely in the alienation endemic to modern life, but also in excessive American-Jewish self-satisfaction. He cited a letter by Heinrich Heine in which Heine explained to his friend why magnificent churches were no longer being built in the modern era. Heine argued that in the past people had acted on convictions, whereas today they merely held opinions: "it requires something more than an opinion to build a Gothic cathedral," he asserted (Heine 1837; 1976, 344). Silver continued,

> We modern Jews have a good opinion about our Judaism, but no strong enough convictions. We need a renewal of that massive religious earnestness which gave to our ancestors their patent of nobility. (Silver 1957g)

The passionate religious Jewish commitment that Silver advocated was one informed by a dialectic process that transformed the process of acculturation into a source of religious inspiration rather than impoverishment of religious faith. One example of this is an address dedicated to American Jewry's tercentenary that Silver delivered in two versions: a complete one, at The Temple in Cleveland on April 2, 1954, and an abbreviated one, in Detroit, Michigan, on October 17 of the same year (Silver 1954d, 1954f). Silver noted that the secret of American Jewry's vitality was that its acculturation and social integration had promoted a commitment to its own Jewish heritage. The synagogues and communal institutions that the American Jews had built, and the solidarity that they had cultivated, were essentially derived from the process of integrating into American society.

This latter view had direct relevance to Silver's position on American Zionism and its standing vis-à-vis Israeli Zionist doctrine. In a speech that he delivered in February 1955, at a special conference organized by the ZOA marking three hundred years since the arrival of the first twenty-three Jews on American shores (Silver 1955k), Silver portrayed American Jewry's solidarity with Israel as rooted in the discovery of America (Silver 1958a). According to Silver, Columbus had laid the groundwork for the development of an American heritage that was committed to nurturing the distinctive collective identities of the various immigrant groups who arrived there. The Jews, in particular, were deeply attached to their separate collective identity and regarded integration within American society as the ideal means of cultivating their distinct identity. The practical conclusion to be drawn from Silver's Zionistic tercentenary speech was that of American Jewry's duty to cultivate, via its synagogues, a Hebrew culture whose main importance lay in its being an instrument for progress and integration:

> The Hebrew language is not only the repository of our most glorious cultural trophies. It has been a powerful instrument for progress and renewal in Jewish life and the bond of union and the chain of continuity. The Hebrew language served our people as the weapon with which to batter down the spiritual and intellectual walls of the ghetto. It was the highway along which our people moved into the modern world. (Silver 1955k)

Quite expectedly, Silver's emphasis on Hebrew culture was an important component of his criticism of the prevailing Israeli assumption that no hub of creative Jewish life could exist outside of Israel (Silver 1952a). He presented Hebrew culture as a prime means of ensuring the existence, side by side, of two such hubs—an Israeli and an American one. In this discussion, Silver was speaking as one who worked extensively, over the course of many years, to promote Hebrew cultural activity among American Jews and to turn it into a vehicle for intra-Jewish reform.[9] He assigned the ideal of Hebrew culture in America a major role in realizing his Diaspora-Zionist ideology. He stressed that Hebrew culture was a vital component of the shared creative endeavor that had subsisted over the course of three thousand years between the diverse centers of Jewish life. Rather than conceiving of Hebrew culture as a manifestation of the primacy of the Israeli-Jewish hub, Silver saw it as the medium for a cultural-pluralist

9. As a teenager, he had made Hebrew the official language of the Herzl Zion Club that he and his brother had founded in 1904. This had placed him in conflict with the adult leaders of the Jewish Educational Alliance, on whose premises the club held its meetings, and whose "melting pot" ideology required that the meetings be conducted in English. Even more indicative were his educational activities at The Temple in Cleveland, which up until his arrival in 1917 had been a bastion of opposition to the use of Hebrew. One of his first acts as a young rabbi was to restore Hebrew to The Temple's prayer service and the curriculum of its affiliated religious school. Throughout his rabbinical career, Silver worked to develop The Temple's Hebrew school, seeing it as one of his greatest achievements (by 1949 the school was offering sixty classes for two thousand pupils of different ages). Silver himself spoke Hebrew at a native level. In 1910, at the age of seventeen, he addressed the Federation of American Zionists, calling in elegant Hebrew for greater funds to be invested in Zionist youth activity. Later, during his studies at HUC, he had been chosen to thank a distinguished guest speaker, the Zionist activist Nahum Sokolow, on behalf of his fellow students; years later his close friend and contemporary at HUC, Rabbi Solomon Freehof, recalled the amazement of all present when Silver answered Sokolow in fluent and eloquent Hebrew far superior to that of which his fellow aspiring rabbis were capable. Silver demonstrated his command of the language at various other opportunities, particularly on his visits to Palestine; audiences were frequently surprised by the fluency of his Hebrew. He also strove to instill in his two sons a sense of the language's importance; many years later, his younger son, Raphael, recalled the weekly Hebrew quizzes given him and his brother by his father as a formative experience (see correspondence with Julian Morgenstern, January 14, 1946, AHSP I; Freehof 1967, 4; Gal and Shiff 1999; Kulber 1993; Neumann 1976, 34–35; Orian 1982, iv–v, xiii, 172; Raphael 1989, 6–7, 51, 64–65).

Jewish "orchestra." This "orchestra" could not have been dominated by a single instrument—neither Israeli nor Jewish American; rather, it needed to emerge from an egalitarian dialogue between the various Jewish centers of Israel and the Diaspora.

In accordance with this Diaspora-Zionist ideology, Silver viewed Jewish acculturation into American society as the positive basis for a post-Holocaust Jewish cultural flowering. In his speech on Hebrew culture as an important force for cultivating Jewish life in the United States, he emphasized that the idea of having autonomous national-minority status in the Diaspora was foreign to American Judaism and unsuited to America's democratic political culture. The American Zionists, he declared, rejected this idea out of hand, seeking instead equal rights and freedom from any form of discrimination within American society. This being the case, American -Zionist solidarity, in contrast to the Israeli variety, was not a manifestation of post-Holocaust disappointment with emancipation and the idea of full Jewish integration into the surrounding environment. The opposite rather was the case: American Zionism needed to cultivate Hebrew culture in such a way as to imbue the promise of emancipation and democracy with authentic Jewish content.

This in turn created an urgent ideological need for Silver to redefine the concept of Zionist fulfillment so that it would not only be expressed in immigration to Israel but also in an internal Jewish religious awakening. In doing so, he aligned himself with a long-standing American-Zionist tradition, which supported the continuation of the Jewish existence in the Diaspora. From the early years of the Zionist movement in America—the end of the nineteenth century and the beginning of the twentieth century—many of its leaders saw Zionism as a moderating tool, which could enable Jewish immigrants from Eastern Europe to undergo a constructive process of Americanization and would not force them to choose between a separatist Jewish identity and an assimilated American one (Sarna 2000; Shiff 1994). Exponents of this aspiration believed it was the duty of Zionism to maintain Diaspora Jewish centers—foremost the United States—alongside the center in Eretz Israel. Many of them shared Silver's definition of Zionism in terms of cultural pluralism. The function of Zionism, according to this definition, was to make it possible to nurture the

"Jewish melody" so that it might contribute to the harmony of the larger American orchestra.

It was this approach that also gave rise to the famous motto of American Zionism, which became identified with the Zionist leadership of Louis D. Brandeis and stated already at the beginning of the twentieth century: "the more Zionist you are, the better an American you are." Diaspora-Zionist views of this sort continued to be characteristic of American Zionism throughout its history, and became most prominent in the first years after the state's founding. Mordecai Kaplan asserted in *A New Zionism* (1955) that after the founding of the State of Israel, the main function of Zionism was to become a means for American-Jewish vitality. Similarly, an article written in 1949 by Daniel Frisch, president of the ZOA, sought to establish a positive role for Diaspora Zionism, whose members choose not to immigrate to Israel even while its gates were open to them. For this purpose, he called for a Jewish education that fostered a view of Jewish existence in the Diaspora as a legitimate Zionist goal (Frisch 1949; Kaplan 1955).

What made Silver's Zionism unique was that he turned this doctrine into a commitment that bore the nature of a religious imperative. Paradoxically, the roots of this religious view lay in the classic anti-Zionist American Reform heritage. The internal pre-Holocaust "theological" Reform debate on Zionism was centered on the question of whether there was a contradiction between religious faith in enlightenment and Jewish national identification. This was a clash between anti-Zionist Reform views that denounced the phenomenon of Jewish nationalism as un-American, promoted by reactionary worldviews that sought to overturn the achievements of enlightenment, and Reform Zionists that saw a binding reciprocal relationship between progressive religious Jewish beliefs and a national-Zionist faith. Accordingly, the meaning of the victory of the Reform Zionist camp in the late 1930s and 1940s was that the support for a Jewish state became not only a basis giving legitimacy to Jewish continuity in the Diaspora, but first and foremost a clear expression of religious identification with the path of enlightenment and democracy (Shiff 2005, 125–58).

For Silver, this approach crystallized into a religious imperative requiring the American Jew to identify the State of Israel's existence with an optimistic faith in the promises of democracy despite the Holocaust and the continued threats to the State of Israel. An example of this can be found in the address he gave to the ZOA on June 2, 1954 (Silver 1954a). He stated that there was a fundamental difference between the problems that characterized the period prior to the founding of the State of Israel and those that characterized the period afterward. The problems in the pre-state period stemmed from an abnormal situation of persecution and displacement. Conversely, the problems that marked the period following the founding of the state—even if grave and serious—constituted "normal" problems with which every nascent state is forced to deal. The recognition of the normalcy of the problems that arose after statehood should have imbued the experience of coping with them with a sense of new Jewish self-confidence, which would crystallize into a religious mission, directed inwardly within Judaism and outwardly toward non-Jewish society.

PART TWO

In Retrospect

Silver's Pre-State Zionist Career

4

Silver's Early Struggle against Anti-Semitism and Nazism

How much of Silver's post-statehood Zionist stance could be traced to the early pre-1948 years of his career? At first glance, Silver's Zionist leadership during the 1940s appears to take an opposite direction, emphasizing anti-Jewish hostility and expressing mistrust toward the non-Jewish American surroundings. In that period, Silver frequently attacked his political Zionist rivals for refraining from exposing the "conspiracy of silence" on the part of the American administration toward the European Jewish victims. On their part, Silver's political rivals saw his combative advocacy as implying a lack of faith in American democracy. Is this not how one should interpret Silver's response to the statement of support sent by President Franklin D. Roosevelt, prior to the November general elections, to the ZOA conference in Atlantic City on October 15, 1944?

> The world was silent at the ruins and outrage of a whole people. . . . A ten year cycle of slaughter and assault at the hand of a people and a government . . . which sacked and ravaged a thousand Jewish communities, slew 3 million men, women and children in horrible human abattoirs and crematories and filled the highways of the earth with herds of frightened feeling refugees, evoked from the civilized world, from the democracies, from our own country, a few perfunctory acts of rescue which resulted in little more than nothing . . . all our representations to our government to help save our doomed people in any way whatsoever resulted in pitifully little. . . . With all my supreme admirations for the great personalities who are our friends . . . I still say, unto you, what the Psalmist said long ago: "Put not your trust in princes. . . ." (Silver 1944)

And yet, it is my claim that a different interpretation of Silver's speech must be employed. One may explain Silver's popularity among American Jewry in the 1940s not in his ability to raise the flag of suspicion and lack of trust in non-Jewish America, but precisely the opposite: his bellicose style of Jewish leadership was seen by his supporters—many of them striving to enter the American middle class—as the only way that could enable them to vigorously pursue their deep feelings of American patriotism without forgoing their Jewish sense of solidarity. This dual, complex quest was shared by many American Jews of that period, who, similar to Silver, bore witness to a tense encounter between the American ethos of individualism and equal opportunity and the deep-rooted, Old World Jewish collective heritage that was still a powerful force in the American-Jewish immigrant ghetto and the Jewish neighborhoods of the early twentieth century. One might say that the simultaneous all-encompassing claims of their Jewish and American surroundings amounted to a formative experience of an inability to choose between Judaism and Americanism. Mordecai Kaplan described this dual existence as one of living simultaneously in "two civilizations," while Silver, in his memoirs, employed the metaphor of "New World" bottles bubbling over with the ferment of "Old World" ideas (Kaplan 1934; Silver 1963a).[1]

The 1920s and 1930s were a challenging period for those who, like Silver, wished to cultivate this complex two-civilization identity. Popular anti-Semitic sentiment both at home and in Europe was particularly threatening. It left many American Jews suspended between the immigrant ghettos, whose walls had already been breached and could no longer impart a full sense of belonging, and the non-Jewish exterior environment that suddenly seemed closed and nonaccepting. Against

1. One may view Silver's rabbinical studies, from 1911 to 1915, as well as his service in the upper middle-class synagogues of Wheeling (1915–1917) and Cleveland (1917 to the end of his life), as socialization apparatus and entry tickets into the American middle class. Each of these early points in Silver's rabbinical career could be seen as enforcing the "two civilizations" experience, that is, his sense of belonging to an all-encompassing Jewish religious-ethnic culture and, simultaneously, of being integrated into an American middle-class culture at the social and cultural levels.

this background, it is easy to understand not only the difficulties faced by those seeking to cultivate a two-civilization approach, but also the degree to which the struggle for that approach's validity appeared urgent in their eyes. It was the struggle to ensure the cultivation of the two-civilization approach that lay behind the dual activism that was characteristic of many American Jews of that period: both an activist struggle of Jewish solidarity vis-à-vis the external pressures of anti-Jewish intolerance and, no less important, a patriotic American stance vis-à-vis the intra-Jewish threat of self-segregation from the non-Jewish environment. The way in which the young Silver tried to strike a balance between concern for Jewish collective survival in the face of anti-Semitism, and the hope for equal participation in general American society, was what would ultimately evolve into his popular combative Zionist leadership of the 1940s and his "bridges and walls" advocacy of the 1950s.

Early intimations of that pattern could be discerned already in the first stages of Silver's rabbinical career. One instance was a sermon in which he described the ideal of the "American Jew of Tomorrow" (Silver 1918). Where there is Jewish faith and pride, he proclaimed, discrimination and anti-Semitism cannot prevail. Silver was not talking about the kind of Jewish pride that disparages the non-Jewish world and opposes integration within it. On the contrary, Silver challenged any tendency to exclude Jews and other "aliens" from American discourse in the name of American "patriotism." American society, he noted, was undergoing a formative process to which each immigrant group made its own contribution. Any attempt to suppress the characteristic traditions of immigrant groups, merely in order to ensure their compatibility with the cultural worldviews of earlier groups, endangered the ongoing project of building a thriving American civilization. Americanization, according to Silver, did not mean obliterating immigrant cultures, but rather the opposite. It meant nurturing the special attributes of each ethnic group and engaging them for the common pluralistic American discourse. Silver drew a distinction between the kind of superficial, distorted Americanization seeking to impose national uniformity and true Americanization that encouraged each immigrant group to make its own unique contribution to American culture:

> The man who speaks English brokenly but works honestly, rears his children . . . with love for American ideals and institutions, is a spiritual kinsman of Lincoln. . . . But the man who exploits American society for selfish ends, who is a bigot in religion and in politics . . . is a foreigner to his polished finger tips even if his ancestors were sea-sick on the Mayflower. (Silver 1919a)

As Silver saw it from the early days of his career, the American-Zionist approach did not reflect any exclusionist tendency, but rather a desire to create an American society characterized by the universal values of humanism and democracy. This Zionist approach obliged the young Silver to oppose not only intolerance in general American society, but also isolationist tendencies within the Zionist camp, particularly those that doubted whether Zionist solidarity could become a vehicle for equal participation in general American society. Silver repeatedly cautioned that Zionism's main goal was not to intensify the sense of Jewish victimhood and distrust, but rather to eradicate the long-held sense of alienness that still existed within the Jewish community:

> The real tragedy of the "golus" is not to be found in massacres . . . and anti-Semitism. . . . The real tragedy of the "golus" is not to be found in the yellow badge which your forefathers were compelled to wear on their shoulders. The real tragedy of the "golus" is to be found in the yellow streak which your children are compelled to carry within their souls. (Silver 1920)

Based on this approach, the young Silver also avoided overemphasizing Zionism's political goals. In a 1917 letter to Rabbi Moses Gries, his predecessor at The Temple in Cleveland and a leading proponent of classical Reform Judaism (Meyer 1997, 13–14),[2] Silver explained that it was Judaism's prophetic spirit that lay at the heart of his Zionism and that he did not find the Zionist political objective of creating a small Jewish state in Palestine particularly inspiring. Rather, he noted, this objective was secondary to the major spiritual and religious challenges then facing American Jewry.

2. Silver to Moses J. Gries, April 26, 1917, Stephen S. Wise Papers, AJHS.

A decade later, when Silver had already established himself as The Temple's chief rabbi, he expressed the same opinion in a contribution to a 1929 memorial anthology honoring Theodor Herzl (Weisgal 1929, 256). In his article, Silver distinguished between the prophetic mission of *tikkun olam* that he regarded as the authentic form of Jewish messianism, and the national messianism that had developed only later with the loss of sovereignty. In Silver's eyes, the national vision took on less importance than the prophetic vision, mainly because it reflected the pessimistic worldview of an oppressed people whose sufferings prevented them from attaining the high moral level of the prophetic outlook. Clearly, Silver had developed this thesis under the influence of classical Reform attitudes that still prevailed among the Hebrew Union College faculty while he was pursuing his rabbinical studies. In keeping with this approach, the founders of Reform viewed the rise of Jewish nationalism as a process that ran counter to the prophetic-universalistic ideal. Silver embraced these ideas virtually in toto, including the conception of Jewish nationalism as a late and inferior development. However, rather than adopting an anti-Zionist stance, he championed the idea of Jewish nationalism as a mere first stage in the realization of higher prophetic-universalist ideals:

> Nationalism is not enough. It is a minimum requirement, not a maximum program. . . . Nationalism is a means, not an end. "What is great in a man," said Nietzsche, "is that he is a bridge and not a goal." This is true also of men collectively of nations and of national cultures. Nationalism will not suffice the eternally questing soul of our people. (Weisgal 1929, 256)

In his 1929 lecture, Silver appeared to have become impatient to reach this advanced universalist stage. "It is well that the political phase of Jewish Messianism is coming to a close in the upbuilding of the National Homeland," he declared, adding that, once statehood was achieved, "we shall not have to lay so much stress in the future on the importance of nationalism" (Weisgal 1929, 256). Given this anticipation, one can understand why, during the 1920s, Silver did not view the Zionist movement as his main area of endeavor and preferred to identify his leadership with social-economic causes, particularly in the area of labor legislation in Ohio.

The hub of this activity was The Temple, as evidenced in the motto over the entrance to the new and impressive synagogue building whose construction in 1923 was meticulously supervised by Silver. The synagogue's logo, visible on several of the building's floors, was composed of two concentric circles—the internal one symbolizing Jewish solidarity, the external one symbolizing identification with humanity as a whole. Silver put into practice the idea embodied by this logo by turning the Jewish synagogue into a focal point for nonsectarian social activity; the building served as a venue for meetings on social legislation attended by Jewish and non-Jewish leaders from all walks of life in Cleveland. Silver also institutionalized the Sunday sermon as an event with resonance in the general public sphere; the sermons' progressive orientation attracted thousands of Jews and non-Jews on a weekly basis. In one of these sermons from November 1928 (Silver 1967b), Silver described the democratic impulse as the central defining theme of Jewish history, from the forty-year sojourn in the desert through the Age of Enlightenment; accordingly, he argued, any effort to strengthen Jewish faith and tradition necessarily entailed Jewish participation in the general American struggle to implement democratic precepts in all areas of life.

> A real Jew is a passionate democrat, not only in regard to political life but in regard to economic and social and religious life. In all the departments of the world he seeks . . . expansion, growth, freedom opportunity for all the children of God.

In the wake of the 1929 stock market crash, Silver's emphasis on social and progressive issues took on an even more radical character. Although during the 1940s and 1950s he would often support the conservative Republican Party, during the Depression years Silver called for the penalization of financiers and captains of industry who, he felt, had undermined the labor unions. In 1930, he published a pamphlet entitled *Religion in a Changing World,* in which he outlined a radical socioreligious plan. In an April 1932 Sunday sermon at The Temple (Silver 1932b), he set forth his personal social philosophy. Marshaling detailed information on unemployment, the minimum wage, healthy nutrition, child poverty, and overall poverty rates for Cleveland and the United States, he presented a socioeconomic plan aimed at addressing what he referred to as the impact of unfettered capitalism on the institution of the family and social ethics. In addition to calling for massive federal financial assistance and for the government to take responsibility for creating jobs, Silver decried the concentration of wealth in the hands of too few people and urged a more equal distribution through higher wages for workers and a large tax increase for those in the highest income brackets:

> There is too much wealth in the hands of too few people . . . if these billions of dollars had been widespread among the millions of workingmen in the country, the depression would have lifted itself all over the land.

This focus on social issues that characterized Silver's early career reversed itself quite dramatically as the Nazis rose to power in Germany and a wave of anti-Semitism inundated the United States.[3] Silver did not cease his involvement in progressive political causes of an American national character, as demonstrated by his continued activity on the national committee of the American Civil Liberties Union and his participation in the struggle for unemployment legislation. However, if up until this point the Jewish sphere had been secondary to Silver's activity in the social and economic sphere, from now on the situation would be reversed, and Silver would come to be associated first and foremost with causes directly related to the American-Jewish community and its collective response to anti-Jewish sentiment in the United States and abroad.

Silver's 1932–1933 sabbatical from The Temple, which he spent in Europe and Palestine, was a watershed year that distinguished between his early "American" struggles of the 1920s and his activity on the "Jewish" front during the 1930s. The very fact that he traveled to Europe and Palestine during a particularly stormy election year was perceived by many of Silver's colleagues as an abandonment of the political-social arena of Cleveland and Ohio. Still, despite this major change in orientation, Silver remained loyal to his universalistic-American approach; now it became most pronounced in his understanding of the nature of the

3. For an early example of this shift, see Silver (1932a).

existential threat facing Judaism. Two specific points along his sabbatical itinerary—a visit to Germany where he witnessed Nazi persecution and Hitler's rise to power firsthand and a meeting with Czechoslovak president Tomáš Masaryk—were major signposts pointing not only to the intensifying Jewish orientation of the causes for which Silver fought, but also to the universalist American meaning with which he invested these causes.

Silver arrived in Berlin on January 22, 1933. In the days that followed, he witnessed pro-Nazi marches as well as anti-Nazi demonstrations by the Communists and Social Democrats in the streets (Shafir 1994, 35–36; Silver 1932-1933, 1963a). Within a short time he reached the conclusion that the Nazis' anti-Jewish legislation threatened Jewish survival and that a full-fledged campaign should be mounted to oppose it. When, several months later, he was interviewed by the American press on the situation in Germany (Shafir 1994, 38–44; Silver 1934a, 1934b, 1934c), he described the German persecution of the Jews as more evil and dangerous than the pogroms of tsarist Russia. The real threat posed by Nazism was, for Silver, that of Jewish exclusion from German society. As he saw it, this isolation of the Jews was a spiritual death sentence, one that surpassed in wickedness all of the pogroms that had ever been perpetrated against the Jews throughout history. For him, the inability to participate equally in the various social and civil circles of the non-Jewish society was a kind of suffocation—that is, a loss of human status.

Immediately upon leaving Germany, Silver traveled to Czechoslovakia, where he met for an hour with President Masaryk, leader of the Czech independence movement and Czechoslovakia's first president (1918–1935). The Czechoslovak leader embodied, for Silver, the hope that Nazism could be combated through faith in the ultimate victory of progress and democracy. The humanistic values that Masaryk advocated represented the appropriate context in which to understand Nazism's threat to the Jewish people. In Silver's view, the danger posed by Nazi isolation of the Jews should be seen as part of a comprehensive agenda of destroying the foundations of democracy. Silver's report on his interview with Masaryk made this abundantly clear:

> "What do you, Mr. President, think of the future of democracy?" ... We were holding our interview a few days after Hitler's rise to power in Germany. His answer came, without a moment's hesitation, clear and decisive, "democracy is passing through a crisis but crisis does not mean defeat. ... All dictatorial experiments are impressive but ephemeral. ... The world needs a new mind and a new devotion to spiritual values bound up with a realistic program of social progress. (Silver 1963a)

Upon his return to the United States, Silver spearheaded Jewish efforts to counter rising anti-Jewish sentiment; at the same time, he advocated a liberal, Masaryk-style response to this danger. Such a response entailed viewing opposition to Nazism as part of an overall struggle to fortify the ethical basis of the democratic way and as an expression of unconditional faith in the ultimate triumph of democratic values. Thus, five months after the Nazis rose to power, and immediately upon his return to the United States, Silver began giving press interviews in which he stressed the danger of the civil suffocation that was being imposed on six hundred thousand German Jews. The gravity of this state of Jewish isolation was also what drove Silver to assume the leadership of an emergency movement to boycott Nazi Germany.[4] This was the first time that Silver led a nationwide Jewish struggle; from Silver's point of view, his anti-Nazi combative efforts were entirely devoted to ensuring equal participation for the Jews in American national life. As he saw it, a combative collective Jewish mode of action vis-à-vis Nazism did not in any way change the approach symbolized by The Temple's concentric-circle logo. On the contrary, the need to focus during that period on the inner Jewish circle actually entailed further emphasis on the outer, humanistic circle.

At first glance, the inner Jewish circle of mass demonstrations against the Nazi regime drew the main attention; speakers at these demonstrations did not hesitate to stress the fearsome danger embodied by the anti-Jewish legislation in Germany. Silver led this combative Jewish effort

4. For more on the boycott movement, see Arad (2000, 104–9); Berman (1990); Cohen (1972, 161–66); Gottlieb (1982).

despite harsh criticism from American-Jewish establishment organizations, such as the American Jewish Committee, B'nai B'rith, and the Union of American Hebrew Congregations. These organizations opposed what they viewed as a dangerous emphasis on the Jews' marginal status—a tactic liable to harm German Jewry and be used as a weapon by American anti-Semites. Silver mounted a vigorous rebuttal to this criticism, which he believed indicated a lack of confidence in Jews' ability to participate equally, without forfeiting Jewish identity, in American national discourse.

At the same time, however, he was also striving to position the anti-Nazi campaign within the broader American circle. This approach was already evident immediately after his appointment as chairman of the movement. The boycott movement had been founded in May 1933 by Abraham Coralnik and Samuel Untermyer. Silver was appointed chairman of the movement's board of directors six months later in November 1933, and his first acts were to change the organization's name and obtain registered association status for it. The movement's original name was the American League for the Defense of Jewish Rights; when it became a registered association, Silver changed it to the Non-Sectarian Anti-Nazi League to Champion Human Rights. Clearly, in this new name Silver was careful not to call attention to the collective, sectoral character of the struggle on behalf of Nazism's victims or to identify those victims as Jewish. In a similar way, the association's charter declared its primary goal to be that of promoting human rights and fighting religious and racial discrimination; the struggle on behalf of German Jewry was not mentioned at all.

The measures taken by the boycott movement were all in a similar spirit, addressing Jewish interests in a combative manner, but in a universalistic grab. This duality was exemplified in a mass rally—attended by some fifteen thousand people—that took place in Chicago in December 1933. The public resolution with which the rally concluded, while affirming the danger that Nazism posed to freedom and to Western civilization, failed to mention the concrete threat that it posed to European Jewry. Moreover, most of those invited to address the demonstrators were non-Jews, and this further contributed to the nonsectarian image that the organizers wished the rally to project. At the same time, however, Silver's choice of words, while delivering the keynote speech, indicates that the event took place in an emotional atmosphere of pained and anxious intra-Jewish dialogue:

> Just why are we so aroused, so deeply stirred? Just why are we so passionately indignant at what has happened and is happening in Germany? After all, we are not unaccustomed to persecution. Many pages of our history are red with the blood of Jewish martyrs. What makes this latest chapter in the story of the age-old persecution of Israel so much more horrible and dreadful? (Silver 1963a)

In answer to the above question, Silver was careful to identify the Nazi threat to Jewish survival as unprecedented in terms of the denial of social participation. For the first time in history, Silver maintained, Jews were being confined within a medieval-style ghetto not by a backward, dictatorial society, but by a society that, on the face of it, had already passed the point of no return of establishing its attendant democratic institutions. For Silver, this precedent seemed especially dangerous because it raised the possibility that democracy, once achieved, could be abandoned and social progress reversed. Should the Nazi precedent come to fruition, then American Jews would no longer be able to take their civil status for granted; they would have to resign themselves to permanent marginality. From Silver's point of view this was an intolerable scenario, and American Jews, he proclaimed, must not reconcile themselves to it.

One finds a similar outlook in yet another of Silver's speeches, this time at a gala dinner held in early 1934 by the boycott movement in honor of William Green, president of the American Federation of Labor. In an address honoring the labor federation leader, Silver sought to persuade his listeners that the boycott movement's struggle against Nazi anti-Jewish legislation was, essentially, a struggle aimed at safeguarding democratic institutions as such.

> It is . . . no accident of history that Nazism, which is the implacable foe of the Jewish people, is also the implacable foe of organized labor. . . . The Jewish people is, therefore, fighting in self-defense against this rising tide of political reaction, national chauvinism and racial intolerance. But other groups, too, must wage a similar defensive war against this

> self-same menace, particularly trade unions which are the first to succumb whenever Fascism triumphs. . . . For every anti-Semite, is under the skin, an enemy of freedom and of the working class. (Silver 1963a)

As Silver was making a reputation for himself in the sphere of Jewish activism, he increasingly found it more important to dissociate himself from possible isolationist forms of that activism. As the decade wore on, Silver's tendency to focus his Jewish-oriented efforts on promoting Zionism, rather than on combating Nazism and anti-Semitism, offered him an efficient means of implementing this duality. Zionism, from his point of view, provided American Jews with a context for opposing Nazism and anti-Semitism combatively, but without highlighting Jewish otherness. On the contrary, it projected images of indigenousness and belonging that connected Jews with American society as a whole and legitimized their integration within that society.

Thus, as Silver became increasingly involved in the anti-Nazi American-Jewish struggle, he became more aware of the need to adopt an alternative American-Zionist approach—one that fought against labeling the Jew as foreign and different. An ostensibly surprising example of this trend can be found in a Purim sermon given in 1936 (Silver 1967a). In the title of the sermon, "But Mordecai Bowed Not Down" (Esther 3:2), Silver sought to convey a message of collective Jewish activism, one that was necessary in light of the mounting anti-Semitic Nazi decrees in Germany. According to Silver, the lesson that should be learned from the book of Esther was that the rescue of the Jewish people from Haman's schemes was a result of the courage that Mordecai displayed in his faith and refusal to bow down; these were also the qualities that would have to mark the Jewish people's struggle in contending with Nazism: "The Jew in these trying times must remember the lesson and not . . . bow down to untoward circumstances." In Silver's view, the Purim holiday represented a recurring story in history, from the days of Pharaoh to the days of Nazism—a story of a Jewish minority living peacefully until its fate was reversed without warning. On the face of it, this was a view that presented anti-Semitism as a recurring historical phenomenon that periodically threatened Jewish life in the Diaspora. However, in the second part of the speech, Silver completely turned around this deterministic message. In his view, it was incumbent on the Jews to fight courageously like Mordecai and Esther; however, they had to do so by expressing their faith in the universalistic values of democracy: "any Jew, who . . . does not fight for democratic human life, is underwriting his own suicide." Silver described this latter struggle as an objective much more critical than the Zionist objective of bringing the Jews from Nazi Germany to the shelter being built in Palestine. He called on the Jews of Germany to remain in place lest their immigration be perceived as abandoning the principled liberal struggle for democracy.

In order to understand the significance of this statement regarding the lesser value of immigration to Palestine, it should be compared with an opposite statement made by Ben-Gurion about two years later. In December 1938, Ben-Gurion was to speak out sharply against Britain's refusal to permit some ten thousand Jewish children from Austria and Germany to immigrate to Palestine, and instead to permit a similar number of children to enter Britain. Ben-Gurion, who, similar to Silver and despite the rhetoric employed by the two, still could not imagine the fate of annihilation that would be suffered by the Jews if they should remain in place, viewed the attempts to save the children from the decrees of the Nazi regime as of lesser value than the possibility of their immigration to Palestine. He therefore declared at a meeting of his labor party's Central Committee that "if I knew that it would be possible to save all the children of Germany by moving them to England, and only half of them by transferring them to Palestine . . . I would choose the second option, because we have to take into account not only these children, but also the historical balance of the Jewish people" (Ben-Gurion 1938). Silver also assigned great importance to the "historical balance of the Jewish people"; however, in his eyes, at least in 1936, before the Holocaust, the supreme collective interest of the Jewish people did not lie in immigration to Palestine, but rather in the equal participation of the German Jews in all realms of life in their non-Jewish surroundings. He feared that the attempts to rescue the Jews of Germany and bring them to Palestine would convey a message of despair concerning the ability of the Jews in Germany or any other country to fully participate in their non-Jewish surroundings. He therefore disapproved of the solution of leaving Germany and argued that the activism and courage required of the Jews in light of the mounting Nazi decrees should be manifested in conveying a message of uncompromising battle against seclusion and prejudice.

> Even if we get two or three million Jews out of countries of Europe and settle them in Palestine that does not solve the problem for the rest of the Jews who are going to remain in the Diaspora. . . . The Nazis prepare destruction for the Jewish people, but there is a law of history which operates not only in Shushan but in Berlin. And that law of history says that in the long last, bigotry, intolerance and hate do not win the day . . . in the long last, it is the ideals of freedom, good will and tolerance that will win in these days.

Silver continued to call on the German Jews not to flee from Germany in a number of sermons given during that period (Silver 1935, 1936b, 1938a, 1938b). In his view, the main danger with which the Jewish collective had to contend at the time was the peril of surrendering to the anti-Semitic demand to push Jews out of civil society. He preached a Diaspora-Zionist message, which viewed the strengthening of a national Jewish consciousness as a means of ensuring the equal participation of Jews in German civil society, and emphasized the shared interest of all enlightened forces in the existence of a society in which every individual and every group had the right to equal participation. However, as the situation deteriorated and the danger of the annihilation of European Jewry began to materialize, it became extremely implausible to continue to preach that the Jews of Germany should continue to adhere to a diasporic national struggle aimed at defending their right to equal participation in German society. This difficulty was liable to reinforce deterministic assumptions of despair at the promises of emancipation. Silver was well aware of this danger, as can be seen in his speech at the B'nai B'rith convention of May 1937 (Silver 1937). Throughout the speech, he attacked those who saw the rise of Nazism and anti-Semitism as a deterministic trend. He called for a shift from a "negative" emphasis on anti-Jewish hostility to a "positive" emphasis based on fostering a Jewish life that was integrated with its non-Jewish surroundings.

> It is the easiest thing in the world . . . to stampede people into joining temples and societies and into giving money for relief by frightening them with anti-Semitism . . . but it's the most dangerous thing in the world, because . . . ultimately you will give the Jew in America a feeling . . . of being in every sense different from every other citizen in the United States. . . . You will be forcing him, psychically, into a self-made spiritual ghetto. . . . We ought to stop thinking of ourselves apprehensively as an isolated camp in the midst of a hundred and twenty millions of other people. . . . We ought to continue to think of ourselves . . . as being integrally and essentially part and parcel of this great America.

Silver's approach was not unusual among American Jews of the time. The rising contrast between the expectations of social acceptance and the anti-Semitic threat created immense pressure among American Jews to promote a response to anti-Semitism that was not based on the vantage point of a "victim" on the margins of social discourse (Shiff 2009). One of the popular initiatives that reflected this trend was the "quarantine treatment" approach led in those years by Solomon Fineberg, a Reform rabbi and member of the American Jewish Committee. The path of action recommended by Fineberg was to avoid at all costs battling against anti-Semitism from a sense of fear and affront that was characteristic of the victim, and instead to view anti-Semitism as a kind of social disease that all citizens, Jews and non-Jews alike, must struggle against and isolate (Fineberg 1943; Shiff 2005, 141–47). Although in the course of the 1940s this approach gradually became the main path for most American-Jewish organizations battling against anti-Semitism, in Silver's view, this represented a "hush-hush policy" and an attempt to refrain from drawing attention to collective Jewish concerns. Consequently, the dilemma that Silver faced was between the danger of overemphasizing the different nature of the anti-Semitic Nazi threat facing Jews as opposed to non-Jews, and the fear that refraining from pointing to this difference would be interpreted as expressing Jewish self-effacement (Silver 1967d, 116).

Early evidence of Silver's attempt to cope with this dilemma can be seen in his 1936 speech in Chicago on the occasion of the seventy-fifth anniversary celebrations of the founding of the Sinai Congregation, one of the oldest and most respected Reform synagogues (*Chicago Jewish Chronicle* 1936; *Sentential* 1936; Silver 1936a). He spoke immediately after a speech by James McDonald, who at the time was the most prominent non-Jewish American figure identified with the struggle for the European refugees. Between 1933 and the end of 1935, he served as Lord High Commissioner for Refugees for the League of Nations. He resigned from this post about ten months before the speech at Sinai Congregation, issuing a sharp condemnation of the racist policies of Nazi Germany and equally condemning the indifference of the free world. Based on this reputation, McDonald could appear confidently at a festive Jewish event and criticize the insufficient mobilization of the American-Jewish community on behalf of the Jews of Germany. In McDonald's eyes, the greatest peril lay in the indifference of the enlightened world and the reluctance of the Jews to combat this indifference. At first glance, McDonald's speech appears to express a view similar to Silver's, and yet when Silver alluded to the internal Jewish awakening that was urged by McDonald, he focused his attention elsewhere. Indeed, at this difficult time, many Jews returned to the synagogue, he asserted. Now, when they picked up the prayer book, they no longer saw it as a collection of anachronistic prayers, but as a relevant book, in which the prayers for mercy and the mentions of slavery and persecution touched the heart and the mind. However, it would be a serious error for the return to Jewish heritage to be based on the current bitter experience of Jewish life.

> We have synagogues *not because* of anti-Semites but *in spite of them*! We are Jews *not because of* but *in spite* of persecution! It is the positive, the life giving, spirit-sustaining ideals imbedded in our religion . . . which have sustained and inspirited our people through these long centuries, none of which ever mind a Hitler! (emphases in the original) (Silver 1936a)

Silver regarded as dangerous the idea of turning the identification with the suffering of the Jewish refugees into a means of Jewish mobilization. He considered this a "negative" response, which could build up walls of suspicion and deviate from Jewish heritage as he interpreted it. This was still not, however, as cohesive an outlook as Silver's "bridges and walls" outlook would become in the 1950s. At this stage, it mainly referred to expressions of unease and opposition to turning the identification with the suffering of the refugees into a "negative" motive for strengthening Jewish solidarity. This unease was to mount as the question of the Jewish refugees became increasingly desperate and as the indifference of the democratic world to their suffering became more blatant.

The challenge posed by this issue was particularly heightened in the second half of the 1930s, after the arena of philanthropic activity on behalf of the victims of Nazism became the focus of American-Zionist activity and, in particular, the focus of Silver's Zionist leadership. In 1935, he was appointed as chairman of the Cleveland Jewish Welfare Fund and continued to serve in this post for about six years. At the beginning of 1938, he was appointed as president of the United Palestine Appeal (UPA), and was later chosen as deputy chairman of the United Jewish Appeal (UJA). Silver's position as president of the UPA was his first national leadership position in the American-Zionist arena. The centrality of the refugee issue turned Jewish Palestine into the most popular fundraising cause among American Jewry, and this had ramifications for the rise in the standing of the Zionist movement versus non-Zionist organizations.[5] The popularity of Jewish Palestine as the only possible sanctuary for refugees was the main factor in the reestablishment of the UPA at the beginning of 1936, and it helped Silver in late 1938 to push from a position of strength toward renewed cooperation with the non-Zionists within the UJA. It was this popularity that also helped him in 1941 in his struggle to thwart the attempts of non-Zionist organizations—the JDC (Joint Distribution Committee) and later of the CJFWF (Council of Jewish Federations and Welfare Fund)—to limit the percentage of funds intended for Jewish Palestine. Certainly, the concern among the American Jews for the Jewish refugees, many of whom were immediate relatives, was the driving force behind the increased popularity of the Zionist issue among American Jewry and a central component of Silver's Zionist activity at the time.

5. Between 1933 and 1939, the membership of the American-Zionist movement grew from nine thousand to forty-three thousand; the Hadassah Zionist women's organization grew from twenty-four thousand to forty-three thousand (Halperin 1961, 32).

This centrality of the refugee issue compelled Silver to contend with pessimistic conclusions of Jewish foreignness and inability to integrate outside of Jewish Palestine. Early echoes of this could be heard in his inauguration address upon assuming the post of UPA president on January 22, 1938. In his speech, Silver warned against Zionist propaganda that focused on the sphere of humanitarian aid to refugees, and instead called to make the building of Jewish Palestine into an educational tool that would encourage the American Jew to take part in American society and not to see himself as separate or isolated from it. Another testimony to Silver's attitude on the refugee issue can be found in two radio broadcasts that he made in 1939 and aired on NBC's national network. Silver appeared on the radio broadcasts in his capacity as one of the deputy chairpersons of the UJA. The first broadcast was given on March 11, 1939 under the heading "the morals of aid to refugees" (Silver 1939) and quite surprisingly made no mention of the Jewish identity of the refugees "who are wandering tonight . . . in quest of new homes." Instead, it focused on the broad common denominator of all the refugees, "young and old, Jewish and Christian, Catholic and Protestant." Silver underscored that the indifference of the world to the suffering of the refugees posed the main danger to human society, and rather than alluding to anti-Semitism as the reason for this indifference, he focused on the bloody series of wars since the start of the twentieth century, which had "brutalized the world and rendered it callous and indifferent . . . to human sufferings." The impression arises that focusing attention on the different status of the Jewish victims still appeared to him as contradicting the proper path required to cope with Nazi barbarism. He maintained that "the response we make to the plight of the world's refugee today will be the measure of our devotion to a united humanity, of our recognition to human solidarity and inter-dependence."

Only a week passed between the first radio address and the second broadcast on NBC, but the difference between them was striking; this time Silver spoke explicitly about the problem of the Jewish refugees (Silver 1967d). He listed three events that separated the two broadcasts. The first event was the final occupation of Czechoslovakia by Nazi troops on March 14, an event that Silver described as a defeat suffered by the democratic world in its battle against fascism. The second event pertained to reports about the intensification of anti-Jewish legislation in Hungary. This time Silver expressed the fear that many of Hungary's Jews would be forced to join the mounting wave of Jewish emigrants trapped on European soil with no way out and no real help from the free world. The third event was the most worrying according to Silver. Following the failure of the Round Table Conference convened by the British colonial secretary at St. James's Palace in London, Britain published its proposal on the issue of Palestine—a proposal that was to become its official White Paper policy within two months on May 17. The main points of the plan, referring to a reduction of Jewish immigration to Palestine to an annual average of fifteen thousand over five years, were already published in March, and in Silver's eyes this was tantamount to blocking the only place of refuge that could save the Jewish refugees from the stranglehold tightening around them. From his perspective, the ramifications were not limited to physical dangers, but also included the danger of exclusion, which he felt threatened not only the Jewish refugees in Europe, but also Jews as a group everywhere, including in the United States.

Against this background, Silver felt that he has no choice but to directly address the Jewish identity of the refugees. Still, he took care to caution that the tragic fate of Czechoslovakia should make it clear that the organized attack on the Jewish people was not an isolated occurrence, but rather part of a broad and malicious plan to attack the rights and the independence of all minority groups, which was a guise for a cunning strategy aimed at destabilizing from within all liberal societies. Silver called on the citizens of the United States to view the struggle against Nazism as part of "a bitter skirmish in the age-old irrepressible conflict between the religions and moral traditions of mankind, as represented in Judaism and Christianity . . . and the indurate traditions of paganism symbolized in the concept of state idolatry." He promised that although the state of the democracies appeared dire, "in the long run, man will accept no substitutes for the autonomy of his spirit." In the two concluding paragraphs of the broadcast, he elucidated this message and urged his fellow Jews "to see our problem against the background of the entire world's problem . . . for us Jews . . . this age of surge and thunder, of suffering and menace, should be a compelling and undeniable challenge, not disillusionment or despair."

Evidence of Silver's call to view the Jewish question in the broader context of the assault on Western civilization can be seen in another speech he gave at Sinai Congregation in Chicago, just one day after the United States entered World War II (Silver 1941–1942).[6] Silver explained that Jewish heritage defined as a "crisis" only an event whose impact exceeded the concrete danger posed to the Jewish people; therefore, it was incumbent upon the Jews to understand the current situation as expressing a crisis that pertained not only to them, but also to the very existence of enlightenment and democracy. "A whole continent of social values which we regarded as the very quintessence of civilized living—peace, justice, brotherhood, freedom, intellectual freedom, elementary human decencies . . . seems to have dropped out of the world like some lost Atlantis." The reason the Nazis had invested such great resources in disseminating the hatred of the Jews did not stem from their hostility toward several hundreds of thousands of Jews in Germany, but because they viewed anti-Semitism as an effective means of weakening the internal solidarity of democratic societies. This larger context pointed to the proper way for Jews to perceive the issue of Jewish survival:

> We do not fight to survive. We will survive anyhow . . . we can accept the role of passivity . . . and creep into crook and crevice and wait and hope for the passing of the wrath . . . [But there is] too much of the . . . prophetic urgency of our tradition, for us to take that road . . . We know why we are being attacked. We know that we have become the symbol in this war. Hitler knows it . . . It is the ancient struggle between the jungle man, the man who lives by his sword and for his sword . . . and the man who selects spiritual values and good will and collaboration with all other human beings. (Silver 1941–1942)

This call for a combative Jewish struggle bearing universalistic messages was not unusual in the Reform discourse of the time. An example

6. For an earlier version, see Silver (1941b, 13–52).

of this can be found in a speech given by the president of Hebrew Union College, Julian Morgenstern, back in October 1934, at the start of the institution's academic year (Morgenstern 1934). Morgenstern, who defined himself as a non-Zionist and at times even as an anti-Zionist, described in similar universalistic terms the necessary courageous Jewish fight against Nazi Germany:

> Judaism versus . . . Hilterism! The antithesis is complete and antipodal. The struggle is titanic and beyond all compromise. The stake is the world and the continued life of humanity and the progress of human culture. . . . Intuitively, perhaps with the unreasoning instinct of the beast, Nazism had rightly singled out the Jew and Judaism as it truest basic, uncompromising antagonist. . . . Very well! Judaism takes up the challenge. . . . The battle will be long and bitter and the suffering great. But again we are enlisted in the cause which our fathers hallowed; again we bear our heritage proudly and with heads erect.

Morgenstern's anti-Zionist affiliation was not accidental. In the internal Reform discourse, the combative universalistic approach was often related to a tone of disapproval and criticism toward Zionism, at least toward such aspects of Zionism that were liable to paint the proactive Jewish struggle in hues of seclusion and suspicion toward the promises of emancipation. Indeed, Morgenstern himself did not hesitate to point out the lines of similarity between Zionism and Nazism. He described the Zionist reaction to Nazism as reminiscent of the Jewish behavior in the days of the reforms of Ezra and Nehemiah and argued that these reforms, particularly the expulsion of the foreign wives and their children, were one of the darkest and most shameful events in all of Jewish history. This was a show of nationalist isolationism so extreme that it was equaled in intensity only by Nazi ideology. He warned against the deterioration of Zionism to a similar extreme reaction and argued that a reclusive response of this kind effectively reflected the adoption of views that were foreign in nature to Judaism.

Silver was not as outspoken as Morgenstern in his criticism of the reclusive trends in Zionism and would not have thought of comparing them to Nazi ideology. However, he certainly saw a real danger in the separatist Zionist views that became popular in those years against the backdrop of the wave of Nazism and anti-Semitism. At the same time, however, more than ever before, Silver presented Zionism as the only sphere of action that enabled a combative universalistic Jewish effort to contend with the Nazi threat.[7] An example of this ever-growing emphasis can be seen in a Hanukkah sermon Silver gave to his congregation on December 21, 1941, about ten days after the United States joined the war against Japan and Germany (Silver 1941a). At this peak hour of American patriotism, the parallel between the historical national struggle of the Maccabees and the American battle was given center stage. It pertained not only to the shared objectives of freedom and democracy, but also to the fact that America, like the adherents of Jewish nationalism, viewed its struggle against Nazism as based on the reciprocal relationship between its own particular interests and the struggle toward universal justice and liberty. "America today is fighting not only for America, but just as the Maccabees for the spiritual Americas all over the world."

Silver explained the reasons for the downfall suffered by the United States at Pearl Harbor by the attitude of indifference and cynicism toward the democratic way that had overtaken American society as a result of the atmosphere of plenty and life of comfort. This phenomenon, he said, was equivalent to the Hellenism that the historical spirit of the Maccabees had to overcome, much as the national Zionist advocacy of his own time had to do in its attempt to overcome the defeatist Jewish mentality. The spirit of Zionism that fought for an inner spiritual revolution in the Jewish people should serve as a model for America upon the start of the war against Japan and Germany. Zionist activism, if it should act as the spearhead in the battle for the values of liberty and general human fraternity, could become a model for the American patriotic struggle against the winds of today's "Hellenism."

7. When the United States began to gradually abandon its neutrality policy at the end of 1940, Silver was among the first to establish a Zionist stance according to which the British policy of turning away the refugee ships that tried to reach Jewish Palestine undermined the very legitimacy of the war against Nazism as a struggle for enlightenment and democracy (Gal 1991).

Silver honed this idea in a sermon given toward the end of February 1942 (Silver 1942). He discussed the wave of internal criticism that swept over the United States against the backdrop of military defeats to the Japanese army, mainly the fall of Singapore, and presented this type of complaint as similar to the slave and exilic defeatist Jewish mentality. Only people who are free in spirit are willing to assume responsibility in the struggle for freedom and do not look for people to blame after every setback or failure. Thus, the Zionist aspiration to cultivate the mentality of Jews who were free in mind and in spirit, rather than a reclusive mentality that casts the blame on the world's hostility, was supposed to become a model for the general American patriotic struggle.

As the war escalated, along with the unfolding of the terrible news about the fate of European Jewry, the universalistic messages of the Diaspora-Zionist approach were to become increasingly crucial and meaningful for Silver and his American supporters. Without them, they might face an intolerable option of turning the most basic feelings of Jewish solidarity into a source of suspicion and mistrust in general American solidarity. From this standpoint, the meaning of the Diaspora-Zionist struggle was summed up in the need to refute the contention that there was an unbridgeable gap between Jewish solidarity and American patriotism, and in the effort to transform the Jewish response to the Holocaust from a struggle that might emphasize Jewish marginality into a struggle that highlighted general American affiliation and patriotism.

5

The 1940s

The Holocaust as Political Leverage

THE 1940S were Silver's peak years as a Zionist leader. During this period he based his Zionist stance on an idealized hyphenated American-Jewish identity—one that affirmed the reciprocal relationship between Jewish solidarity and American patriotism. This stance was in tune with the unique challenges faced by American Jews of that era: America's entry into World War II dictated a form of American patriotism from which any deviation was perceived as treacherous; at the same time, the Holocaust intensified an urgent sense of American-Jewish solidarity. Silver's growing popularity among the American-Jewish public was rooted in his presumption to devise a reaction to the Holocaust that turned feelings of growing Jewish solidarity into legitimate and proud expressions of American patriotism.

This is how one should understand the stance Silver took in leading the opposition to the American-Zionist leadership under Wise—a leadership perceived by many as hesitant to confront the Roosevelt administration and demand concrete action on behalf of European Jewry (Feingold 1995). Silver's main allegation against Wise was that, by failing to challenge the administration, he had unwittingly promoted an approach that distinguished between so-called narrow Jewish interests and legitimate American interests. The troubling reports that began to arrive in late 1942 regarding the annihilation of European Jewry made this distinction an intolerable one, both to Silver and to large portions of American Jewry. The message that one risked conveying by failing to confront the government was that Jewish existential concerns, however urgent and fundamental, had no place within the framework of mainstream America.

Silver's public strength lay in his success at using Zionism as a means of transforming American-Jewish concerns into a determined demand on behalf of American-Jewish citizens for thoroughgoing rectification of Jewish marginality. This is exemplified in a speech delivered on May 2, 1943 at the National Conference for Palestine (Silver 1943a). In the speech, Silver linked Zionist demands with opposition to American policy in Algeria subsequent to the latter's liberation from Vichy forces in November 1942; he protested the fact that the Vichy regime's anti-Jewish laws continued to be upheld under American auspices.[1] Silver connected American acquiescence in Algeria's continued enforcement of discriminatory legislation with the American policy of evading the issue of a Jewish national home. In both cases, Silver felt, America had allied itself with the enemies of democracy and weakened those striving to ensure democracy's ultimate triumph over Nazism. He cautioned that, should the United States maintain such policies, its war against the Nazis risked transformation into a mere power struggle. He maintained that only by conducting itself justly toward the Jewish people—a national group lacking any power and the one destined to emerge the most severely devastated by the war—could the United States pretend to be acting out of unselfish determination to safeguard democratic values as its primary objective in the war against Nazism.

Silver's address was delivered against the background of disillusionment and disappointment that prevailed among American Jews in the wake of the April 1943 Bermuda Conference. Despite previous hopes, no rescue plans were seriously discussed at the conference, and the American and British participants rejected all proposals that might involve diverting resources from the war effort.[2] In contrast to Wise, who cautioned

1. Silver expressed fury that, even after American pressure had forced General André Giraud to annul the racial laws in November 1943, he continued to implement a policy of discrimination against Jews.

2. On the disappointment expressed in American Jewish public discourse regarding the results of the Bermuda Conference, see Gorny (2009, 161–62, 168–69).

against any public statements that might cast Roosevelt in the light of an enemy of the Jewish people, Silver took the opposite line, decrying Roosevelt's empty condemnations of the Nazis and declaring him disloyal to his own stated cause of safeguarding justice and democracy (Silver 1943a). In order to grasp the real significance of Silver's struggle against the conciliatory tactics practiced by the Zionist establishment under Wise, one must distinguish between the recriminations exchanged between the two and the tragic reality of American Jewry's powerlessness. As the Bermuda Conference demonstrated, no camp, neither the more activist nor the more moderate, possessed the degree of influence necessary to propel the American government into action. Silver essentially acknowledged this in an account of the failed struggle to create a Jewish army. He admitted that the efforts would have been unsuccessful whether they were led by the American-Zionist establishment or by the much more militant Bergson Group.[3] Silver himself played an active role in the Jewish army initiative and was one of the key figures behind the Reform movement's groundbreaking endorsement of the issue—one that caused a major rupture within the Reform camp.[4] Still, he was forced to admit that, regardless of the tactics employed, the various Jewish groups involved had run up against the same brick wall.

It is against the background of this collective powerlessness that Silver's brand of Zionist activism may be appreciated in all its complexity. Silver's combative rhetoric notwithstanding, he was fully aware that the combative option could bring no immediate relief to European Jewry. His Zionist efforts to lift the White Paper immigration restrictions, whether conducted diplomatically and behind the scenes or combatively and publicly, were relevant primarily to the postwar period. Silver's criticism of Wise had very little to do with the issue of immediate aid to European Jewry, but rather with the way in which American Jewry should acknowledge its inability to take immediate and concrete action on behalf

3. For information about the Bergson group, see Wyman and Medoff (2002).

4. The anti-Zionist American Council for Judaism was founded as a result of the Reform decision to support a Jewish army resolution.

European Jewry. Silver felt that this powerlessness should be openly acknowledged and used as a vehicle for protesting Jewish marginality and demanding far-reaching change.

In order to illustrate the kind of struggle that the Jews, in their impotence, would need to wage, Silver quoted Marshal Ferdinand Foch's famous words just prior to the Second Battle of the Marne during World War I: "Hard pressed on my right. My center is yielding. Impossible to maneuver. Situation excellent. I attack." Disdainfully alluding to Zionist timidity under Wise, Silver praised Marshal Foch's approach as precisely the one that a responsible Jewish leadership should be adopting at that time. On the face of it, this made little sense. The fact that Silver's combative alternative would not have brought about a tangible change in American policy might actually have accentuated American Jews' sense of marginality, underscoring the discrepancy between their mobilization for the war effort and their inability to pressure their own government to rescue the Jews of Europe. In this context, Silver's speech of May 1943 is particularly important. A close reading of it indicates the effort that Silver invested in turning Jewish powerlessness into a weapon in the Zionist struggle to resolve the problem of Jewish marginality and helplessness. Silver ended his address with a kind of "call to arms"; if earlier he had quoted Marshal Foch's battle cry, now he delved even deeper into military history, finding inspiration for the Jewish struggle in a quote attributed to the mythic fifteenth-century Czech hero Jan Žižka. The latter is said to have made a deathbed request that his skin be used for war drums to lead the Hussite troops into battle. For Silver, Žižka provided a model for the way in which American Jews should be using the Holocaust in their Zionist quest. Silver was calling for the battle to be waged despite the complete absence of hope: no "Miracle of the Marne" was going to bring about the immediate deliverance of European Jewry. Indeed, Silver regarded Zionism not as a means to directly resolve the immediate problem of aiding European Jews, but rather to conclusively end the fundamental problem of Jewish helplessness. His allusion to Žižka—his call to transform the suffering of the Holocaust victims into the "battle-drum" of Zionism—was an attempt to turn the cry of despair into a fearsome weapon that would be capable of transforming a flawed reality in which the world could look with equanimity on the murder of Jews and in which the United States could fail to treat the existential concern and solidarity of its Jewish citizens with due seriousness.

This activist approach differed from that of Ben-Gurion and the Yishuv leadership. Silver, like Ben-Gurion, saw the creation of a Jewish national home as the key to ending Jewish marginality. However, he differed from the latter by not taking a deterministic view of Jewish marginality outside of a future Jewish state. On the contrary, he was determined to use the demand for a Jewish national home as a means of remedying Jewish marginality not just in Palestine, but in the Diaspora as well. The foregoing provides the perspective necessary for an understanding of the American intra-Zionist struggle between Wise and Silver, which culminated in the competition between the two for leadership of the AZEC in August 1943. Silver's supporters turned the saying "Put not your trust in princes" (Psalm 146:3) into Silver's campaign slogan.[5] Although they were referring to Roosevelt and his administration, they were not by any means expressing distrust of American society. Had that been the case, they would automatically have been rebuffed by the American-Jewish public, which was then undergoing a process of integration into that society. The slogan became popular because it appeared to warn against a conciliatory approach that, by seeking favors from the government, perpetuated Jewish marginality. The mass appeal of Silver's alternative was that it utilized maximalist Zionist demands in order to transform a minority group's quest for tolerance into a struggle that called for the conclusive resolution of Jewish collective marginality.

Silver's activist stance was expressed most emphatically at the American Jewish Conference of August 1943, an event whose purpose was to generate broad support for Jewish demands for action to aid European Jewry.[6] Even prior to the conference, the non-Zionists who led the American

5. Silver's supporters were headed by Emanuel Neumann and Rabbi Irving Miller (Neumann 1976, 203–4).

6. The preparatory conference took place in Pittsburgh on January 23–24. Thirty-two organizations participated, declaring that the goal of the conference was to secure Jewish status in the aftermath of the war.

Jewish Committee tried to ensure that it took place in an atmosphere of caution and moderation. The head of the Committee, Judge Joseph M. Proskauer, attempted to persuade Wise to pressure Henry Monsky, president of B'nai B'rith and organizer of the American Jewish Conference, to postpone the conference by a year. To justify the delay, he quoted government officials on the undesirability of Jewish preoccupation with narrow group interests while the United States was at war. During the conference deliberations, as fear grew that Wise might strike a deal with the American Jewish Committee, Silver was summoned urgently before the plenum (Neumann 1976, 208–9). In a speech that would later be remembered as one of the most important of his life, he electrified the hundreds of conference delegates and led them to near-unanimous support for maximalist Zionist demands—namely, that the White Paper be annulled and that the Jewish people's right to a national home in Palestine be recognized (Silver 1943b). The fundamentally American meaning that Silver attached to the demand for a Jewish national home—and the one that enthralled his audience, moving many of them to tears (Orian 1982, 104–6)—urged a paradigm shift from preoccupation with Jewish powerlessness vis-à-vis the destruction of European Jewry. Silver cautioned his audience against the tendency to fixate on the European tragedy; this would constitute a form of self-flagellation, a continual reopening of wounds. Instead, he urged the delegates to see their highly charged identification with European Jewry not as something that relegated them to the status of charity-seekers vis-à-vis the American government, but rather as an authentic expression of American patriotism and civic responsibility.

This latter approach is also the proper context in which to understand Silver's two-year struggle to bring about a joint resolution by the Senate and House of Representatives on Palestine.[7] On the face of it, the goal of this struggle—to reaffirm the support expressed by Congress in 1922 for the creation of a Jewish national home in Palestine—hardly justified the tremendous effort invested in it. Silver fought relentlessly, even in the face

7. The congressional struggle, which included three rounds, started on January 1944 and ended on December 19, 1945.

of opposition mounted repeatedly by senior figures in the administration, including the secretary of state, the secretary of defense, and the US Army chief of staff, who personally attended meetings of the foreign affairs committees of both houses of Congress to warn of the negative implications that the proposed resolution would entail for American security interests. Silver stood steadfast,[8] despite the political harm that this entailed for the Zionist cause and the political price that he had to pay for it.[9] In later years, Silver and his supporters would describe their congressional efforts as the foundation for broad public and political support that ultimately led President Truman to back the creation of the State of Israel. This hindsight, however, is insufficient to explain the importance attached to the resolution campaign while it was going on. Specifically, it does not explain Silver's willingness to stick with the struggle despite the hostility that it elicited from the administration and its potential political damage to the Zionist cause—damage feared not only by Wise, but also by Ben-Gurion, who raised doubts regarding Silver's political acumen. In this context it is also important to note that when the resolution was finally passed by the Senate and the House of Representatives in December 1945, it had little public resonance and almost no practical political repercussions.

Despite first appearances, the goal of the congressional struggle was not merely to advance political Zionist interests. In retrospect, one finds evidence of this in an address from March 2, 1945 at an event held in Silver's honor by a group of loyal political activists. This group, in the wake of Silver's resignation from the AZEC, had founded a new organization, the Zionist Policy Committee. Silver's speech before the committee was intended to put forth his oppositional stance vis-à-vis the Zionist leadership under Wise (Silver 1949c). In his speech, Silver attached primary importance to the congressional support for a Jewish state. Referring to the indifference to Jewish pleas for action on behalf of European Jewry, he declared that only a reaffirmation of the mandate's intention to establish

8. About Silver's stance, see American Zionist Emergency Council (1944).

9. Silver was obliged to withdraw from the chairmanship of the AZEC for the first half of 1945, following a second failure to bring the proposed resolution to a Senate vote.

a Jewish national home could ensure the emergence of a new attitude toward the collective concerns of American Jews. Silver feared that in their quest to help their European brethren, American Jews would become permanently entrenched in the position of a favor-currying minority. By contrast, the cause of Jewish statehood constituted a political demand, formulated in the spirit of American democracy, to decisively address the problem of Jewish marginality. For Silver, the "success" of the pro-Zionist congressional resolution lay in the very fact that an overt political struggle had been waged vis-à-vis the president and his administration. In order to be true players in the American democratic game, American Jews would have to abandon the ignominious path of conciliation and forge a power base of organized public opinion.

From Silver's perspective, Congress was the ideal arena in which to pose Zionist demands in a manner that emphasized Jewish participation as legitimate players in the American democratic political game. Rather than asking for consideration on the part of the "authorities," Silver preferred to lead an all-out political struggle by a Jewish electorate. It should be noted that the joint-resolution battle was merely the culmination of wide-ranging political activity led by Silver with the participation of thousands of Jewish activists from all over the United States. This activity was based on an extensive network of local emergency councils that Silver had founded throughout the country. By early December 1943, the number of these councils had already passed one hundred; by January 1945, they would swell to four hundred. Together, they formed a well-oiled publicity machine that reached nearly every Jewish community of any consequence and aggressively pressured relevant congressional representatives. These operations also included a newspaper editorial campaign that generated hundreds of articles, radio broadcasts, and innumerable petitions mounted by intellectuals and academics. All of these efforts cast Zionism in the light of a broad, openly Jewish political cause during a period in which the pursuit of "narrow" Jewish ethnic interests was regarded by Jews and non-Jews as illegitimate. For Silver, and for the thousands of American Jews who took part in the campaign, the very fact that democratic mechanisms were being employed in order to place Jewish issues on the agenda was itself liberating; from this point of view, the public campaign was far more important than its results. Participation in the campaign was an act that enabled American Jews to express their particular concerns in a way that affirmed their integral role in mainstream American discourse.[10]

The value of the joint-resolution campaign was particularly evident on the partisan political front. The effort vis-à-vis Congress made it possible to portray Zionism as a bipartisan cause that transcended narrow Jewish interests. This effort reached its peak just prior to the November 1944 elections. Disregarding the strong reservations of Wise and then president of the ZOA, Israel Goldstein, Silver led an AZEC majority to approve a plan aimed at having pro-Zionist clauses included in the platforms of the Democratic and Republican parties whose conferences were being held in Chicago during June and July of that year. To ensure implementation of this decision, Silver personally oversaw the effort to have a Zionist clause included in the Republican Party platform. He installed himself, with a team of assistants, in a hotel facing the party headquarters, and over the course of a month interacted continuously with the platform committee, taking advantage of his strong personal relationship with Senator Taft, the committee chairman, and his ties with New York Governor Thomas Dewey, the Republican presidential candidate. This constituted a significant deviation from the main path of Jewish political activity as practiced during that period. Most American-Jewish leaders, first and foremost Wise, identified American-Jewish interests with the liberal-progressive approach of the Democratic Party. From their point of view, Silver's affiliation with the Republican Party ran counter to Jewish interests. They particularly focused their anger on the Republican Party platform's Zionist clause, which criticized Roosevelt's equivocation on the subject. They saw this intermingling of American state policy and "ethnic politics" as illegitimate. Silver counterattacked by calling his adversaries' commitment to the Democratic Party excessive; the implication was that it was they who were guilty of pursuing narrow partisan interests by hindering efforts to identify the Zionist cause with American state interests that transcended any partisan dispute.

10. On Silver's view of the struggle, see Neumann (1976, 218); Orian (1982, 144–45); Silver (1949g, 1963a).

The conflict intensified after Roosevelt's victory in the November 1944 election. From Silver's point of view, his effort to place the Zionist cause within a bipartisan consensus had enjoyed outstanding success. As he saw it, the pro-Zionist clauses embedded within the Republican and Democratic platforms, as well as the explicitly pro-Zionist statements made by both parties' presidential candidates, were direct outcomes of the political pressure that he had exerted. Silver was therefore determined to adhere to this tactic and to resubmit the resolution bill on Palestine to both houses of Congress. This time the Zionist establishment mounted a major rebellion; the ZOA and Hadassah made any new initiative conditional on the approval of the State Department or the president. Silver, for his part, refused to accept the ZOA leadership's authority, arguing that the current initiative had become at this stage a bipartisan one, not subject to the particular interests of any faction, whether Jewish or non-Jewish. At this point the inner Zionist conflict escalated beyond control, with each side trying to pull the Senate Foreign Relations Committee in the opposite direction. On December 11, the day of the decisive committee meeting, the conflict reached its peak. At the meeting, the secretary of state conveyed a personal statement from the president asking that the resolution not be approved; the committee members, who had already been receiving mixed messages from the warring Zionist factions, voted not to bring the bill before the Senate plenum. At this juncture, Wise and Silver were obviously pulling the AZEC in opposite directions. After several days of resignations and impeachment attempts, it became clear that a majority of the Zionist leaders opposed Silver's approach, and Silver was forced to resign. Silver, for his part, remained steadfast; in a December 20 address before the AZEC leadership, he explained that, although he had not acted in literal conformity with AZEC decisions, he had nevertheless expressed the will of the Jewish masses. He attacked Wise's conciliatory approach and called for Jewish relations with the administration to be reestablished on a basis of political power and the rules of the American democratic process.

This conflict between Silver and Wise exemplified two very different attitudes toward the democratic political game. Wise felt that the long-term Jewish interests would be best served through the realization of the Democratic Party's liberal-progressive platform, even when this entailed concession regarding collective Jewish interests. He believed that the Democrats' liberal ethos constituted the best possible safeguard against all forms of discrimination and injustice. This was the mindset that enabled him to accept the administration's contention that the best way to address the massacre of European Jewry was to mobilize a joint effort to overcome the Nazi threat to American democracy and to end the war as quickly as possible. Silver represented an almost completely opposing view. As he saw it, any state policy that did not make rescuing Jews its first priority would not be living up to America's humanistic-democratic ideal; it was thus a patriotic duty to fight such a policy. This is what explains Silver's readiness to confront the upper political echelon head on—not merely in the name of Zionism, but first and foremost in the name of America's democratic values.

For a short time it had seemed that Silver's resignation in late 1944 heralded a recovery for Wise's conciliatory approach. However, with Wise having been relegated to a symbolic role, Silver's resurgence on July 21, 1945 as the sole head of AZEC indicated that it was actually Silver's more combative form of Zionism that was now emerging as the dominant trend in American-Jewish public life. A major catalyst for this process was President Roosevelt's death on April 12, 1945 and the ensuing sense that a Zionist strategy based on Wise's relationship with Roosevelt was no longer viable. The feeling that the Zionist movement had lost its influence in the corridors of American power intensified when, because of US-British pressure, the "San Francisco Conference," at which the United Nations Charter was created, prohibited any official Zionist participation and refused to address the issue of Palestine.[11] In the eyes of many American Jews, this was seen as continuation of a policy of ignoring the collective Jewish plight—a policy that now, after the war, was more problematic than ever

11. Silver expressed his disappointment in a manifesto issued by the American Zionist Policy Committee on May 28, lamenting that even the rivers of Jewish blood that had recently flooded Europe were not enough to change British policy regarding Palestine. Silver's disappointment in their approach notwithstanding, Wise and Goldmann garnered major victories, most notably the frustration of an attempt by the Arab countries to annul the provisions of the League of Nations mandate system.

before. The inability to change their government's stance, even after the magnitude of the Nazi atrocity had been revealed, threatened to reinforce their sense of marginality. It was the combative approach espoused by Silver that provided a framework for expressing the growing frustration experienced by American Jews during the post-Holocaust period. Thus, in a speech at the AZEC Executive Committee, Silver affirmed that the stance to be taken vis-à-vis the American administration would not be one of supplication or reliance on its goodwill. Rather, the destruction of European Jewry would be employed as the most terrible and persuasive moral argument ever utilized in the history of the human race by a nation seeking to exercise its historical rights (Silver 1945b).

Silver's audacity in positing the Holocaust as a legitimate political tool provided an outlet for the growing number of American Jews who felt compelled to actively express their solidarity with the victims and survivors but who wished to do so without reinforcing their sense of collective powerlessness. The solution that Silver offered American Jewry can be found in a particularly clear form in his speech at the forty-eighth annual ZOA convention, held in Atlantic City on November 16–19, 1945 (Silver 1945a). After being introduced by his rival, Stephen Wise, as the sole candidate for the job, it was at this convention that Silver was elected to his first term as president of the ZOA. In his inaugural speech he presented a particularly accusatory line: the presentation of the Holocaust as iron-clad evidence against the United States for having allowed European Jewry to be massacred and for continuing, even after the war, to deny their legitimate claims.

> Our six million dead are a tragic commentary on the state of Christian morality and the responsiveness of Christian conciseness. . . . The contribution of our own country in the face of this greatest single human holocaust in modern history consisted . . . in sending away from its shores a shipload of helpless human beings to find their ultimate doom in the gas chambers of Auschwitz. . . . Many of these six million innocent victims might have been saved . . . if our government . . . had pressed Great Britain in the name of America's moral and legal commitment in the matter of Palestine to open those doors.

Ostensibly Silver's preoccupation with battling the American government reinforced Jewish self-perceptions of marginality and helplessness: "We were slaughtered by our enemies. We were betrayed by our friends. There was nothing that we could do," Silver admitted. He then immediately launched into a discussion of the post-Holocaust period: "So we turned our attention quickly to the remaining survivors. Surely these would be now saved." Silver did not present Jewish inaction during the Holocaust as an indication of inherent communal impotence, or even as grounds for Jewish guilt; rather, he portrayed it as yet another count in the indictment being mounted by enraged citizens against an ongoing failure of their elected government. Moreover, the second half of the statement posited concrete objectives for action, which was now in the power of American Jews to take on behalf of the surviving few. In effect, the possibility of present action made it legitimate for American Jews to avert their gaze from the spectacle of their powerlessness during the war. One might say that, by calling for collective Jewish mobilization to halt the government's policy of inaction, Silver was offering American Jews a chance at "atonement"; in effect, they were now presented with another opportunity to wage the struggle that they had been unable to launch during the Nazi era.

In accordance with this approach, Silver sought to delineate an American-Zionist mode of action that would position American Jews as legitimate and powerful actors on the political stage, demanding a total reversal of their government's attitude toward their collective concerns. Silver's reactions to several statements made by President Harry Truman, almost immediately upon taking office, are outstanding examples of this approach. As Silver himself admitted on several occasions, Truman's statements testified to a deep humanitarian commitment to resolving the Jewish displaced persons (DP) problem, and even to an understanding that this resolution would have to be based on the socioeconomic framework developed by the Jewish community of Palestine.[12] And yet, Silver

12. Thus, at a press conference held on August 16, after his return from the Potsdam Conference, Truman announced his desire to enable the largest possible number of Jews to enter Palestine and that this objective would be pursued via diplomatic negotiations with

refused to see these statements as heralding a turning point in American policy. Rather, from the earliest days of the Truman administration he denounced any governmental measure that could be interpreted as placing the Jewish question solely in the light of a humanitarian issue. What was demanded, rather, was recognition of the Jewish question's political nature as a story of ongoing disenfranchisement that had reached its peak during the Holocaust years and now required a thorough rectification.

Thus Silver consistently opposed all measures, however tactical or pragmatic, that might prove detrimental to the maximalist political goal of a Jewish national home in Palestine. At the September 10, 1945 AZEC meeting, he brought about a decision to launch a public protest against the government, in light of what he regarded as American cooperation with British attempts to freeze the plan for a political solution in Palestine. The mass protest rally staged in New York on the first of October, and the week of activity that preceded it, constituted the most impressive evidence to date of the Zionist movement's organizational capacity and, no less important, of the Jewish public's willingness to adopt a combative approach that rejected even generous humanitarian gestures as insufficient. During the week prior to the rally, the White House was inundated by a quarter of a million telegrams demanding American involvement in the effort to reach a political solution in Palestine. Some seventy thousand participants attended the protest rally, and Silver, who delivered the main speech, promised to give the White House no quarter until the doors of Palestine opened to Jewish immigration and a Jewish state was established.[13]

Great Britain and the Arabs. In another instance, on August 31, Truman responded to the Harrison Report, which had been submitted to him ten days earlier and which roundly criticized British White Paper policy, with a personal letter to Clement Attlee, the newly elected British prime minister, in which he called for the immediate issuing of one hundred thousand certificates for immigration to Palestine. In addition, the report's criticism of the way in which the American occupation forces were treating the displaced persons prompted Truman to send a letter of reprimand to the military governor of the US occupation zone, General Dwight D. Eisenhower.

13. The intensive nature of the struggle spearheaded by Silver may be inferred from Truman's reaction, expressed at a meeting with the heads of the American Jewish

Silver's combative approach was particularly pronounced during his struggle against the Anglo-American Committee of Inquiry. The committee had its beginnings in a British initiative aimed at neutralizing the Palestine issue. On October 19, 1945, the British ambassador to Washington submitted an official proposal to the US secretary of state that a joint commission of inquiry be created to address the problem of displaced persons. A few days later, President Truman responded favorably on condition that the immigration to Palestine of one hundred thousand displaced Jews occupy a high position on the committee's agenda. Silver objected to this almost immediately, insisting that cooperation with such a committee be conditional on recognition of the Jewish right to establish a national home in Palestine; he likened a committee that failed to recognize this right to a ship sailing the seas without a compass (Silver 1963a). His opposition increased in vehemence after the joint declaration on November 13 by President Truman and British Foreign Secretary Ernest Bevin regarding the creation of the Anglo-American Committee of Inquiry. Bevin's speech was a particular target of outrage. Silver forcefully denounced the British Foreign Secretary for insinuating that the Zionist movement was promoting racism among the Jews of Palestine. He explained that the demand for a Jewish majority in Palestine was rooted not in a quest for exclusivity, but rather in a desire to solve the continuous problem of Jewish marginality, which stemmed from the fact that Jews were a minority wherever they lived, even in the land of their fathers. He therefore called for a solution that would sidestep the trap of the humanitarian gesture. Such a gesture, however valuable, would only serve to perpetuate Jewish marginality (Silver 1945a).

Silver's opposition to the Anglo-American Committee of Inquiry was fervent and consistent. The day after the joint Truman-Bevin announcement, a plenary meeting of AZEC was held with the participation of

---

Committee. He deplored the pressure being exerted on him by the Zionists to intercede on behalf of a Jewish state in Palestine—a task that he saw as potentially capable of unleashing a third world war. A clear indication of Silver's success in mobilizing the American Jewish public for struggle on behalf of Zionist political demands may be found in the Elmo Roper polls conducted in autumn 1945, according to which 81 percent of American Jews supported the Zionist solution of a Jewish state.

Chaim Weizmann, who had arrived several days earlier from London. Silver proposed that Weizmann resign in protest and that the Committee of Inquiry discussions be boycotted altogether; indeed, Silver refused to testify before the committee, even when most other Zionist leaders in the United States and elsewhere agreed to cooperate with it, if only for tactical purposes. Echoes of this dispute could also be heard at the forty-eighth ZOA convention in Atlantic City. Silver voiced objection to the Jewish Agency's demand of the previous June for a hundred thousand immigration certificates, contending that the humanitarian agenda that the Committee of Inquiry was trying to advance could never have seen the light of day had the Zionist movement itself not advanced a similar agenda; he warned that cooperating with the committee would be tantamount to obscuring Zionism's political objectives.[14]

Silver took the same uncompromising tone during the Zionist leadership deliberations that were held intermittently in Palestine from November 28 to December 14. Although Ben-Gurion also made a speech denouncing Bevin and the Anglo-American Committee of Inquiry,[15] during the actual deliberations he expressed willingness to cooperate with the committee. This difference between Silver and Ben-Gurion had nothing to do with a pragmatism that the latter purportedly possessed and the former lacked, but rather with differing frames of reference for the Zionist struggle. In Silver's eyes, Zionist activism embodied American Jewry's struggle for equal status within the American democratic framework; thus he displayed pragmatism regarding any measure likely to advance that aim. This strategy was most strikingly in evidence during the summation stage of the committee's work. The recommendations were divided into those of long-term (that neither a Jewish nor an Arab state should be

14. Similarly, in a speech given on March 31, 1946 at the Bnai Zion hall (the Bnai Zion organization had voted him world Zionism's "Man of the Year"), Silver called the Committee of Inquiry a British plot to liquidate the Jewish national home (Orian 1982, 288).

15. Ben-Gurion opened his speech by proclaiming: "I want to tell Bevin and his associates that we are prepared to die rather than compromise on three things: on free Jewish immigration, on our right to build up the wilderness of our homeland, and on our people's political independence in its land" (Ben-Gurion 1956, 9–32).

established) and short-term (the immediate immigration to Palestine of a hundred thousand displaced persons). In Silver's view, a linkage of the two represented a real danger that a short-term humanitarian solution would be made conditional on renouncement of the long-term political solution. Thus, although Silver continued to boycott the committee deliberations, he took part in the preparation of a compromise formula to be submitted to the president's advisors for use in a statement by Truman supporting the immediate implementation of the short-term recommendations but deferring discussion of the recommendations regarding Palestine's final status (Neumann 1976, 237). On April 30, 1946, British pressure notwithstanding, Truman did issue such a statement, rejecting Britain's stipulation that action on the short-term recommendations be linked to implementation of the long-term recommendations. This constituted a success of sorts for Silver; Truman's willingness to authorize a compromise with Silver—with a view toward the November 1946 congressional elections—constituted an acknowledgement of the power of the American-Zionist movement, now understood to represent a population that had overcome its wartime impotence and had become a force to be reckoned with.[16]

At the same time, this qualified success did nothing to soften Silver's combative stance toward the American government. To the contrary, in Silver's view, the Truman administration's attempt to ingratiate the Jewish voter without changing its fundamental policy actually underscored the administration's intention to limit public discussion of the Zionist enterprise to the humanitarian realm. Silver saw the Truman administration's humanitarian gestures not as marks of deference for Jewish public opinion, but rather as a scheme to divert Jewish attention. In this spirit, he denounced the president's statement regarding the Committee of Inquiry's recommendations—a statement that he himself had a hand in drafting.

16. In a June 12 speech at the protest rally in New York, Silver responded to Bevin, who accused the American government of supporting the immigration of the DPs to Palestine in order to prevent their arrival in New York. Silver denounced what he regarded as Nazi libel on Bevin's part against the entire American populace.

He took care to add a personal message to AZEC's statement welcoming the distinction between the short-term and long-term recommendations; in this message, he warned against any attempt by the administration to keep the long-term recommendations' troubling implications out of public debate. A few months later, while delivering his annual report to the forty-ninth ZOA convention,[17] Silver cautioned that Truman's support for the immigration to Palestine of one hundred thousand displaced persons should not be regarded as heralding a favorable policy change. Rather, he disapprovingly noted the president's insistence on the humanitarian basis for this support as well as Truman's simultaneous assurances to Arab leaders that American policy regarding Palestine remained unchanged.

During June and July 1946, Silver was engaged in yet another campaign—one intended to ensure that Congress attached conditions to a $3.75 billion loan sought by Great Britain from the United States. Silver claimed that it was in the administration's interest to represent the American-Zionist political demand as striving illegitimately to conflate American humanitarian concerns with matters of foreign policy. He therefore deplored the administration's insistence that this loan remain out of bounds with regard to the American-Jewish political struggle, inasmuch as it was in the highest interest of the United States to ensure the stability of the Western Allies during the postwar period. He also reproached his American-Jewish colleagues for objecting to Zionist interference in the pursuit of American foreign policy.[18] Silver appealed to Congress "as a Jew, as a Zionist, and as an American citizen," and demanded that American

17. The forty-ninth ZOA convention was held on October 25–29, 1946, just prior to the November 1946 congressional elections (Silver 1946).

18. In the plenary AZEC deliberations of June 21, Wise and Goldmann objected to Silver's demand. Wise sent a public letter of support for the loan to Sol Bloom, chairman of the House Committee on Foreign Affairs. He noted that this support reflected his position as an American citizen concerned for the country's vital interests—despite his opposition to British policy. Wise's letter was published on July 3 in *The New York Times*. On the same day, the *Times* also published a declaration of support for the loan by twenty-six heads of Jewish organizations, including the heads of the American Jewish Committee and the American Jewish Joint Distribution Committee.

taxpayer money not be given to a British government that had become the enemy of the Jewish people and, thereby, of the American people (American Zionist Emergency Council 1946).

A few months later, in late October, while reviewing the campaign to attach conditions to the loan (Silver 1946), Silver called for Great Britain's Palestine policy to be accorded the same antidemocratic—and, by implication, anti-American—rating that Czechoslovakia and Poland had received during the congressional debate over their economic aid requests. This endeavor to have conditions attached to the British loan constituted an escalation of the struggle that Silver had launched against the Truman administration. In the earlier case of the Anglo-American Committee of Inquiry, Silver had merely sought to keep the United States from explicitly supporting the linkage of a solution for the displaced persons to the withdrawal of Zionist political demands. In the instance of the loan to Great Britain, Silver raised the bar of expectation: he declared his anticipation that the United States would become an active supporter of the collective concerns of its Jewish citizenry and thereby affirm the integrality of these concerns to national American interests.[19]

> The Government of the United States is after all our government. As citizens we can turn to it for redress . . . and also for an explanation and an accounting . . . that is why we have placed so much importance on persuading our Government not to treat the Palestine problem as an incident on the periphery of its world-wide diplomatic activities . . . but to put it along with the other major political questions of the hour at the very center of its foreign policy. (Silver 1946)

Silver faced yet another challenge in July 1946 as details began to surface of a new British-American agreement, eventually known as the Morrison-Grady Plan, aimed at engineering an additional compromise on the Palestine issue. Under this plan, the Jewish and Arab areas would

19. This opinion was expressed in a letter by Silver to the press and in a statement by the ZOA administration; Silver repeated it in his report to the forty-ninth ZOA convention in October 1946.

have cultural autonomy, while the British would remain responsible for matters of foreign policy, security, justice, transportation, and the maintenance of public order. Key figures in the administration hoped that their support for a Jewish autonomy proposal, in addition to the proposal for a hundred thousand displaced persons to immigrate to Palestine, would satisfy Jewish voters and prevent any political damage to the Democratic Party. The fact that the autonomy being offered was limited both geographically and practically was perceived not as a drawback but as an advantage, inasmuch as this would prevent the regional instability that, in the State Department's view, might ultimately harm American interests in the Middle East. By contrast, from Silver's perspective, the Morrison-Grady Plan was the most dangerous version of the president's humanitarian policy. Silver was concerned that by offering a limited answer to Zionist demands, the Truman administration would cause the movement to settle for a solution that was mainly humanitarian in character. This danger was particularly palpable in light of Truman's caustic remarks about acting in the vital interests of the United States—not those of New York Jewry—and being tired of the demands of the Jews, Poles, Irish, and others who appealed to him with their narrow interests rather than on behalf of the national good.[20]

Silver responded with a relentless public campaign against the Morrison-Grady Plan. He saw to it that Democratic candidates for public office were kept under continual pressure; these candidates informed Truman that, should the plan be approved, it would be futile for any New York Democrat to run for Congress in the November 1946 elections. At a July 30 Washington rally that had been organized in protest of the president's anticipated statement on the Morrison-Grady Plan, Silver warned that support for the plan would trigger Jewish mobilization to topple the Democratic administration responsible for such an anti-American policy.

20. Truman made these statements at a July 17 meeting with Democratic senators and James McDonald, who vehemently criticized the Morrison-Grady Plan. Truman angrily responded that he was acting in America's vital interests, not in the interests of the New York Jews whom it was impossible to satisfy. Later, on July 30, he expressed similar sentiments before a protest delegation of Democratic congressmen (see McDonald 1951).

The crude political force exerted by Silver finally did produce results; Truman was obliged to tell British Prime Minister Clement Attlee that he was rejecting the plan. Nevertheless, Silver became more determined than ever to fight what he perceived to be a hidden agenda of neutralizing Zionism's political aspirations.

This combative stance vis-à-vis the administration grew increasingly popular among the Jewish public. By late 1946, purchasers of the Shekel (the Zionist organizational membership fee) numbered 960,000, indicating that support for Zionism did not remain confined to the traditional centers of Jewish life. For example, in Carmel-by-the-Sea, California, nearly two thousand of the town's five to six thousand Jews purchased the Shekel. In San Francisco, a known stronghold of the anti-Zionist American Council for Judaism, some six thousand Jews acquired the Shekel out of a Jewish community of forty thousand. United Jewish Appeal data also heralded a turning point for the Zionist movement. In 1946, $101 million was collected throughout the United States, nearly three times the figure of $35 million that had been collected in 1945, and over seven times the $14 million collected in 1941. The forty-ninth ZOA convention was yet another manifestation of the dominance that Silver and his combative stance had attained within the Zionist movement. The convention convened on October 25–29, just prior to the congressional elections, and unanimously elected Silver to another term as ZOA president. The rise in ZOA membership from 140,000 at the previous convention to 250,000 also testified to Silver's influence and the transcendence of the traditional boundaries of the American-Zionist movement.

The growing popularity of Silver's combative leadership was the basis for his retaliatory voting initiative during the midterm congressional elections of November 1946. On September 10, he presented a plan before the AZEC plenum aimed at punishing the Democratic Party for its failure to support Zionist demands. He stressed the role of such a measure in affirming the political maturity of the American-Jewish public—a public unafraid to fight openly for the causes it embraced. As expected, the plan encountered intense intra-Jewish opposition: Wise contended that it was in American Jewry's long-term interest to vote for the Democratic candidates, while Hadassah President Rose Halprin objected to the idea of judging candidates solely from a Zionist perspective. However, this stance was by now the rearguard position; Silver's contrary claim—that a candidate's loyalty to national American values ought to be measured in terms of his commitment to Jewish communal concerns—garnered widespread support.

This approach also guided Silver's attitude toward Truman's famous "Yom Kippur statement," made just prior to the start of the Yom Kippur fast on October 4, which hinted at presidential support for the creation of a Jewish community in Palestine. Although indications could be found in the speech that Truman was edging closer to recognition of Zionist political demands (Silver was later to make use of the speech while fighting for US approval of the UN partition plan), at this point Silver chose to address the speech's negative aspects. He noted that the speech sought merely to stem the tide of American-Jewish dissatisfaction with the Democrats—particularly in light of the statement of support that the Republican governor of New York was expected to issue two days later. In the final analysis, it was clear that, from Silver's point of view, the primary issue was the position of power to which the Jewish community had acceded. To Silver and the Jewish electorate, it was a fitting reversal of Holocaust-era Jewish impotence—a most effective way of removing the stigma of Jewish collective powerlessness.

From this latter point of view, Silver's strategy was a resounding success. Even before the midterm elections were underway, a *New York Times* commentator described Silver as a leader who had enabled American Jewry to exploit the democratic system in a way that no other American ethnic group had ever dared to do. The Republican electoral gains in the November 1946 elections were indeed impressive proof of Silver's success. Although the Democratic losses in both houses of Congress—the first suffered since 1928—were not due entirely to the Jewish vote, nevertheless this retaliatory tactic made an unmistakable dent in Jewish Democratic strongholds, most notably New York. The importance of the election outcome did not go unnoticed by Joseph M. Proskauer, head of the American Jewish Committee. His opposition to Silver notwithstanding, Proskauer was forced to admit that the election results constituted a defeat for

American-Zionism's "moderate" camp and a major turning point for the entire American-Jewish community (Orian 1982, 358–59).

Silver's stance was also a major sticking point between him and Ben-Gurion, and 1946 marked a turn for the worse in their relationship. Ultimately Ben-Gurion was unable to count on Silver to subordinate the American-Zionist struggle to Yishuv strategy. This rift between Silver and Ben-Gurion[21] deepened over the Jewish Agency's partition initiative, which was approved at a meeting of the Zionist Executive in Paris on August 5 in Silver's absence. In Ben-Gurion's view, the main danger posed by the Morrison-Grady Plan related to the possibility of the Yishuv and the Zionist movement finding themselves isolated, without the endorsement of a great power.[22] For this reason, it seemed expedient to build on Silver's success in thwarting American support for the plan, and finding a means of strengthening Zionism's status vis-à-vis the American government. Ben-Gurion therefore supported the Zionist Executive's decision to send Goldmann to the United States with a partition proposal as a means of improving relations with the American government and persuading it to pressure Britain. Silver drew the opposite conclusion from his success in torpedoing the Morrison-Grady Plan. In his view, compromise on the Biltmore Program's maximalist Zionist demands was a slippery slope, one liable to undermine American Jewry's new political power and to return it to its conciliatory tactics and wartime impotence. At the August 12 AZEC meeting, he referred to Goldmann's venture as a humiliating exercise in Jewish conciliation. Two days later he sent a letter to Ben-Gurion in which he announced his resignation from the Jewish Agency administration. Ben-Gurion, for his part, had trouble understanding the rationale behind Silver's behavior. The latter's willingness to endanger

21. Although Ben-Gurion agreed with Silver's call for an aggressive stance vis-à-vis Great Britain, he felt that continued conflict with the administration over the British loan was excessively risky, and thus counseled moderation.

22. Ben-Gurion viewed the Morrison-Grady Plan as the continuation of a plan drawn up by Nuri as-Said, the pro-British prime minister of Iraq who sought changes favorable to the Arabs in the partition plan recommended by the Peel Commission of 1937 (Tevet 2004, 796–98).

Zionist relations with the American government annoyed Ben-Gurion, who doubted Silver's political acumen (Neumann 1976, 240–42; Orian 1982, 361–62).

The two different viewpoints of Silver and Ben-Gurion became strikingly evident at the twenty-second Zionist Congress, which convened on December 9, 1946 in Basel, Switzerland. Attesting to this was the political dispute surrounding continued negotiations with Great Britain via the London Conference to which Jewish and Arab representatives were to be invited in late January 1947. Silver's opposition to participation in the conference was perceived by many as an extreme and dangerous view that moved combativeness from the realm of tactics to that of ideology. Accordingly, Weizmann warned the congress against false prophets. Ben-Gurion, despite his shared interest with Silver in the struggle against Weizmann, derided the stance that glorified militancy. He distanced himself from Silver's position and took the intermediate stance between Silver and Weizmann of "neither Massada nor Vichy," leaving the door open to participation in the London Conference. Ultimately it was Ben-Gurion's position that won out. Although the congress, by a slim margin and despite the threat of Weizmann's resignation, approved the decision of the political committee under Silver to oppose participation in the London Conference, it nevertheless ruled that, should the situation change, the Zionist Executive would be authorized to determine whether conditions had become suitable for participation. In the wake of this vote, Weizmann resigned in protest; in the Zionist Executive discussions that began immediately afterward, Ben-Gurion fortified his position as chairman of the Jewish Agency for Palestine and, thereby, as chairman of the World Zionist Organization, while Silver settled for a position created especially for him—chairman of the Jewish Agency's American section. Silver returned to the United States with a sense of missed opportunity. Despite the sanction given by the congress to the decisions of the political committee that he headed, it was Ben-Gurion's Yishuv-oriented pragmatism that had effectively been endorsed.

The source of Silver's popularity with the American-Jewish public was his ability to turn Zionism into a sociopolitical demand for integration and equality in America. However, this approach, which was so meaningful to American Jews, was perceived by the non-American Zionist leadership as merely a tactic that could be changed whenever necessary. Thus, at the first plenary meeting of the Zionist General Council under Ben-Gurion in London immediately after the Zionist Executive deliberations had concluded, Ben-Gurion supported Goldmann's proposal that participation in the London Conference be raised with the British. Silver, on being informed of this immediately upon his return to the United States, convened the newly appointed Jewish Agency administration there and denounced Ben-Gurion's decision.[23] Ultimately, however, he was forced to watch from the sidelines as unofficial negotiations with Britain were held, with brief interruptions, from January 22 until their collapse in mid-February.[24] This situation provided additional evidence that the main Zionist agenda was informed by a perspective overwhelmingly oriented toward strengthening the Yishuv as a state in the making and was relatively uninterested in Silver's American-Jewish perspective.

On the face of it, the situation appeared to undergo a complete reversal after Bevin's announcement that the talks regarding the London Conference had broken down,[25] and that no choice therefore remained but to submit the matter of Palestine to the United Nations. In the wake of this announcement, the center of gravity of the Zionist struggle eventually returned to the American public arena, whose influence on the United Nations was critical. In this arena Silver was a dominant power; it would have been reasonable, accordingly, to expect this dramatic new reliance on Silver's leadership to place his American-Jewish agenda at the center of the world Zionist stage. However, in retrospect one might say that the opposite occurred. Despite Silver's vital role in the 1947–1948 Zionist political struggle, it was precisely this historical juncture that was to

23. Later, in his autobiography, he was to express a more moderate opinion, noting that Ben-Gurion's decision was based on a legitimate interpretation of the congress's resolutions.

24. As he had done in connection with the Anglo-American Committee, Silver boycotted these negotiations, yet he remained in constant contact with Emanuel Neumann, who participated in them (Neumann 1976, 253–59; Tevet 2004, 888–903).

25. For Silver's discussion of the London Conference affair, see Silver (1963a).

underscore the marginality of the American-Zionist agenda vis-à-vis that of the Yishuv. Paradoxically and, from Silver's point of view, rather tragically, the greater his success in advancing Zionism's political objectives, the more he actually did to fortify the Yishuv agenda's dominion over the Zionist movement and make irrelevant the American-Diaspora brand of Zionism that he himself championed.

6

1947–1948

An American-Jewish or a Pan-Jewish Leader?

BY FEBRUARY 17, 1947, even before Bevin's proposal to bring the issue of Palestine before the United Nations had been authorized by the British Parliament, Silver had proclaimed the opening of a new chapter in the Zionist endeavor. The current challenge, he declared, was to ensure American support for the founding of a Jewish state. Without such support the effort vis-à-vis the United Nations was destined to fail. The understanding that statehood had finally become a tangible objective constituted the fulfillment of a dream that he had cherished since childhood; his Zionist leadership thus took on a historical dimension far transcending the American-Jewish arena. As chairman of the Jewish Agency's American section he soon found himself the de facto representative of the Jewish people (and not just of American Zionism) to the nations of the world. This latter role became apparent after a few days of procedural UN deliberations, when the General Assembly decided to appoint the Jewish Agency as the Jewish people's sole recognized representative before the General Assembly on issues relating to Palestine, thus reaffirming its previous designation as such by the League of Nations. This effectively catapulted Silver to an entirely new status. All at once, he became the authorized representative of a pan-Jewish national entity in the making—an entity striving to secure recognition and exercise its rights in relation to the nations of the world.

The need for unity in the name of a future Jewish state became the new basis for Silver's leadership. The revolutionary nature of this new mode of action could be seen in Silver's definition of the common denominator characterizing the Reform movement. From 1945 to 1947, until just a few months before the start of the UN effort, Silver had also served as head of the movement's rabbinical body, the CCAR. During most of that period, he had been careful not to draw this key Reform institution into Zionist/anti-Zionist conflicts. This reflected his consistent approach throughout his rabbinical career of viewing the Jewish religion, rather than Zionism, as the unifying force within Judaism and, thus, as the decisive shared feature that ought to bind Zionists, non-Zionists, and anti-Zionists within the Reform movement. However, in June 1947, at the fifty-eighth annual CCAR convention, which marked the end of his term as president, Silver brought about a decision authorizing him to take any measures necessary to ensure a united American-Jewish front vis-à-vis the United Nations, and to demand, in the name of the Reform movement, that the United States actively support a UN resolution guaranteeing the Jewish people's basic right to a national home in Palestine. This amounted, essentially, to making the issue of support for Jewish statehood something that transcended any internal religious or political disputes within the Reform movement.

Silver's first speech as the Jewish Agency's representative before the UN's Ad Hoc Committee on Palestine was yet another indication of his new self-perception as a representative of the overall national interests of the Jewish people. This first, historic address had been scheduled for May 8 at 11:00 a.m. Ben-Gurion, as the Zionist movement's most senior figure, had been the originally designated speaker; however, a telegram the day earlier announced that he would be arriving in the United States only during the afternoon. At a joint meeting of the Jewish Agency Executive and AZEC, it was decided not to request that the deliberations be postponed but to let Silver deliver the historic address. Though by now a seasoned public speaker renowned for his oratorical skills, Silver was to recollect later that he did not sleep the entire night before. His speech underscored the importance of the Jewish Agency as the Jewish people's representative body; Silver insisted that, as the representative of the Jewish Agency, he spoke "not merely for the organized Jewish community of Palestine," but rather on behalf of the entire Jewish people (Neumann 1976, 261; Silver 1949a, 1963a).

As the UN campaign intensified, Silver increasingly focused his activities on the single, supreme goal of obtaining worldwide recognition of the future Jewish state. When this new prioritization required that he abandon practices that up to then had seemed to him basic and unassailable, he did so without hesitation. This may be seen in his stance regarding the partition plan, which only a few months earlier he had regarded as unacceptable. Now Silver marshaled all of his political and rhetorical skills on the plan's behalf. This turning point involved the majority recommendation issued by the United Nations Special Committee on Palestine (UNSCOP). UNSCOP, which became operational on June 16, wavered between a partition plan that called for two independent states linked by a common economic system and a binational federative solution. By August 25 (a week before the UNSCOP recommendations were announced), the Zionist General Council had convened in Zurich to deliberate on the anticipated recommendations. From various sources it was learned that a UNSCOP majority would be recommending the partition plan option, and that in the event of such a recommendation, the plan stood a good chance of being approved by the United Nations General Assembly. Based on this expectation, Silver announced that, however uninspired the plan left him, he would support it unequivocally. A week later, when UNSCOP's eight-to-three decision in favor of the partition plan was announced, Silver gave his official concurrence to the UNSCOP majority report. On his return to the United States, and in advance of the UN General Assembly deliberations scheduled to begin on September 16, he announced that the intra-Zionist debate had come to a close and that the sole task remaining for the movement was that of securing a two-thirds General Assembly majority in favor of the partition plan.

A few days later, when Silver addressed the UN Ad-Hoc Political Committee on October 2, 1947, he went a step further: he portrayed the partition plan as the Jewish problem's ultimate solution. In response to the UNSCOP report's assertion that "any solution for Palestine cannot be considered as a solution of the Jewish problem in general," Silver summoned all of his oratorical powers in order to cast the partition plan in the light of a definitive solution to the problem of Jewish homelessness and marginality:

> We are at loss to understand the meaning of this recommendation. . . . The "Jewish problem in general" is not a problem of Jewish immigration or of refugees. It is the age-old problem of Jewish national homelessness. There is but one solution to this problem, a national home. (Silver 1949f, 143)

Still, although he had not been asked to do so, Silver also made sure to emphasize that the Jewish Agency had no objection to the immigration of displaced persons to other countries. On the contrary, the Jewish Agency hoped that the nations of the world would open their gates to those displaced persons who wished to enter them. Silver's antagonists in this instance were not the non-Zionists,[1] but rather those Yishuv leaders who adhered to the "negating the exile" approach. One might say that as Israeli statehood inched closer to realization, Silver felt all the more compelled to emphasize an American-Zionist belief in the compatibility of territorial and Diaspora Zionism. This tendency would become increasingly pronounced, and it pointed to an inherent difficulty in Silver's position. Now that a Jewish state was just over the horizon, American Jewry's Zionist activism took its cue from the deeds and declarations of the Yishuv leadership, most of which was aligned with an anti-exilic ideology. This in turn raised real concerns for Silver—namely, that the Diaspora-Zionist approach would take a back seat as his own Zionist effort became focused exclusively on obtaining international recognition for the Jewish state.

Moreover, by adopting the Yishuv leadership's order of priorities, Silver relegated himself to a secondary role as an assistant to the Yishuv leadership, rather than that of the driving force behind American Jewry's "emancipation." Paradoxically, the fortification of Silver's position as undisputed leader of the political struggle vis-à-vis the United Nations underscored his marginality vis-à-vis the Yishuv leadership. This became all the more pronounced in the aftermath of the November 29 resolution,

1. The comment, which Silver sought to add to the recommendations of the UNSCOP report, reflected a different stance from that of the American Jewish Committee and the non-Zionist leaders, who, for their part, took care to stress that their support for the partition plan had no bearing on their loyalty to the United States (Ganin 2005, 59–62).

which immediately catapulted the Yishuv to the status of a sovereign state in the making and, inevitably, placed the existential challenges facing the Yishuv at the top of the Zionist agenda.

Silver became painfully aware of this turn of events in early January 1948, when he arrived in Jerusalem to participate in a Zionist General Council meeting. In stark contrast to his exalted status in the aftermath of the historic victory in the November 29 UN Partition Resolution, and after having been praised by both supporters and rivals within the American-Jewish leadership as the architect of this victory, on arriving in Israel he encountered a new reality that, almost inevitably, dictated new priorities and overshadowed his own political agenda. Upon landing at Lydda Airport, he was obliged to wait for the British military to authorize his travel by convoy to Tel Aviv, where he then had to wait again before traveling with a Haganah convoy to Jerusalem. The deliberations of the Zionist General Council began on January 19, when most areas of the city were under attack and Jerusalem was faced with shortages of food and other provisions. Silver was taken aback by the situation, which gave him an all too concrete sense of the Yishuv perspective—namely, that the Jewish statehood question would ultimately be decided not in the corridors of the United Nations, but on the Palestinian battlefield. From this perspective, the Zionist role of Silver and American Jewry in general was simply to support the main effort spearheaded by the Yishuv leadership.[2]

And indeed, immediately after Ben-Gurion inaugurated the deliberations with a deferential nod to Silver, "who, more than any other American Zionist, was responsible for the greatest political achievement in the history of our people since the Second Temple was destroyed—the UN's recognition of our right to establish the State of Israel," the discussion moved on to the existential security challenges facing the Yishuv (Orian

2. Silver's parents, who had immigrated to Palestine in 1927, were living at that time in Jerusalem. Silver first saw them, after eight years of not visiting Palestine, in 1945, while participating in the Zionist General Council (November 28–December 14). Already during this early visit, he had discovered that their health was deteriorating. His mother would pass away on February 20, 1948, two weeks after Silver's return to the United States. His father would pass away on November 1, 1948.

1982, 452). Although Silver tried to contribute to the deliberations, his relative lack of experience in security-related issues left him at a loss. His proposal that American-Jewish military experts be called on for assistance raised eyebrows among some of the participants and angered others. As Ben-Gurion saw it, the only forms of assistance that could be expected from American Jews who chose to remain in the United States rather than fighting shoulder to shoulder with their Yishuv counterparts was that of pressuring the US government to lift its arms embargo on the region and fundraising for arms purchases. Ben-Gurion and other participants failed to comprehend yet another proposal of Silver's—that of creating, under UN supervision, a mixed Jewish and non-Jewish militia, whose prospective volunteers would be motivated to aid the Yishuv by their shared identification with the United Nation's progressive agenda of justice and democracy. It was obvious that most of those present at the meeting neither understood nor seriously considered this characteristically Diaspora-Zionist idea. A few of the participants ridiculed the proposal, in which they detected a tone of panic, as though the Yishuv needed the United Nations to save it from physical annihilation. Others merely insisted that Silver's place was in the United States, where he could be more useful by leading the political and financial effort that American Jewry needed to undertake on the Yishuv's behalf. It was clear from the deliberations that the Yishuv leaders viewed American Jewry's role exclusively in terms of financial support and political lobbying; they were certainly opposed to any intimation that American Zionism might possess a valuable Zionist agenda of its own.[3]

Silver returned to the United States in early February and, as requested by the Zionist Executive, dedicated himself to winning over American public opinion and exerting influence on the US government, primarily regarding the withdrawal of American support for the partition plan in

3. Silver raised the proposal for a UN-sponsored international force in several different versions since the Zionist Executive meeting of January 1948. Immediately after returning to the United States, in early February, he proposed to send a UN force composed of small and neutral countries. He repeated this proposal in his speech on March 5, 1948 to the United Nations General Assembly (Silver 1949d).

favor of a renewed British trusteeship in Palestine. As the head of AZEC and chair of the Jewish Agency's American section, Silver unquestionably made a major contribution to the cause. He organized and participated in press conferences aimed at swaying public opinion against the Truman administration's stance; convened local AZEC chapters across the United States and spoke at their meetings, exhorting them to pressure their representatives in both houses of Congress; recruited and deployed public figures such as Thomas Mann, former First Lady Eleanor Roosevelt, and leading Christian clerics; was responsible for inundating the White House with hundreds of thousands of protest telegrams; and took part in huge demonstrations and rallies, such as a march by fifty thousand Jewish war veterans on April 4 along Fifth Avenue in New York City, protesting the president's announcement a week before that the United States would be rescinding its support for the partition plan.

However, despite of all of these activities, it was clear that his status and function had undergone a radical change. He was no longer the leading actor, and even in the moments when he did take center stage, he was merely the director of a lobby on behalf of the future Jewish state rather than the independent leader of a religious-ethnic group vying for its place within the American democratic political culture. And thus, during the months that remained until the British Mandate's termination date and Israel's declaration of independence on May 14, Silver found that the representatives of the state in the making (primarily Moshe Sharett and Eliyahu Eilat—the future Israeli foreign minister and the first Israeli ambassador to the United States, respectively) had become the principal negotiators with the administration. Despite his formal standing as head of the Jewish Agency's American section, he was now forced to suffice with reports on the meetings that were being held; sometimes he found out about them only after the fact. To a great extent Silver had become a lobbyist for the Yishuv struggle, working on behalf of the Palestinian Zionist leadership.

The inherent difference in status between Silver and the Yishuv leadership became particularly tangible during the intra-Zionist deliberations on the question of whether to postpone the new state's declaration of independence. On April 26, Assistant Secretary of State Dean Rusk submitted to Sharett and Proskauer an armistice proposal, to enter into effect on May

1. On May 2, Rusk posed an ultimatum—this time to Sharett and Goldmann—regarding a ten-day ceasefire and at least a ninety-day postponement of any declaration of Israeli statehood. The reward for assenting to this ultimatum would be guaranteed American assistance in repelling the anticipated Arab attack; the punishment for refusal would be the Yishuv's possible abandonment in the face of that attack and an intensification of the American arms embargo on the region. During deliberations of the Jewish Agency Executive in the United States, Silver was among those most vehemently opposed to yielding to the ultimatum. He discounted the fear expressed by some of the participants that the Yishuv would collapse in the wake of an Arab attack should no aid be forthcoming from the United States. As the declaration of statehood approached, Silver exhibited in many ways a level of decisiveness similar to that of Ben-Gurion. However, the shared characteristics of this resolve actually underscored the contextual and positional differences between the two leaders. By deciding not to postpone the declaration, Ben-Gurion was acting in his capacity as the leader of the Yishuv's military campaign; it was he who would bear the weighty responsibility of that campaign's outcome. Certainly Silver also felt a sense of tremendous responsibility, as he had played a decisive role during the early period of the UN effort, but now, in the final stages of the struggle for statehood, he was dependent on factors that lay beyond the American-Jewish arena—factors for which he bore no responsibility and over which he had no real influence. Essentially, he had no choice but to rely on the authority and leadership of Ben-Gurion. This new situation was pointedly expressed by Silver's most loyal colleague, Emanuel Neumann, who recollected having asked himself whether he would have had the ability to face the dangers entailed by the fateful step of declaring Israeli independence. Neumann candidly answered that at that critical juncture he had completely trusted Ben-Gurion's resolve and leadership (Goldmann 1969, 246–47; Neumann 1976, 276–78; Silver 1949e).

The new reality became all too apparent in the wake of Israel's declaration of independence. Silver was later to describe the day of Israel's establishment as the most important and exciting of his life. On receiving word from Tel Aviv that statehood had been declared, he movingly announced it in a news conference at the United Nations. His exhilaration intensified later in the day on hearing that the United States had been the first country to grant the fledgling state de facto recognition. However, this pinnacle of achievement was also a turning point: from the moment that Israeli statehood had been declared, Silver, as an American citizen, was clearly not eligible to be that new entity's foremost spokesperson. This was particularly true in light of the Israeli demand for exclusive loyalty to the newly established state as a kind of litmus test indicating the degree to which Zionist leaders abroad were committed to the cause. Abba Eban, who from April 1947 until Israel's declaration of independence had been a junior member of the Jewish Agency's UN delegation, described the day of Israel's founding as the one on which Silver was forced to reach a decision that until then he had been able to evade—whether to become an Israeli citizen and renounce all other loyalties, or to retain his American citizenship and thereby become, overnight, ineligible to represent a "foreign country." From Eban's perspective, Silver's embrace of the latter option could be likened to abandoning ship at the journey's most critical juncture. For Eban, it was unsettling how, all at once, American Zionism's preeminent leader and charismatic spokesman suddenly got cold feet and let it be known that the endeavor underway was not one to which he felt personally committed. Thus, as demonstrated by Eban's account, Silver's decision to remain in the United States after the achievement of Israeli statehood was a testament to the weakness of his Zionist allegiance (Eban 1977, 117–18; Silver 1949b).

From Silver's perspective, however, the situation was more complicated. Even at the height of the political struggle for statehood, while he had taken upon himself the de facto role of spokesman for the state in the making, he had been unwilling to view this role as the sole manifestation of his Jewish leadership and never intended to shirk his duties as an American-Jewish religious leader. He took care to return each weekend to Cleveland to perform his various functions there as the community's rabbi, even though the transportation conditions entailed considerable personal exertion and sacrifice. These efforts indicated the degree to which he regarded his Zionist mission as intertwined with his obligations as an American religious leader. Still, as Eban noted in his memoirs, to the non-American members of the UN delegation, this attitude constituted problematic evidence that Silver was not exclusively committed to the Zionist struggle in Palestine. Now that statehood had been achieved, the problem, as they saw it, had only worsened. Silver needed to decide whether he was prepared to become a full-time Zionist and subordinate his other obligations and loyalties to the demands of the Jewish state (St. John 1972, 188). As far as Silver was concerned, the real question was not one of abandoning his American-Zionist ideology but, rather, how that ideology could be made compatible with the Israeli state agenda. The question that Silver had to face was whether the American-Zionist perspective could continue to exist within a Zionist arena that was now subordinate to the Israeli state agenda.

Silver's answer to the above question was hinted at in the "two centers" speech, which served as his flagship Zionist address from August 1948 through late 1952 and posited a dialogue between Diaspora Jewry and a sovereign Jewish center in Israel as the ultimate expression of pan-Zionist Jewish solidarity. Silver was not content merely to advocate the existence, side by side, of two Jewish centers, an Israeli and an American one; rather, he called for a dialogue of equals between two Zionist models (see, e.g., Silver 1950a). However, Silver soon realized that any attempt on his part to oppose Israel's exclusive control of the Zionist agenda would be highly problematic. This difficulty came to the fore in early July 1948 during the fifty-first ZOA convention held in Pittsburgh. The convention opened just a month and a half after Israel had declared its independence; however, rather than the atmosphere of exhilaration that might have been expected in the wake of that historic achievement, a sense of divisiveness prevailed regarding the *hafrada* (separation) initiative that Silver and Neumann were advocating. Silver and Neumann proposed that, henceforth, the Zionist movement in the Diaspora function on a completely separate basis from the State of Israel; in order for this to happen, it would be necessary to reorganize as a "Friends of Israel" movement that would merge all of the American-Zionist political parties into one large and cohesive federation (Neumann 1976, 288–89).[4]

4. On the attitude of the American Jewish Committee to the separation initiative, see Report on Meetings of Zionist Actions Committee in Israel, September 17, 1948, AJHSA, RG-347.17 Gen-12. On Ben-Gurion's attitude to this same initiative, see Meeting of Israel

As the American-Zionist parties that Silver and Neumann wished to subsume within a larger organization were for the most part branches of the Israeli-Zionist parties, the proposal thus sought to reorganize the American-Zionist movement not on the basis of Israel's domestic political agenda, but as a Diaspora movement and on the basis of an American-Jewish program that would engage the Israeli-Zionist agenda in a dialogue of equals. However, the proposal was perceived by many American Jews as antagonistic to the State of Israel and, therefore, illegitimate. For most American Jews, the great attraction of solidarity with the State of Israel was its monopoly on Zionist discourse. As long as Zionist ideology could be regarded as an external, non-American phenomenon, it could continue to serve as a unifying focus of pan-Jewish identification. When Silver attempted to undermine this Israeli monopoly, he was perceived as trying to drag the external unifying Zionist symbol into the internal disputes of American Jewry.

This inability of Silver to lead an American-Zionist opposition against the State of Israel became strikingly evident in early 1949, when Silver was ousted from his various positions in the Zionist movement by the Israeli-Zionist leadership under Ben-Gurion. A series of dramatic confrontations culminated in Silver's loss of control over the United Jewish Appeal; this in turn doomed any effort on his part to lead an independent American-Zionist movement, one capable of engaging in an equal dialogue with the Israeli leadership. Despite the widespread support that he still enjoyed within the Zionist activist community, Silver thus found himself obliged to resign from his leadership positions in the Jewish Agency and AZEC. During his farewell meeting at AZEC, he declared that, despite the unjustifiable Israeli interference in internal American-Zionist affairs, he could not endorse insubordination to Israel, which was even from Silver's perspective the acknowledged representative institution of Jewish unity (Orian 1982, 512–13).

First Temporary Government, November 10, 1948, Israel State Archive; Executive Meeting of Mapai Party, April 22, 1949, Ben-Gurion Archive; Ben-Gurion Diary, April 21, 1949, Ben-Gurion Archive.

In this way a clear demarcation line came to be drawn between the period of Silver's Zionist leadership during the 1940s and the leadership model to which he adhered during the last decade and a half of his life. As Silver saw it, the State of Israel had a dual function to fulfill for American Jewry: it had to be both an undisputable source of unity and solidarity and a source of inspiration for an internal American-Jewish awakening, with its own distinct agenda and mission. Now that the Israeli-Zionist viewpoint was threatening to monopolize the entire Zionist agenda, the danger arose that a fundamental contradiction would emerge between these two functions. It was a real concern that the State of Israel would become a point of identification that, while fostering American-Jewish pride and cohesion, nevertheless suppressed any possibility of an autonomous American-Jewish creative endeavor. Silver's efforts during the last decade of his life to maintain his Zionist leadership mandate would thus become the story of a search for a new balance between the internal and external American-Jewish functions fulfilled by the State of Israel—between a deep commitment to Israel as the supreme expression of a Jewish collective identification and an equally deep need to turn this commitment into a force for intra-Jewish awakening and for the creation of an American-Jewish agenda distinct from the Zionist agenda emerging at that time in Israel.

PART THREE

Israel Becomes an Ideological and Political Challenge

7

In the Wake of Israeli Statehood

THE COMPLEXITY of the dilemma faced by Silver in the wake of Israeli statehood is illustrated in the speech he gave on June 16, 1949, following a five-month leave of absence from his post as chairman of the American Zionist Emergency Council (AZEC). Not only did this speech officially terminate his tenure in an official Zionist capacity, but it also effectively marked the end of the activity of the AZEC, which thereafter became a strictly pro-Israel lobby group named the American Zionist Council (AZC). Silver spoke nostalgically about the struggle in the United Nations and the hard work done by people with opposing worldviews. He presented this accomplishment as an ideal model of American-Jewish unity, which drew strength from identification with the Jewish state endeavor. Although this was a painful moment of parting, Silver refrained from pointing at Israel as having sabotaged a successful Diaspora-Zionist model. On the contrary, he felt compelled to link the model's success to the commitment and unconditional loyalty—on his own part and on the part of American Jewry—to the Jewish state endeavor. It was clear from his statements that he did not do this merely in a perfunctory manner, but rather with deep conviction and inner awareness. Silver thus found himself speaking words of love and commitment to Israel and its leadership, even though they, and their Israel-centric ethos, had ultimately led to his fall from power and removal from his post (Orian 1982, 513).

In retrospect, Silver's sincere effort to base his quest for an independent Diaspora-Zionist leadership on unconditional loyalty to the State of Israel points at a fundamental and perhaps unresolved quandary. At this early stage, however, it was still too difficult for him to decide whether to see his resignation as a final retirement from official positions in the

Zionist movement, or to view it only as a temporary setback and tactical retreat. This lack of clarity lasted four years until the end of 1952. An early example of the ambiguity that existed can be found in a letter Silver sent in March 1949 to James McDonald, who had recently been appointed as the first US ambassador to Israel. Silver updated the ambassador on the internal Zionist debate that had triggered his resignation. He explained that although the debate pertained to an issue that was ostensibly of limited scope and only concerned the United Jewish Appeal's manner of operation, it represented, in fact, a struggle over the very existence of an American-Zionist movement. He summed up the issue by a firm statement that even though the "first battle" may have ended in failure, he was certain that in the overall course of the "war," the American-Zionist movement would prove its vitality and its ability to exist independently. As he would also do on many other occasions, in this letter Silver contributed to the impression that his Diaspora-Zionist leadership was still relevant and that he had not yet given up the struggle to preserve the independence of the American-Zionist movement. At the same time, however, he did not clarify—nor was he apparently able to do so—what this meant in practical terms.[1]

This vagueness regarding his intentions would be characteristic of Silver's activity throughout this period; it was particularly true for Silver's supporters among the grassroots activists in the American-Zionist movement, who found it difficult to accept the sudden disappearance of their admired leader. An example of this can be found in correspondence carried out in 1950–1951 between Silver and Rabbi Jerome Unger, who had just been appointed as the AZC's executive director. This correspondence demonstrates that, although Silver was succeeded in his post as chairman by the veteran Zionist leader Louis Lipsky, he continued to receive ongoing reports about the council's activities. Thus, in a letter dated February 6, 1950—a full year after Silver's effective retirement—Unger sent Silver

1. Letters between McDonald and Silver, March 16 and 18, 1949, General Correspondence (D3-02-X364) Silver, Abba Hillel, 1949–1960, the Papers of James Grover McDonald, the Herbert H. Lehman Papers of the School of International Affairs, Columbia University.

a detailed report about the AZC's activity on two main issues: a protest against supplying arms to Arab states while a US embargo on supplying arms to the State of Israel remained in force, and the struggle against the internationalization of Jerusalem. In his report, Unger elaborated the AZC's activities vis-à-vis the Vatican, the United Nations, and the two houses of Congress, detailing names of people approached by the AZC, and when, in Unger's opinion, support speeches could be expected by certain members of the Senate and House of Representatives. Unger also took every opportunity to express the hope that Silver would return to his official position as the movement's leader. In a letter dated April 7, 1950, Unger reported to Silver about preparations for the State of Israel's Independence Day ball, and implored him to attend. Silver declined, apparently in order to avoid an awkward situation in which he would be overshadowed by the guest of honor, Ambassador Abba Eban. Eban, who had been a junior member in the Jewish Agency's delegation to the United Nations headed by Silver, had risen seemingly overnight to become the most popular spokesman for the State of Israel. Instead, Silver chose to give the keynote speech at a mass Independence Day rally held on May 14 in New York's Madison Square Garden. The next day, Unger quickly sent an emotion-filled letter of thanks to Silver for his speech; he emphasized that everyone who expected Silver to return to his position of leadership was filled with hope upon hearing his words.[2]

It appears that Unger indeed believed that the speech marked Silver's intention to officially reassume the leadership position, and he therefore urged Silver to attend an AZC conference on the issue of the American arms embargo held on June 4–5 in Washington. This was an attempt to re-create a pattern of activity that Silver had instituted during the period of the prestate struggle, during which local Zionist activists would "descend upon" Washington, convening for two concentrated days of lobbying and applying pressure to Senate and House members from their respective states and districts. Unger urged Silver to be present throughout the two-day conference and assume once more the active and invigorating role he had filled

2. "American Zionist Council," AHSP I (February 6, 1950–May 18, 1951).

in the past. Eventually, the conference was canceled as a direct outcome of intervention by Silver, who at that point had not held any official position in the council or the Zionist movement for nearly a year and a half.

On May 25, a statement was issued on President Truman's behalf regarding a tripartite British-French-American agreement to adopt a coordinated policy of equal treatment in supplying arms to Israel and the Arab states. In light of this statement, Silver concluded that there was no point in conducting the concentrated lobbying activity in Washington. The next day, he called the council's head office from his office in Cleveland to inform Unger of his decision. Immediately upon receiving the message, Unger decided to postpone the conference. The announcements were signed by Lipsky, but in characteristic fashion, the wording of the press release was reported to Silver the same day (American Zionist Council 1950).[3]

Ironically, this continuous deference to Silver served to highlight the impasse he faced. It appeared as if Silver's loyal supporters—those who wished in vain for him to return to an official position of leadership—inadvertently underscored their leader's paradoxical situation. Ostensibly, the road back to leadership was open for him to take. However, as the leader of a lobby organization whose sole purpose was to serve the Israeli agenda, this position of power would have further amplified Silver's marginal standing and reduced stature. This problematic position in relation to Israel can be observed in a report written by Eliezer Livneh (Liebenstein). Livneh, who served in the first and second Knessets (Israel's parliament) on behalf of the ruling party, Mapai, was among the few members of that party who openly supported Silver's return to the Zionist leadership. At the beginning of 1950, he was sent to the United States by Ben-Gurion in order to ascertain the state of the Zionist movement there. He soon developed an independent position on the American-Jewish issue. Livneh pointed to the irony that the founding of the State of Israel had considerably weakened the standing of the American-Zionist

3. American Zionist Council, correspondence between Unger and Silver, May 26, 1950, AHSP I.

movement, attributing this state of affairs to the utter dependence on Israel that American-Zionism had developed. Livneh regarded this as a dangerous process that was leading to a disintegration of the ideological-political element of the American-Zionist movement. He stated that in the short term the Israeli leadership might feel more comfortable with Jewish supporters who never questioned its policies, but warned that these supporters could vanish at the first sign of difficulties. Livneh concluded that the American-Zionist ideological movement headed by Silver should be revived. He described Silver's great popularity among grassroots Zionist activists, and stressed that many of them hoped for his return to a position of official leadership. Livneh also correctly analyzed the practical political options Silver confronted, arguing that Silver would be unable to return to any leadership position without the blessing of the Israeli leadership. He therefore proposed that Ben-Gurion take advantage of Silver's distress, give him the post of chairman of the Zionist General Council, and thereby make Silver indebted to Mapai.[4]

Ben-Gurion's rejection of Livneh's proposal reflected not only his ideological objection to Diaspora Zionism, but also his personal political distrust of Silver. However, even if Ben-Gurion had approved Livneh's proposal, it would still have been unacceptable to Silver. Livneh was mainly concerned by forecasts of a drop in UJA revenues in 1951, and even more important, he feared that the Council of Jewish Federations and non-Zionist bodies such as the American Jewish Committee would demand a larger portion of the donations be channeled into local needs. He argued that the amounts designated for Israel hinged on the hegemony over the UJA of an ideological Zionist organization with Silver at the helm. He hoped that Silver could be turned into an ally who would, by means of the UJA, transform the federations into strategic fundraising sources and thus guarantee the funds would be channeled into Israel rather than used for local American-Jewish needs.

4. Livneh voiced his position in a speech given to American-Zionist activists on March 28, 1950 in New York, (AHSP I), and later stated it in a report he wrote for Ben-Gurion upon his return to Israel (Ganin 2005, 62–67).

In effect, Livneh's approach did not differ from that of Ben-Gurion. He, too, was looking for the most effective way to mobilize American Jewry in support for the State of Israel's financial and political needs; he diverged from Ben-Gurion only in his tactics. Livneh was not party to Ben-Gurion's opinion that the best way to harness American Jewry for the benefit of the State of Israel was to neutralize the American-Zionist movement and establish a direct relationship with the American-Jewish masses. Instead, he believed that the best tactic was to maintain a strong ideological American-Zionist movement.[5] For Silver, both positions were unacceptable, as they both forcefully illustrated that, from the Israeli perspective, the American-Zionist leadership would eventually be relegated to serving as mere executives of an Israeli-determined agenda, which would essentially disregard the local needs of American Jewry.

Against this backdrop, Silver gradually came to see that even with all of his influence in the American-Zionist arena, he would only be able to return to a genuine leadership position by finding a way to effect a fundamental perceptual change within the Israeli leadership. In Silver's view, the American-Zionist agenda was not supposed to replace the Israeli-Zionist agenda, but rather to establish a dialogue of equals. From the Ben-Gurionist perspective, however, such a demand challenged the Israeli presumption of a monopoly over the definition of Zionism. At this stage, it appears that Silver still nurtured the hope that it would be possible to convince Ben-Gurion and the Israeli leadership to legitimize the coexistence of an Israeli state agenda and that of the Diaspora. He soon discovered that the Israeli leadership's willingness to tolerate a distinct Diaspora-Zionist agenda was limited. This is reflected, for example, by Ben-Gurion's angry reaction to the resolutions of the Zionist General Council, which convened in April 1950 in Jerusalem. In Ben-Gurion's view, these resolutions deviated from the legitimate objectives of the Zionist movement. They stated that, besides encouraging immigration, Zionist activity in the Diaspora should foster the Jewish and Hebrew education

5. See also a later report by Livneh (1952), which described the relations between Israel and American Jewry in the same vein.

of Jewish youth. Ben-Gurion was also displeased by the resolution of the Zionist General Council to establish an institution to coordinate between the Jewish Agency and the government, and saw this as acceptance of an unjustified demand by the American Zionists for recognition of the legitimacy of a Zionist ideology that was not solely dedicated to immigration to Israel. Because of the need for the Jewish Agency's help in absorbing immigration, he agreed to honor the resolution and set up the coordinating institution, but this did not prevent him from declaring his opposition as a Zionist. He also took care to arrange that Jewish Agency representatives in the coordinating institution would consist exclusively of Israelis.[6]

Ben-Gurion's objection to recognizing the legitimacy of a separate American-Zionist ideology was exemplified most vividly in the memorandum of understanding reached at approximately the same time, in August 1950, between Ben-Gurion and Jacob Blaustein, the head of the non-Zionist American Jewish Committee. In this document, Ben-Gurion was ostensibly willing to agree to all the principles to which he was adamantly opposed when it came to a possible understanding with the American-Zionist movement. In his letter to Blaustein, Ben-Gurion declared his recognition that American Jews owed loyalty only to the United States, and promised that Israel would refrain from intervening in the internal affairs of American Jewry. However, as a number of researchers have already explained (see, e.g., Feldstein 2003, 57–61), this declaration did not constitute a retreat from Ben-Gurion's ideological views. On the contrary, because this was not part of the inner Zionist discourse, Ben-Gurion was able to regard the understandings with Blaustein as a tactical move designed to secure the economic and political support of American Jews for the State of Israel. In his eyes, the memorandum of understanding with the non-Zionists was part of a pragmatic policy that took into account that Zionist propaganda for immigration would lead to friction with the masses of non-Zionist American Jews and, therefore, would needlessly damage the economic and political support that could be obtained from

6. For a speech that expressed Ben-Gurion's stance regarding the need for total Israeli control over Zionist discourse and the activities of the Jewish Agency, see Ben-Gurion (1950).

them. In contrast, an ideological dialogue with the American Zionists required legitimizing the existence of the Diaspora-Zionist ideology, which Ben-Gurion firmly opposed.

This was also an important reason for Ben-Gurion's refusal to invite Silver to the economic conference that he convened in Jerusalem at the beginning of September 1950. The gathering of forty-four Diaspora Jewish leaders was designed to lay the foundations for the Israel Bonds campaign. Ben-Gurion's initiative came during a turnabout in Israel's foreign policy and considerable economic difficulties that arose after implementing an economic austerity policy and following the great wave of immigration. During the economic conference, Ben-Gurion explained to the Jewish leaders that Israel would have to absorb some two hundred thousand immigrants annually over the coming three years; in order to do so, along with its other economic and security needs, it would require $1.5 billion over the course of the coming three years.[7] Despite the urgency of mobilizing American Jewry to help underwrite Israel's economic needs, Ben-Gurion delayed inviting Silver until the last moment. An important reason for this was Ben-Gurion's objection to Silver's Diaspora Zionism. In fact, he saw the initiation of the Bonds campaign as a means of neutralizing this ideology, which despite Silver's ousting still represented a strong current within the UJA. Ben-Gurion was interested in a funding machinery that would be totally subordinate to the Israeli administration (i.e., the Israeli treasury office) and its economic needs.

While it is true that there were those in the Israeli leadership who disagreed with Ben-Gurion's attitude toward Silver, these differences of opinion were only tactical. Thus, in meetings convened by Ben-Gurion at the end of July in advance of the economic conference, a number of people, including Foreign Minister Sharett, Ambassador Eban, and Eliyahu

7. The austerity policy was instituted following the huge deficit in the balance of payments and the constant foreign currency shortage from the total sum of $1.5 billion. Israel hoped to raise $1 billion from foreign sources, partly through a US loan and partly through donations and investments by American Jews (Feldstein 2003, 51–65; "Israel Cabinet Meeting Today on Economic Crisis; Experts from Various Groups Participate," August 20, 1950, AHSP I).

Dobkin, head of the Jewish Agency's Organization Department, spoke in favor of recognizing the unique contribution of the American-Zionist movement and encouraging cooperation with it. However, the speakers' reasons were solely focused on the benefit that the American-Zionist movement could bring to the State of Israel. Sharett, for example, suggested that the ideological branch of American Zionism was Israel's most loyal and reliable ally. Accordingly, he suggested a definition of Zionism that was not solely based on immigration to Israel, but was rather focused on loyalty and commitment. He defined as a Zionist anyone "who identifies with all his heart and soul with the State of Israel, someone who can be trusted at any difficult hour of the state . . . and will later search for a way to explain and resolve this position with . . . his formal duty towards his government" (July 25, 1950, Israel State Archive 45 c-5563; quoted in Feldstein 2003, 56).

Needless to say, in sharp contrast to this latter definition, Silver viewed loyalty toward the United States as more than a formal obligation that must be reconciled with Zionist loyalty. For Silver, the tension created by viewing the United States and Israel as two homelands was a positive and vital component of his Diaspora Zionism. In the context, when at the very last moment Sharett and Eban succeeded in persuading Ben-Gurion to invite Silver, Silver fully understood that, if he wished to maintain his political independence, he could not accept the invitation. Three days before the start of the conference, on August 28, Ben-Gurion empowered Ambassador Eban to send a personal invitation to Silver; Foreign Minister Sharett added a personal message, imploring him to accept the invitation. In his response, Silver mentioned his heavy workload, and asked Eban to convey the message that if the prime minister should wish to consult him at a later date, he would be glad to make a special trip to Israel.[8] In retrospect, it is clear that it was exactly because of his dependence on receiving legitimization from Ben-Gurion that he could not accept the invitation. Silver understood that his acceptance would communicate his

8. For Silver's report from about nine months later in a speech at the Commercial Club in Tel Aviv regarding his response to Ben-Gurion's invitation, see *Ha'aretz* (1951c).

willingness to relinquish his presumption to the unique status of a leader of an independent ideological Zionist stream within American Jewry.

On his part, Silver perceived the rise in strength of the Israel General Zionists Party at the end of 1950 as perhaps the last opportunity to try to compel the Israeli leadership to acknowledge the equal status of American Diaspora Zionism. The rise in the strength of the Israeli General Zionists Party received its first electoral expression in the municipal elections of November 1950, against the backdrop of the government's increasing difficulty maintaining its austerity policy of rationing and price control. The municipal elections were held in the face of public complaints that the austerity regime had failed, and that the attempt to manage the economy through directives from above was unsuccessful. The General Zionists skillfully expressed this sense of protest, and when the polls closed, it became apparent that they had succeeded in garnering an impressive 25 percent of the vote. These results positioned them as the second-largest party after Mapai, and constituted a huge leap in comparison with the 6 percent that the party received about two years earlier, in January 1949, in the first general Knesset elections. The results placed the General Zionists in a position that appeared to threaten Mapai's rule, especially in light of a governmental crisis and the second general Knesset elections that were scheduled for July 30, 1951. What contributed to the sense of euphoria among the General Zionists were the results in certain places such as Tel Aviv, where they gained a victory of 31 percent of the vote versus only 23 percent for Mapai. And so, although sober commentators stated that there was a high probability that the results of the general Knesset elections would be much more positive for Mapai, some harbored hopes that the General Zionists would be able to replicate or even better their achievement, and thus become a much more significant player in Israeli politics.[9]

9. In the municipal election, Mapai received 92,589 votes, which constituted 27.9 percent of the total votes and a decline of 6.7 percent in comparison with the first Knesset election in January 1949. The General Zionists received 80,202 votes—24.9 percent of the total vote and an increase of 17.8 percent in comparison with the 1949 election (Shacham 1991, 64).

Silver himself had no illusions regarding the possibility of a change of government, but he hoped that the rise in the General Zionists' strength would force the Mapai leadership to legitimize his status in the Zionist arena. He consequently cultivated close ties with the General Zionist leadership, hoping to benefit from their increased strength. However, when rumors occasionally arose as to his intentions to personally participate in Israeli politics, he took care to clarify that his interest was focused solely on the American-Zionist arena. An example of this could be found in his reaction to the telegrams that he received from leaders of the General Zionists at the conclusion of the municipal election day on November 14, 1950. Party leader Peretz Bernstein was the first to write to Silver. Immediately after midnight, even before the vote tally was complete, Bernstein sent the following telegram message: "Overwhelming victory achieved, details tomorrow." Over the course of that night and the next morning, Silver received telegrams from lower-level party activists, detailing the results in Tel Aviv, Jerusalem, and Haifa, and announcements about the party's demand to hold new Knesset elections. Silver was not indifferent to the results, but in the congratulatory telegram he sent to Bernstein the next day, he focused on the new possibilities he hoped would develop in the American-Zionist arena. He was especially pleased by the fact that the General Zionists gained strength relative to the Progressive Party, which had split off from them in 1948, and in the United States was identified with his rivals in the ZOA. Silver hoped that a union between the two parties in Israel would create a large Israeli political camp that would be under the control of the General Zionists. He believed that in such a case, Mapai would have no choice but to include the unified camp in its coalition, and that this step would in turn bring him legitimization from Israel's government and thus stymie the internal American-Zionist opposition to him.[10]

10. Elias Epstein, "The Municipal Election in Israel," AHSP I; Telegram from Rosenblum to Silver, n.d. (probably February or March 1950), AHSP I, Israel General, 799; Israel State Archive, A 122/123; Telegram to Silver from Bernstein, November 15, Israel; Telegram to Silver from Rivilin, November 15, 1950; Telegram to Silver, November 15, 1950 (not signed), AHSP I; Text of cablegram to Dr. Peretz Bernstein, November 16, 1950, AHSP I.

In the following months, between the municipal elections of November 1950 and the second Knesset elections of July 1951, Silver closely followed political developments in Israel; he took a number of steps to take advantage of the expected gain in the strength of the General Zionists. The first significant step was taken in March by Neumann, Silver's loyalist, who hoped that the political developments would lead to a reconciliation between Silver and Ben-Gurion, and that this would enable Silver to return to the WZO Executive and receive a key position in the twenty-third Zionist Congress, scheduled to convene in August 1951, about a month after the Knesset elections. As part of this move, Neumann asked Eban to propose to Ben-Gurion that Silver be invited for an official visit to Israel, but Ben-Gurion unequivocally refused. "No invitation will be sent to Silver in any form," he wrote to Eban. Along with this, Ben-Gurion sent a telegram to Benjamin Browdy, president of the ZOA, in which he denied reports by *Ha'aretz* to the effect that he harbored a personal grudge against Silver, and voiced confidence that as all other American Zionists, Silver would be committed to helping the State of Israel. From Silver's standpoint, the implications of this indirect reaction were harsher than a direct debate with Ben-Gurion. It meant that Ben-Gurion refused to acknowledge Silver's special status, even as an adversary, and in general assigned to the American Zionists the limited role of assisting Israel's interests (Silver 1932-1933; see also Feldstein 2003, 74).[11]

Ben-Gurion's response strengthened Silver's evaluation that engaging the former in dialogue would have to be done from a position of political power. In other words, it would require strengthening the alliance with the General Zionists. This conclusion led him to accept the request of a delegation headed by Yosef Serlin, deputy speaker of the Knesset from the General Zionists, to come to Israel in April–May as the party's guest, and to personally participate in the election campaign on its behalf. Despite this, Silver understood the limits of his power, and was careful to make it clear that the goal of his visit was not involvement in the election battle

11. Correspondence between Ben-Gurion and Eban, Israel State Archive, March 28, 1951; Correspondence, March 2, 1951, Ben-Gurion Archives.

against Mapai, but rather to contribute to achieving a union of forces between the General Zionists and the Progressive parties. He wrote to this effect in a private communication to Neumann, and spoke in a similar manner at the farewell party held in his honor prior to his departure for Israel. During the party, Browdy, ZOA's president, presented him with a gold pen and voiced the hope that it would serve him after his election at the twenty-third Congress in August as president of the World Zionist Organization. Silver responded by saying that he was unable to understand why bitterness had built up between the American Zionists and the government of Israel and blamed this on his rivals, the supporters of the Progressives in the United States. It was clear that from Silver's point of view his decision to actively contribute to the General Zionists' election campaign was not intended to challenge Ben-Gurion, but rather to force the latter to acknowledge his standing as an independent leader of American Zionism (Gelblum 1951; *Yiddish News Digest* 1951, 2).[12]

Silver arrived in Israel on April 25, 1951. Despite his statements, both the General Zionists and Mapai viewed his visit as directly connected to the political rivalry between them. The General Zionists styled the event as an official state reception, which only underscored the demonstrative absence of all representatives of the ruling party, Mapai, from the ceremony. Israeli newspapers spanning the political spectrum described the extraordinary reception on their front pages and reported that, prior to the visit, the General Zionists had appointed a special public committee comprised of all their leaders to receive their guest. A day before Silver's arrival, a preparatory parade was held near the airport with the participation of bands and youth movement members. Early the next day, the welcoming convoy, consisting of between one thousand and fifteen hundred people, headed to the airport. The reception was conducted according to all the rules of protocol, and included a band that played "Hatikva" and a speech by Silver (in Hebrew) that was broadcast on IBA radio. After the ceremony, Silver and his escorts traveled in a motorcycle-led convoy followed by a detachment of riders; the convoy passed through the streets of

12. Letter from Silver to Neumann, 19 April 1951, Zionist Central Archive, A 123/206.

several cities that were controlled by the General Zionists. In each of these cities, honorary stages were set up with bands and welcoming speeches. In Petah Tikva, Silver was received with a traditional bread and salt ceremony. In Ramat Gan, national flags were raised over the municipality buildings, and the deputy mayor declared, "we ask you to stand at the head of the Diaspora Jews." In Tel Aviv, in Mugrabi Square, the largest reception of all was held, after which many members of the audience accompanied Silver to his nearby hotel, which was decorated with banners in Hebrew proclaiming: "Abba Hillel Silver, welcome to Israel."[13]

Silver was not a passive player in the political show of force organized by the General Zionists. As can be observed from his speeches, he was certainly pleased by the extraordinary reception; in his public statements he made it clear that he viewed the warm welcome as a personal vindication and a kind of revenge for Ben-Gurion's refusal to invite him officially to Israel. Thus, in a speech he gave at the Commercial Club in Tel Aviv on his first evening in Israel, he contrasted what he described as the puzzle elicited by the incongruity of Ben-Gurion's refusal to officially invite him with the warm welcome he received from the citizens of Israel. However, Silver also made it clear that he had not come for a confrontation, but rather for dialogue and partnership with Mapai. This conciliatory tone was so evident throughout the speech that even *Davar*, the newspaper which was identified with Mapai, reported with a certain measure of surprise that contrary to the political nature attached to the visit by the General Zionists, Silver himself refrained from attacking the labor party and instead severely attacked the Progressive Party for its refusal to unite with the General Zionists. And indeed, during the visit Silver repeatedly reprimanded those who sought to fuel the personal friction between him and Ben-Gurion. He added to this by describing himself as not being motivated by any personal or factional political scores, but rather working in a substantive manner on behalf of Israel. He said that although he had been

13. On the reception and the first day of Silver's visit, see *Al-Hamishmar* 1951a; *Davar* 1951a, 1; *Ha'aretz* 1951a, 1; *HaBoker* 1951a, 1; 1951b, 1; *Hazophe* 1951a, 8; *Ma'ariv* 1951, 3; *Yedihot Achronot* 1951a.

unjustly removed from his positions in the Zionist movement, he rallied as a loyal soldier for the State of Israel's vital interests. He repeatedly noted that he had traveled the length and breadth of the United States in order to raise funds for Israel, and that in the last weeks before his trip to Israel, he traveled some 8,000 kilometers for this purpose. He went on to pledge his full dedication to the success of the Israel Bonds campaign, despite the fact that he was excluded from the discussions in which decisions were made on this issue (*Davar* 1951b; *Ha'aretz* 1951c; *HaBoker* 1951c).

Similarly, he took care to refute his image as an ideological adversary of the Israeli socialist camp. He came out against the propaganda that portrayed him as an American reactionary, an enemy of the workers, and a supporter of the right-wing branch of the Republican Party. He cited his struggles in the United States for workers' rights, and the fact that he was identified with progressive social-economic views and staunch opposition to McCarthyism; he emphasized that he had often been attacked in the United States as a radical and even a Communist. In the same context, he mentioned his firm opposition to hawkish positions on the Cold War and the Korean War, and stressed that in many of his positions—such as his support for American recognition of the People's Republic of China and the dismissal of the commander of US armed forces in Korea, General MacArthur—there were profound differences of opinion between him and leaders of the conservative right-wing branch of the Republican Party. He described the General Zionists Party as the counterpart of the Democratic Party in the United States, and explained that his support for it should not be construed as an attack on the Socialist camp in Israel; rather, it was intended to restore the balance that in Silver's opinion was disrupted between socialism and social-minded approaches that advocated free competition and private capital (*Al-Hamishmar* 1951b; *Ma'ariv* 1951).

In analyzing these speeches, one should not examine whether the high marks that Silver gave himself for his nonpartisan behavior faithfully reflected his true motives. The more important issue pertains to his attempt at using the position of power that he believed the alliance with the General Zionists afforded him in order to reach a dialogue with Mapai's leaders and extract from them recognition of his separate Zionist ideology. In virtually all of his speeches, Silver repeatedly argued that the

State of Israel needed a strong Zionist movement in the United States. He stated that Israel should by no means render American Zionism devoid of content by presenting immigration to Israel as the sole essence of Zionist ideology, nor should it advocate immigration based on the pretext that the situation of US Jewry would deteriorate. Silver objected to this "negation of exile" approach, and called instead to base the Zionist message on the positive vision expressed by the national revival of Israel. He argued that this latter form of advocacy would capture people's hearts, serve as a focus for a new American-Zionist awakening, and ultimately draw young American Jews, who would come to Israel not as a result of propaganda of fear but rather of their own free will. His main contention was that an outlook that did not mobilize support for Israel on the basis of fear required viewing the involvement of American Zionists in Israel not as external intervention but as a necessary and authentic expression designed to influence and contribute to society in Israel.

Did Silver's tactic meet with success? How did Israelis respond to the attempt to present the alliance with the General Zionists as part of the effort to highlight the importance of an independent Diaspora Zionism? In this respect, which was so crucial for Silver, he was met with utter defeat. The main responses to the Zionist statements he made during his visit to Israel ranged from skepticism and lack of understanding, even among his sympathizers and friends, to suspicion that gradually mounted among his rivals. An example of this can be seen in an editorial that appeared in *Ha'aretz*, which usually wrote favorably about Silver and his visit to Israel, but changed its tone while discussing his Zionist ideology. After praising Silver for disappointing those who expected him to behave like a party activist mobilized on behalf of the General Zionists and against the government, the editorial responded with skepticism to the parts in which Silver expressed the universalistic-religious aspects of his Zionist outlook. The editorial noted that Silver did not succeed in explaining how the universal-religious vision of creating a "good society" could be fulfilled, and that he spoke more as a preacher than as a statesman. The writer offered a similar opinion about the role of bringing global peace that Silver envisioned for the State of Israel. He viewed this as a privilege undertaken by a Jewish leader who did not bear the burden of everyday action, and could therefore permit himself to adopt a moral stance that did not take into consideration the limitations of reality (*Ha'aretz* 1951c).

The negative responses to Silver's views became sharper when commenting on his argument that Zionist ideology should not be limited to the issue of immigrating to Israel. An article in *Ma'ariv*, which like *Ha'aretz* generally reported favorably about Silver's visit, mocked Silver's presumption to preach to the Truman administration on foreign policy issues in the name of Jewish morality instead of devoting himself to the sole Zionist obligation of bringing Jews to Israel. The writer of the article questioned Silver's need to interpose himself in the dispute between the Republicans and the Democrats, and asked why he should not instead engage in his duty as an admired Jewish rabbi and go out to his brothers and tell them the truth: "Their eyes have been blinded, and they honestly believe that by giving us dollars, they are saving us. The opposite is true: Let them come to us and leave the Exile—even if this is as difficult for them as parting the Red Sea" (Efrat 1951).

When it came to the Mapai leadership, the skeptical reactions gave way to a hostile and suspicious attitude regarding Silver's political intentions. The Mapai leaders did not respond to Silver's direct and implied proposals for dialogue; instead, they boycotted him almost without exception. This was particularly true when it came to Ben-Gurion, who refused to meet with Silver during his visit, despite many requests. This reached its peak on May 2, when the two leaders did not meet even though they were both at the airport almost at the same time. Silver departed for a visit to Eilat, while Ben-Gurion left for the United States to launch the Bonds campaign. Only Sharett did not boycott Silver. On May 6, he joined Silver's tour as a guest of the Jewish National Fund in the Galilee. At that time, the border dispute between Israel and Syria was at its peak, concerning the Israeli initiatives to dry up the Hula Lake and expand its agricultural use of demilitarized areas in the border region. In his role as foreign minister, it was important to Sharett to update Silver about the need for his participation in the diplomatic struggle to mobilize US support for Israel's position regarding the UN armistice committee. Therefore, his participation in the tour should not be seen as a political statement made by a Mapai leader in favor of dialogue with Silver, but rather as part of the opposite

Israeli outlook, which allotted the activists of the Zionist movement in the United States the role of lobbyists in the service of Israeli interests and policies (*Yedihot Achronot* 1951c).[14]

In retrospect, it can be said that Silver failed in his attempt to use the Israeli political arena in order to force the Mapai leadership to recognize American Zionism's independent status, and this became even more evident during Ben-Gurion's first post-statehood visit to the United States. When Silver returned to the United States, Ben-Gurion was already in the midst of his tour on behalf of the Israel Bonds campaign. From an American-Zionist perspective, Ben-Gurion's trip was a harsh disappointment. In his speeches and meetings, Ben-Gurion demonstratively ignored the American-Zionist movement and its role in the struggle for Israel's establishment. In a dinner held by Jewish leaders in his honor at the end of his visit, Ben-Gurion took care to make it clear that he had not come to the United States to speak with the Zionists, but rather with the masses of US Jewry. Silver was personally offended by the fact that Ben-Gurion did not find the time to meet with him, even when he was visiting Cleveland. On his part, in a speech at the June 1951 ZOA convention in Atlantic City, Silver attacked Ben-Gurion for his preference of the non-Zionists over the American-Zionist movement. He rejected Ben-Gurion's demand for nonintervention of the American Zionists in Israeli politics, and led a resolution by the convention, which announced the endorsement of the General Zionists Party in the coming Israeli election.[15]

Paradoxically, the draft resolution and the discussions surrounding it highlighted even more profoundly the dependence of Silver and American Zionism on the Israeli leadership. In fact, the main internal battle in the ZOA between Silver and his opponents was a tactical debate on how to obtain legitimacy for their separate Diaspora-Zionist views on the part

14. Silver's Diary, May 2 and May 6, 1951, AHSP V.

15. Ben-Gurion's Diary, May 9, 1956; Ben-Gurion Archives, Speeches and Articles (Visit to the United States); Neumann's Speech during the 23rd Zionist Congress, in *The Twenty-third Zionist Congress—A Protocol* (Jerusalem: World Zionist Organization, 1951), 95–98; Zionist Central Archive, A123/206 and A512/44; Silver's Speech in the ZOA Convention, Foreign Office, 118/6, Israel State Archive; Feldstein (2003, 74).

of the Israeli-Zionist discourse. Whether this should be pursued through an alliance with the General Zionists, which became the main opposition party to Mapai, or through an alliance with the Progressive Party, which positioned itself as Mapai's loyal coalition partner (*The American Zionist* 1951). Regardless of these differences, both factions failed in their attempt to gain legitimacy for their separate Zionist ideology, and as a result, both suffered from an ongoing drop in membership and support in the American-Jewish community.[16] This growing weakness of American Zionism became even more evident given the results of the second Knesset elections. The General Zionists gained a sizeable increase in votes, but this was still not enough to make a bid for power. The government that was established on October 7, 1951 was almost identical in composition to the previous government, with the exception that both the General Zionists and the Progressives now found themselves temporarily outside the coalition. Only a coalition crisis with the religious parties about a year later, in December 1952, ultimately led to the two parties' inclusion in the government. However, at this stage it was already clear—both to Silver and to his rivals in the ZOA—that the inclusion of the two parties in the coalition would not change the status of American Zionism in the eyes of Israel's government.

This became quite clear in the wake of the twenty-third Zionist Congress, which convened in Jerusalem shortly after the elections. Ostensibly, the congress passed a majority vote against Ben-Gurion's will and decided to support the "status resolution," recognizing the WZO's special status as the sole representative of the Jewish Diaspora in Israel. As time passed, however, it became apparent that approval of the "status resolution" and, mainly, its manner of implementation were not dependent on the balance of power in the congress, but on government decisions and Knesset legislation. It also became clear that Ben-Gurion and the Israeli leadership would not support or legitimize a special Diaspora-Zionist

16. In the fifty-fourth ZOA convention in June 1951, the ZOA's membership dropped from two hundred thousand to one hundred sixty thousand, and the number of convention delegates dropped accordingly from eight hundred to five hundred.

status. Ben-Gurion took care to promise this to the leaders of the American Jewish Committee immediately after the resolution of the twenty-third Congress on the matter. Indeed, the wording of the "status law" that was passed by the Knesset in 1952 was limited to matters of immigration absorption, and did not recognize in any way a separate Diaspora-Zionist agenda.

This inherent weakness of Diaspora Zionism in relation to the State of Israel was demonstrated even more clearly in the speeches during the congress made by American speakers of the two rival camps within American Zionism. The main differences of opinion between the various American speakers were not in the ideological Zionist realm, but rather with regard to the manner of conduct versus the government of Israel. One approach was expressed in the words of Nahum Goldmann, who succeeded Silver as head of the American branch of the Jewish Agency, and was now elected as president of the twenty-third Congress. Like Silver, Goldmann also spoke in favor of a Diaspora-Zionist agenda that would not settle for a minimalist nationalist-political interpretation of Zionism. However, when he spoke about the nature of the partnership between Israel and the Diaspora, he emphasized that the Zionist movement was unable to act if it were not given the authority to do so by the State of Israel. He even went so far as to say that the Zionist movement, by its very nature, owed unconditional loyalty to Israel, to the point that it would have to cease its activities in case of an unbridgeable conflict with the Israeli government. Silver represented an opposite approach, which viewed the demand for unconditional support of the Israeli government's policies as a demand posed only to a defeated enemy. Silver advocated a partnership of equal status between Israel and the Zionist movement, in which both parties would have the right and even the obligation to critique the other on behalf of their shared interests. And yet, even Silver, when explaining the demand to give special status to the Zionist movement, did not argue in the name of mutual interests of Israel and Diaspora Jewry, but on the grounds that the Zionist movement was the only body within Diaspora Jewry that was truly loyal to the defense and promotion of the State of Israel's interests. In fact, Silver and his colleagues attempted to justify their demand for an independent status by claiming to be the most loyal and committed to Israeli interests among Diaspora Jewry (Ganin 2005, 112–30).[17]

This inherent need of American Zionists of both factions for recognition of their devotion and loyalty to Israel became a powerful weapon in the hands of Ben-Gurion. About a week before the start of the twenty-third Zionist Congress's discussions, Browdy met with Ben-Gurion in another attempt to bring about a dialogue with Silver. Ben-Gurion accepted Browdy's request and invited Silver and Neumann for tea. However, the meeting was devoted to a philosophical conversation about Baruch Spinoza and other lofty matters; Ben-Gurion insisted on refraining from discussing Zionist politics. Neumann also initiated another meeting in which he tried to link the coalition negotiations that were held following the Knesset elections with securing the post of chairman of the Zionist General Council for Silver, but Ben-Gurion rejected this idea as well (*Yedihot Achronot* 1951b).[18] This refusal to recognize Silver as the leader of a legitimate Diaspora ideological stream within Zionism continued to be the most effective weapon that Ben-Gurion employed against Silver a year later, following the Republican victory in the November 1952 elections. There were many American Zionists, and apparently Mapai leaders too, who believed that Silver's ties with the new American administration would lead to a strengthening of his standing in the American-Zionist arena. This is evident in the correspondence between Ben-Gurion and Zalman Aran, the future minister of education, who at the time was serving as a Mapai Knesset member. Aran was in the United States during the November election and in the two months that followed. On November 10, a few days after the elections, he described the defeat of Democratic presidential candidate Adlai Stevenson as a defeat for the American-Zionist

17. *Twenty-third Zionist Congress*, 583–84 (status resolution), 196–98 (Goldmann's speech), 91–96 (Neumann's speech), 146–51 (Rose Halprin's speech), 162–69 (Silver's speech); Ben-Gurion's Diary, March 8, 1951.

18. Ben-Gurion's Diary, August 6, 1951, August 15, 1951, August 21, 1951; Ben-Gurion's report about his meeting with Neumann, Coalition Section, August 21, 1951, Ben-Gurion Archive.

supporters of Mapai. He anxiously predicted that there would be no choice but to cultivate ties with Silver. In a further letter dated November 13, Aran warned that Silver was planning to fill among the American Jews a leadership role equivalent to that of Cardinal Spellman among the Catholic population of New York, and that a seat of power would be created around Silver that would be close to the American administration and hostile toward Mapai.[19]

The sober response that was sent by Ben-Gurion to Aran on December 5, slightly mocking Silver's new leadership presumptions, is particularly enlightening. Unlike Aran, Ben-Gurion dismissed the fear that Silver would become a "Jewish Spellman" as groundless. He explained that rather than comparing Silver with Spellman, it was more reasonable to view the government of Israel as the equivalent of the Vatican in terms of its ability to bestow power and prestige on Silver or any other Diaspora Jew. He therefore made it clear to Aran that he did not intend to utilize Silver's connections with the new US administration. Ben-Gurion fully understood that Silver's only chance of reestablishing a status of "Spellman-like" hegemonic power was completely dependent on the State of Israel's cooperation; he had no intention of giving him such backing. It is interesting to note that, in his correspondence during this same period, Ben-Gurion also addressed the foreseeable difficulties for Israel following Eisenhower's victory: "even if Eisenhower is not a captive in the hands of the supporters of the Arabs, as is alleged about him, it is clear that from now on, greater attention will be paid to gaining the friendship of the Arabs than until now." However, he did not cite this as a reason for the need to take advantage of Silver's ties with the administration.

Along with this, it appeared that Silver gradually began to understand that his ongoing confrontation with the Israeli government was eroding his strength even on his home field within the ZOA. He already discovered this at the fifty-fifth ZOA convention held in June 1952, where

19. Correspondence between Ben-Gurion and Zalman Aran, Correspondence Section, November 10, 1952; November 13, 1952; November 16, 1952; December 5, 1952, Ben-Gurion Archive.

the election for the ZOA presidency took place between Rabbi Irving Miller from Silver's camp and Abraham Redelheim. Ostensibly, the election results confirmed the dominant standing of Silver's camp in the ZOA. A closer look, however, shows the emergence of a strong opposition that received 354 votes versus 594 for the Silver-Neumann-Miller camp and was supported by most of the district presidents.[20] It would appear that at this stage, Silver already understood that in order to reestablish a leadership status within US Jewry and Zionism, he had to find a new path that did not battle against Israel. To a large degree, Silver devoted the last decade of his life to searching for alternative paths of this kind.

20. *Zionist Information Service* (ZINS), vol. 4, no. 54-b-52; Zionist Central Archive, A-512/44.

8

Identification without Subordination

FOLLOWING THE FIRST YEARS after the establishment of Israel, Silver gradually realized that the most challenging problem he faced was that of remaining committed to Israel while advancing an alternative American-Zionist agenda. Compelling evidence of this concern is found in a volume of journal entries in which he reported on Israel-related events. The one-hundred-page document was composed during irregular intervals between September 29, 1949 (shortly after he resigned from his official positions in the Zionist movement) and March 1, 1963 (nine months before his death). In writing this journal, Silver engaged in a conscious process of composition and editing, often recording activities that extended over the course of several days or even weeks. In some cases he took the trouble to attach background documentation pertinent to the events in question. Clearly, Silver did not automatically record every Israel-related event in which he was involved; rather, he thought matters through beforehand, at times deciding to include a particular topic only once he was persuaded of its importance.[1]

1. The document was composed of about one hundred pages with appendices amounting to a similar number of pages. Although there are no original manuscript versions of Silver's journal entries (apart from a single draft devoted to his April–May 1951 visit to Israel, which was appended to the collection without having been edited or printed), his familiar editing style is evident in the texts at hand. The entries begin half a year after he resigned his positions in the Jewish Agency and the Zionist Executive, and a month and a half after a self-imposed leave, followed by an official resignation, from his post as head of AZEC. Silver was not a private person, and his journal entries make virtually no mention of matters of a personal nature.

When we examine the criteria according to which Silver judged topics to be worthy of inclusion in his Israel-related journal, we are immediately struck by the absence of the category pertaining to Zionist politics. Silver, who during the early years of Israeli statehood had been involved in all areas of Zionist politics, made almost no mention in his journal of Zionist political struggles—neither those taking place within the American-Zionist movement nor those between American Zionism and the State of Israel. For example, he refrained from mentioning his behind-the-scenes activity in the American Zionist Council, his involvement in the ZOA, or his involvement in Israeli politics. This decision indicates Silver's desire to distance himself from the oppositional tone that he had taken regarding the Israeli leadership. This approach had led to his resignation in early 1949, and had left him caught in a stranglehold, unable to engage Ben-Gurion and the Israeli government in dialogue. Silver's journal thus reflected his hope of forging a new leadership model that would represent broad pan-Zionist interests. Entries in this style had begun to appear during the period of his early clashes with the Israeli leadership; gradually, and in particular after the Republican victory in the November 1952 elections, the suprapolitical tone became dominant both in Silver's journal entries and in his actual activities.

A partial explanation for this new leadership model may be found on the personal-psychological plane. Silver had a keen sense of personal dignity and disdained any measure that might place him in the light of an ousted leader unable to come to terms with his defeat; he therefore made a point of affirming his continued activity on Israel's behalf despite the unjust means by which he had been expelled from his positions in the Zionist movement. However, as important as the psychological perspective may be, it provides only a partial explanation for Silver's failure to mention his involvement in Zionist politics. For example, it does not explain why he refrained from writing about "positive" events, such as those unmarred by tension or political conflict with the Israeli leadership. Among those events that received no mention in the journal were the impressive welcoming and honorary-citizenship ceremonies held in Silver's honor during his 1951 and 1956 trips to Israel, and the Kfar Silver youth village's opening ceremony, held with Ben-Gurion's participation during Silver's visit to Israel in March 1956. Also absent from the journal were moments of retrospective poignancy such as Ben-Gurion's gracious July 1963 speech honoring Silver upon reaching the age of seventy. The most significant event in this category to be excluded from the journal was Silver's unexpected appointment in 1955 as Chairman of the Israel Bonds Board of Governors. This appointment was the highest profile instance of pro-Israel activity on Silver's part during the last decade of his life.

Notes and correspondence from Silver's private archive indicate that Silver would indeed have been entitled to view the position offered to him as proof of the Israeli leadership's recognition of his unjust treatment in 1948–1949. On the basis of this recognition, he was now being asked to replace Henry Morgenthau, Jr., who had stepped down from the post of chairman. It was particularly significant that the offer was extended at a time when Ben-Gurion had returned to the Israeli premiership after a two-year hiatus. Just a few years earlier, Ben-Gurion and the Israeli leadership had rated the non-Zionist Morgenthau's stature as more valuable to Israel than that of Silver. Only three years before, when the Israel Bonds campaign had been launched during Ben-Gurion's first trip to the United States as prime minister, the Israeli leader had ignored Silver while visiting Cleveland. Now, six years after his ousting from the UJA, Silver might have been gratified to find that the Israeli government was at last heeding his warnings about reliance on parties uncommitted to Zionist ideology. All of this potential gratification notwithstanding, the matter was excluded from Silver's journal.

The timing of this nomination, subsequent to the 1955 Israel Bonds convention in Washington, is also significant. In light of Israel's growing needs and a concomitant decline in UJA and Israel Bonds income, it was clear to the convention participants that the entire bonds fundraising enterprise was in need of revamping, and that one major step in this direction would be the appointment to the Israel Bonds chairmanship of a Jewish figure who was not only highly esteemed in the American public, but also, unlike Morgenthau, unconditionally committed to devoting his time and energy on behalf of Israel and Jewish affairs. Silver was the natural choice, and as a first step, the Israeli Finance Minister, Levi Eshkol, sent him an official letter in which Silver was praised in the most flattering terms. Eshkol affirmed that he was appealing to Silver on behalf of the State of Israel and that he, along with the Israeli leadership as a whole, was fully aware of Silver's special status within American Jewry. Eshkol called attention to the great needs engendered by the recent wave of immigration, as well as by growing tensions with Egypt, and pointed out the necessity of raising, via Israel Bonds, an additional $35 million beyond the funds obtained through the UJA. Eshkol went on to note that American Jewry had always met its commitments to the Yishuv and the State of Israel with exceptional generosity; this was due in great part to the skill of leaders who had awakened and encouraged such action. "The time has come for yet another awakening," he wrote, "and we hope that you will be in a position to lead this awakening under the banner of the Israel Bonds campaign."[2]

On November 7, 1955, two weeks after Eshkol sent his letter, Israel Bonds Vice President Josef Schwartz visited Silver at his home in Cleveland to officially offer him the post. After ten days of correspondence,[3] Silver wrote to Schwartz that, before reaching a final decision, he needed to know the exact duties associated with the job, as well as the position's status within the organization's executive hierarchy. Although he did not put the question explicitly, it is clear that he was seeking a certain kind of protection from the trap into which he had fallen after Israel's establishment in his earlier posts of Jewish Agency American-section chair and AZEC head. Essentially, Silver was reminding Schwartz that he had already held offices of the highest importance within the Zionist hierarchy, and that despite this (or perhaps because of it) he had been faced with an impossible choice between assuming a subordinate role or adopting an oppositional agenda in relation to Israel. Silver sought to confirm that

2. Letter from Levi Eshkol to Silver, October 25, 1955, AHSP I; Israel Bonds, State of Development Corporation for Israel, New York, AHSP I.

3. Letters between Silver and Joseph J. Schwartz, November 8–17, 1955, AHSP I.

the offered position would not draw him once again into the intra-Zionist political vortex. He wished to be viewed as one called upon to serve Israel owing to his high personal stature and independent nonpartisan stance so that his solidarity with Israel would not necessarily subordinate him to the state's agenda.

Schwartz understood Silver's letter in the spirit in which it was intended. On November 15, he responded in detail, noting that the post envisioned for Silver was positioned within the organizational hierarchy in a manner that would ensure its autonomous character. With regard to organizational structure, Schwartz differentiated between the Board of Directors, which bore legal responsibility for Israel Bonds activity as a commercial entity subject to the rules of the New York Stock Exchange and was therefore also responsible for the organization's political operations, and the Board of Governors, which Silver was being invited to head. Schwartz explained that the Board of Governors should be seen as a mediator between Israel Bonds and the American-Jewish community. He noted that Silver would be expected to remain above the political fray, and thereby to embody American Jewry's cohesive power and prestige. Silver would also be expected to inspire and give direction to the Board of Directors and the Israel Bonds organization, and, thereby, to American Jewry as a whole. These latter sentiments were probably intended to flatter Silver and express esteem for his leadership skills, but it was the letter's closing lines that, apparently, won Silver over. Schwartz noted that the position in question had been held by the former secretary of the treasury under Roosevelt, Henry Morgenthau, Jr., and that since Morgenthau had stepped down, the post had remained vacant. He also explained that it was the Executive Committee, chaired by Josef Shulman and himself, as deputy chairman, which was responsible for all of the day-to-day operations, whereas Silver, like Morgenthau before him, was being called on to play the role of an apolitical, inspirational leader. In effect, Schwartz was promising Silver a lofty position far removed from any ongoing disputes regarding Zionist affairs. Silver found these explanations persuasive; on November 17, the day after he received the letter, he made a note to himself in which he stated that he had called Dr. Schwartz that morning and informed him that he would accept the position.[4] It seems that what really swayed Silver was the solution that the offer presented: an apolitical role as head of Israel Bonds that would position him as one whose agenda was not rooted in the authority vested in him by the Israeli leadership. On the contrary, the Israel Bonds chairmanship would cast Silver in the light of a devoted friend of Israel, one to whom the state had appealed for assistance despite—or even because of—its recognition of his independent status.

At the same time, Silver's acceptance also indicated that he well understood that Israel Bonds fundraising consisted of persuading people to support Israel not on an ideological Zionist basis. This non-ideological approach unquestionably ran counter to the stance that he sought to promote in his various leadership posts from the mid-1930s into the early 1950s. As noted earlier, during the 1940s Silver opposed measures that, in his view, risked divesting American Zionism of ideological content and turning it into a humanitarian project. Moreover, the 1949 UJA crisis that ended with Silver's ousting revolved specifically around Silver's arguments regarding the legitimacy of a continued independent existence for the American Diaspora-Zionist approach; it also lay behind the arguments at the twenty-third Zionist Congress in 1951 in favor of conferring special status on the Jewish Agency. It may be said that, by accepting the Israel Bonds chairmanship, Silver was, paradoxically, aligning himself with the non-ideological leadership model with which he had battled for many years within the Zionist movement. Indeed, in his first speech as Israel Bonds Chairman, Silver focused exclusively on the financial aspects of supporting Israel. He pointed out that, in the final analysis, it was Israel's economic might that would enable it to defend itself from military aggression. Silver did not discuss the need for ideological Zionist commitment, or for the importance of such commitment in engendering a Judaic cultural and national awakening within American Jewry. The speech could almost be regarded as fully in line with the approach taken by Morgenthau (Silver 1955–1956).

4. Note in Silver's handwriting, November 17, 1955, AHSP I. The handwritten note was probably intended for his journal, although it never took shape as an actual entry.

These latter characteristics may explain why Silver chose not to mention his Israel Bonds chairmanship in his journal entries of the period. The importance of heading the Israel Bonds organization, in Silver's eyes, lay in the apolitical leadership model associated with it, which would make it possible to express solidarity with Israel in a way that avoided ideological subordination to the Israeli leadership. However, this advantage also reflected the stark disparity between Silver's political standing within the American-Jewish community and that of Morgenthau, his predecessor in the post. An ideologically detached stance regarding Israel-related issues or Jewish affairs indeed suited Morgenthau, who attached little importance to his own standing within the American-Jewish community, but this stance in no way suited Silver. Morgenthau brought to his Jewish leadership positions the prestige that he had acquired in the general American arena. By contrast, Silver's overall status in American society was rooted almost exclusively in his activity in the Zionist and Jewish arenas (his efforts on behalf of labor legislation and civil rights notwithstanding). This being the case, Silver was destined to find in the long run that the aloof and non-ideological status could have torpedoed any aspiration on his part to a leadership position within the American-Jewish community, or to building a self-sufficient, Diaspora-oriented American-Zionist agenda. In retrospect, both Silver's accession to the position of head of Israel Bonds and his care not to make much of it in his journal reflect the depth of the challenge that he faced in trying to adopt a model of American-Zionist leadership that was committed to Israel but was nevertheless free from ideological Zionist dependence.

It is against this background that one should examine the events that surrounded Silver's candidacy for the headship of the World Jewish Congress held in Jerusalem on April 24–May 7, 1956. Just prior to the congress, during the second half of March, Silver visited Israel—his first trip since 1951. Although many of his supporters hoped to see this as a step toward reentering the Zionist political arena, Silver appears to have had the opposite intention. He meant to use the visit to draw a clear line between his role as Israel Bonds chairman and the ideologically and politically charged role of WZO president that he was unwilling to assume. Immediately after his Israel Bonds appointment in late 1955, Silver began to receive letters from supporters anticipating his return to Zionist politics. Most notable of these were the letters that he received from the General Zionist leadership. Party Chairman Peretz Bernstein wrote that, in accordance with a decision of the party directorate, he welcomed Silver back to the Zionist political arena. Bernstein announced his hope that Silver's decision to head the Israel Bonds organization would prove the first step toward a return to the leadership of the WZO. Letters that Silver received from Samuel Landman, a leader of the British General Zionists, were written in an even more explicit style, informing Silver that Landman was mobilizing broad support for Silver's election as president of the WZO. Landman described the initiative as part of a political strategy aimed at forcing Ben-Gurion to form an emergency government that would include Bernstein and Menachem Begin (the head of the main right-wing oppositional party), while also making Silver eligible, in his future role as head of the World Zionist movement, to speak ex-officio before the Knesset on issues related to world Jewry and its relations with Israel.[5]

Silver did not cooperate with these initiatives. In the many letters that he sent in advance of his trip to Israel, he was careful to note that he would not be making political speeches during his two-week visit. In fact, he used his Israel Bonds chairmanship as a means of avoiding any appearance of political involvement in the Zionist or the Israeli arenas. He took care not to give Landman a green light regarding his candidacy; to Bernstein, he responded that he would be happy to meet with him when he arrived for his two-week Passover visit, but that the main challenge before him was that of raising funds for Israel in his capacity as head of Israel Bonds, and of exerting an influence on the US government's Middle East policy. In fact, Silver was informing Bernstein that, as far as his Zionist involvement was concerned, he should not be regarded as an active politician.

The Israeli leadership responded to this message with open arms. Even before he arrived in Israel the newspapers reported on the anticipated

5. Letter from Peretz Bernstein to Silver, December 2, 1955, AHSP I; Letter from George Flesh to Silver, January 17, 1956, AHSP I; Letters from Samuel Landman to Silver, March 9, 1956 and March 11, 1956, AHSP I.

reconciliatory meeting between Silver and Ben-Gurion. The encounter took place at the prime minister's office; that an atmosphere of conflict no longer subsisted between the two could be seen in the invitation that Silver subsequently received to the wedding of the prime minister's daughter. Two days later, the prime minister made a point of attending and speaking at the Kfar Silver opening ceremony; in stark contrast to his former tone of belittlement, Ben-Gurion now declared that Silver was the most loyal and devoted Diaspora-Zionist leader ever. The rest of the Israeli leadership followed suit. In contrast to the near-total shunning that had been imposed on Silver by the Israeli leadership during his previous 1951 visit, this time Silver was invited to meet personally with President Ben-Zvi, Speaker of the Knesset Yosef Sprinzak, and Foreign Minister Sharett; a special reception was held in his honor by Finance Minister Eshkol. Silver, for his part, made sure to affirm his lack of interest in the various political positions that were offered him; he also noted that in his meetings with the prime minister no political issues related to the Zionist movement or to Israel had been discussed.[6] In fact, Silver planned his trip to conclude prior to the twenty-fourth Zionist Congress, with the clear intention of emphasizing the apolitical nature of his activity on Israel's behalf.

Three weeks after his return to the United States, and just a day after the congressional deliberations had begun in Jerusalem, he felt that it was necessary to clarify that no oppositional statement had been intended by his absence. Silver sent a telegram to Zalman Shazar (who would become Israel's third president) after he, along with Eliyahu Dubkin, entreated Silver to participate in the congress. Silver explained that his nonparticipation in the congress had nothing to do with an oppositional Zionist stance on his part. He made sure to mention that during the short time that had passed since his return from Israel he had already taken part in

6. The information about Silver's visit and his meeting with Ben-Gurion were published on the front pages of almost all the major Israeli newspapers, including *Davar*, the semi-official organ of Mapai. For descriptions of Silver's daily schedule between March 21 and April 5, 1956, see *Davar*, *HaBoker*, *Al Hamismar*, *Ha'aretz*, *Hazophe*, *Ma'ariv*, and *Yedihot Achronot*. For a detailed description of Silver's news conference, see *HaBoker* (1956, 1, 3) and *Hazophe* (1956, 3).

two important Israel Bonds campaigns, and that on April 26, during the twenty-fourth Zionist Congress, he was scheduled to meet, on behalf of the Israeli government, with President Eisenhower and Secretary of State John Foster Dulles.[7]

This latter communication may be seen as a point of convergence for the various issues that Silver excluded from his journal and for those that he deemed worthy of mentioning. In theory, there should have been no difference from Silver's perspective between his lobbying activities, which he discussed in depth in his journal, and his activity as the head of Israel Bonds, which he excluded from the journal. In both instances he strove to cultivate the image of a distinguished leader using his connections to advance Israel's interests. However, the main characteristic of the Israel Bonds chairmanship was its distant, uninvolved stance from an ideological-Zionist point of view. By contrast, in his lobbying activity Silver hoped to present his Zionist commitment as a valuable asset to the Israeli leadership; he believed that emphasizing his ideological-Zionist commitment would ensure his reception by the American administration as an authentic leader of the American-Jewish community who had only recently demonstrated his readiness for uncompromising ideological struggle on behalf of Israeli statehood. One should, therefore, view Silver's journal entries up to 1952 as mainly reflecting his aspirations to transform his lobbying activity into a source of strength—one that expressed ideological identification with Israel rather than subordination to it.

Silver's desire notwithstanding, he soon discovered that its implementation was almost impossible. His repeated attempts to persist in this line of leadership—and to report about it in his journal—may reflect the lack of other available options. In this latter context, the first difficulty that Silver faced was that of limited access to the Democratic leadership during the four years that succeeded Truman's surprise victory in the November 1948 elections. Truman and his entourage harbored a deep suspicion of Silver, in particular because of the aggressive public campaign that

7. Letter and telegram from Silver to S. Z. Shazar (World Zionist Congress), April 23, 1956, AHSP I.

he had spearheaded against the Democratic administration during the struggle for Israeli statehood, as well as his close relationship with leaders of the rival Republican Party. Silver's resignation in early 1949 from his leadership positions in the Zionist movement had the effect of further eroding his already limited access to the Democratic leadership. Moreover, the plummeting of Silver's importance in the eyes of the Democratic administration was part of the overall declining political influence of the American-Zionist leadership during the period immediately following the State of Israel's establishment. The main reason for this was that the nascent state's official representatives took over many of the functions that had earlier been filled by American-Zionist leaders. Another reason was that many of the American-Zionist leaders had distanced themselves from Truman and his administration during the 1948 election campaign. The vacuum was filled by the incoming president of the American Jewish Committee, Jacob Blaustein. The president, who confided in Blaustein that he had felt hurt by AZEC actions during the UN struggle and that his de jure recognition of Israel had been despite, and not because of, the aggressiveness of the Zionist lobbying activity, preferred to interact with the Jewish community via the non-Zionist Blaustein rather than through Silver. In the President's view, Blaustein's non-Zionism was an advantage, as, unlike Zionist leaders, he was not regarded as automatically representing Israeli interests and could therefore play the important role of impartial advisor on Israeli affairs (Ganin 2005, 154–58, 162–69).

This difficulty of limited access to the Democratic leadership is reflected in one of Silver's first reports in his journal regarding a telephone conversation on September 28, 1949 with James McDonald, the first US ambassador to Israel. In his journal, Silver portrayed Ambassador McDonald as a sort of confidant who provided him with inside information on White House meetings. According to Silver's depiction, McDonald had made the call from Washington in order to inform him of the problematic attitude toward Israel that prevailed in the White House and the State Department. Apparently, it was not an attitude of intentional hostility toward Israel that concerned McDonald, but rather what McDonald perceived to be the administration's guiding assumption, namely, that in its relations with the Arab world it was up to Israel to make concessions.

In this context, McDonald described Secretary of Defense Louis Johnson as one who bore Israel no preconceived hostility, while Clifford, a presidential advisor, was portrayed as a key pro-Israel member of the White House staff. Finally, the ambassador stated that it would be necessary to "educate" the administration about a more pro-Israel policy, though he felt that public pressure would only harm the cause.[8] Examining Silver's journal report, it should be noted that in contrast to the impression one might have formed from Silver's depiction, McDonald was not a central figure in the Truman administration, and it is doubtful whether his standing would have enabled him to provide Silver with sensitive inside information. McDonald's appointment as ambassador had been a goodwill gesture to the nascent state, but his ability to influence White House policies in a practical way was limited. Moreover, if we look more closely at Silver's journal report we find that, despite the friendly tone, McDonald was saying things of a general nature. For example, McDonald's remarks about the importance of maintaining ties with Clifford were hardly newsworthy to Silver, who until half a year earlier had been in continual and direct contact with Clifford and who was well apprised of the latter's key status within the White House. McDonald's "report" could therefore be described as general, devoid of real news, and lacking in specific information on White House discussions. Thus, in contrast to the importance that Silver attached to it, the conversation with McDonald appears to have

8. McDonald was in Washington at the time; he telephoned Silver a day before his scheduled return to Israel. Tensions between the United States and Israel were high during this period. Two weeks earlier, the Lausanne Conference, which was intended to move past the armistice agreements between Israel and the Arab states and arrive at a permanent peace treaty, had ended in failure, while the previous May, a harshly worded message had been sent by Truman to Israel, threatening that the United States would reconsider its relations with Israel if the latter did not agree in principle to allow a return of the refugees and relinquish some of the territory to which it had gained control beyond the partition plan borders. Truman's threatening letter contributed to a widespread feeling within Israel that the United States saw its primary regional interest as that of enlisting Arab support for itself vis-à-vis the Soviet Union, and that this was the prism through which it viewed the major issues of peace between Israel and the Arabs.

been an exercise in civility between two individuals whose moral status based on past endeavors had garnered them no present political influence.

Moreover, the journal report indicated that McDonald had a political agenda of his own, and that his main objective was to persuade Silver to support Democratic candidate Herbert Lehman in the special Senate elections scheduled to take place in New York a month later in November 1949. Lehman, a Jewish former governor of New York State, would be competing on November 8 against John Foster Dulles for the Senate seat that had been vacated a year earlier by its ailing pro-Zionist occupant, Democrat Robert Wagner. McDonald advised Silver to support Lehman without trying to exact a political price from him, that is, without pressuring him to publicly condemn the administration's insufficiently pro-Israel policies. Lehman and McDonald maintained a close friendship, making it likely that McDonald's correspondence with Silver was in fact a preliminary effort to engage Silver's support for his friend in the Senate race.[9]

This Senate seat fight was again mentioned on October 21, ten days before the elections were to be held in New York. The entry was devoted primarily to Silver's correspondence with the Republican Governor of New York, Thomas Dewey. Like McDonald, Dewey also wished to obtain Silver's support, this time in favor of the Republican candidate, Dulles. Given the background of allegations by Lehman that Dulles had supported the Nazi regime and continued to do business with it until 1935, Dewey hoped to obtain from Silver a "character reference" for Dulles, absolving him of any taint of anti-Semitism. Thus, Silver received appeals for support from political patrons of both candidates, and had to decide whether to side with the Democratic candidate or to continue cultivating his relationships with the Republican leadership.[10] Ultimately, Silver

9. On McDonald's continued commitment to Israel, see his memorandum to Eisenhower and Dulles (McDonald 1954).

10. The battle between the parties was one of prestige. Dulles, who was highly esteemed as a Republican Party powerhouse and one of the party's most outstanding experts on international relations, was a senior Dewey advisor and would have been appointed secretary of state had Dewey become president. After losing to Truman in the presidential elections, Governor Dewey appointed Dulles as the Democrat Wagner's replacement until

answered the appeal of Dewey, the highest-status Republican, rather than that of McDonald, who, though a personal friend, nevertheless lacked real influence in the Democratic Party. Silver's statement of approval regarding Dulles's attitude toward Zionism and the State of Israel would eventually reap a dividend with Dulles's appointment as secretary of state under Eisenhower; however, at this stage it merely reflected the impasse that Silver had reached in relation to the Democratic administration and, more notably, the degree to which his influence and status had declined within the American-Jewish community. In the November 1946 elections Silver had taken a similar stance, leading a retaliatory campaign against the Truman administration. Then as well, Lehman had run against a Republican senator (the non-Jewish Irving Ives); however, at that time Silver and the American-Zionist movement were at the height of their power and the punitive campaign against the Democrats contributed significantly to Lehman's defeat. Now, in the November 1949 elections, when Silver placed the entire weight of his prestige behind Dulles's candidacy, Lehman emerged victorious.

Given this state of affairs, Silver had no choice but to resign himself to the relatively marginal status of liaison between Israel and the Republican Party. The majority of Silver's journal from the Truman years is devoted to a number of isolated instances in which Israeli leaders sought his intervention with the Republican leadership. The first entry along these lines dates from April 21, 1950, and documents a telephone call from Israeli Ambassador Eliyahu Eilat, in which the latter asked Silver to lobby Senator Taft on the inadvisability of supplying Western arms to the Arab world. This was the first time since Silver's ousting that he received an official request to act on Israel's behalf, and his enthusiasm for the task was evident. On the very day of the phone call he set up meetings in Washington, where he arrived four days later. After an early morning meeting with the Israeli Embassy team, headed by Ambassador Eilat with the participation

---

the special elections were held. Lehman had preceded Dewey as governor of New York, and a victory by Dulles was liable to be interpreted as an additional humiliation for Dewey at Truman's hands.

of Eliezer Livneh and Washington Consul Moshe Keren, he attended an afternoon meeting with Senator Taft. The next day he met with Dulles and John Cooper, who, like Dulles, was considered to be a senior Republican figure with expertise in international relations. In these meetings, Silver argued that it would be undesirable to arm the Arab countries at a time when the United Kingdom and the United States were refusing to sell weapons to Israel. It is difficult to estimate Silver's actual contribution to this cause, but one may confidently assert that it was less central than he made it out to be in his journal. In this context it is worth mentioning the activity of Blaustein, the head of the American Jewish Committee, to whom the Israeli Embassy had also appealed for help in this matter. Blaustein did not meet with Republican legislators; rather, he met with President Truman himself. He was thus able to take a certain degree of credit for the authorization of light arms sales to Israel (presumed to be for defensive purposes)—a development for which he was thanked personally not just by the ambassador (as in Silver's case), but also by Ben-Gurion and Sharett (Ganin 2005, 172).

Another affair involving pro-Israeli lobbying activity, one that extended through the entire first half of 1951, was that of the grant-in-aid of $150 million that Israel was then seeking from the United States. The reason why the Israeli ambassador at the time, Abba Eban, requested Silver's assistance was that, in this case, not only was the administration's approval necessary, but also that of both houses of Congress. According to Silver's journal, Eban and Silver held an initial meeting at the Israeli Embassy in Washington on January 22; the very next day Silver met with Taft, who agreed to sponsor, along with the Democratic Senator Paul Douglas, a bipartisan resolution on the matter. Assessing the importance of Silver's involvement, Nahum Goldmann reported to Foreign Minister Sharett that Senator Taft's support had been obtained without the need for Silver's intervention. This, however, was not entirely accurate. Goldmann, who had acceded to Silver's place within the Jewish Agency and still viewed him as a rival, sought to downplay the importance of Silver's efforts. Goldmann's representation of the matter notwithstanding, it was actually Silver who had succeeded in ensuring that the Republican Taft's name would appear on the bill; Ambassador Eban took care to give Silver credit for this achievement not only in a formal letter of appreciation, but also in his own report to Jerusalem.

Nevertheless, despite Goldmann's intentional belittlement of Silver's lobbying efforts, there was some truth to his report. Although one might form a different impression from Silver's journal reports, his lobbying activity had, in fact, not been the key endeavor in the campaign to secure American economic aid for Israel. In November 1950, two months before Eban had contacted Silver, a group of twelve Jewish leaders, including Goldmann, met with Truman and submitted to him a secret memorandum on the matter. Additionally, in February, Pinchas Lavon, then serving as Israel's Minister of Agriculture, made an emergency trip from Israel in order to conduct direct negotiations with the Truman administration. It is also worth mentioning that Israel had mobilized the American Zionist Council for lobbying activity, ostensibly of an independent American-Jewish nature, similar to that of AIPAC today vis-à-vis both houses of Congress. As AZC director Unger was still reporting to Silver regularly on the organization's lobbying activity, Silver clearly knew that his own activity was merely one component of a comprehensive Israeli campaign. He himself reported on his meeting with Taft not directly to Ambassador Eban, but to Isaiah Kenen, the AZC lobbyist in Washington. It may therefore be said that Silver ascribed importance to a lobbying effort that, in retrospect, actually underscored the steep decline in his previous central status, emphasizing his role as a mere "soldier" in Israel's overall lobbying operation rather than the one who designed and implemented it (Kenen 1981, 70–80).[11]

As reflected in his journal, Silver could not easily reconcile himself to the new state of affairs. On February 7, he received from Kenen the congressional draft resolution that had been composed by a team of experts from the Israeli Embassy and Foreign Ministry. Kenen noted that the content of the draft resolution had already been determined and that he was seeking Silver's advice merely on issues of style. Kenen thus made it clear

11. Letter from Abba Eban to Silver, January 8, 1951, FR/O/80e-3, Israel State Archive; Letter to Silver from Jerome Unger, March 16, 1951, AHSP I.

that, in contrast to the period in which Silver had headed AZEC, it was now the Israeli Foreign Ministry and Embassy experts who were setting policy and making decisions. It soon became clear, however, that Silver would not be content to serve merely as a sort of editor. On the same day that Silver received the letter, February 9, he wrote back to Kenen that the problem was not one of style, but rather he vigorously opposed the equation implied by the bill between the desired grant-in-aid and an Israeli commitment to stand beside the United States in case of war with the Soviet Union. He further drove his point home by sending a copy of the letter to Ambassador Eban, and by writing to Senator Taft on the matter. Silver averred that it would be better to formulate the draft resolution in a way that held Israel to no security commitment; rather, emphasis should be placed on the ethical partnership that existed between Israel and the United States.

Silver's attempts to remove the security clauses from the bill continued for several weeks, until the end of February; they testify to his sense of possessing greater expertise on the issue than the experts employed in Israel's Foreign Service. This kind of tension was not unusual between opinionated American-Zionist leaders and official Israeli personnel during the early years of Israeli statehood. Israel's official personnel did not care for the independent status that some of the American-Zionist leaders strove to retain, and they made every effort to bring these leaders into line. Unlike the non-Zionist leaders, the American Zionists were perceived both by themselves and by various parties in the White House and on Capitol Hill as semi-official representatives of the State of Israel; therefore, so the Embassy staff reasoned, their responsibility to carry out Israeli state directives was all the greater. This Israeli attitude produced tension not only with Silver, but with many other American-Zionist leaders who, by virtue of their long years of struggle on behalf of Israeli statehood, felt themselves better qualified than the state's professional Foreign Service personnel to assess and pursue Israel's "true" interests.[12] The latest

12. An early indication of this tension appeared in 1949, after Truman's ultimatum during the Lausanne Conference. Subsequent to the ultimatum, then ZOA President Daniel

example of a similar tension was prompted by Goldmann's follow-up activity to the November 1950 meeting between the twelve American-Jewish leaders and the president. Without consulting Eban, Goldmann decided to publicize the arguments in favor of economic aid to Israel that had featured in the secret memorandum submitted to the president. Goldmann believed that these arguments would help persuade the public of the closeness of Israeli and American interests; however, one of the points made by the memorandum was that Israel, by encouraging Jewish emigration from Eastern Europe, weakened the Communist bloc. By publicizing this argument, Goldmann had, in the Israeli Foreign Ministry's view, demonstrated flagrant unprofessionalism. Goldmann received letters of reprimand from Eban and Foreign Minister Sharett for acting on his own, without going through the proper channels, and for thereby harming the prospects of Jewish immigration from the Soviet Union.

In the case of the interaction between Kenen and Silver regarding the congressional economic aid bill, the ongoing inherent tension served to underscore Silver's separate Zionist agenda. As noted earlier, Silver opposed the Cold War and believed that loyalty to the democratic ethos should dictate an American policy of dialogue rather than one of conflict

---

Frisch met with Assistant Secretary of State for Near Eastern Affairs George McGhee, who made conciliatory remarks regarding America's commitment to Israel's existence, which Frisch then made public. This in turn angered Ambassador Eilat, who, in a report to Foreign Minister Sharett, expressed great frustration over Frisch's failure to coordinate his actions with the Israeli authorities and, in particular, with the lack of professionalism that had caused him to fall into the State Department's trap. In the ambassador's eyes, this situation underscored an inherent lack of discipline on the part of the American Zionists and demonstrated the kind of damage that it could cause to the coordinated and professional pursuit of Israeli foreign policy objectives. Similar tension resurfaced during Abba Eban's tenure as ambassador. In 1952, then ZOA president Benjamin Browdy called for UN mediation between Israel and the Arab countries—an appeal uncoordinated with Israel. He was reprimanded by Eban in a long letter stipulating the basic compliance with Israeli policy to which anyone who called himself a Zionist should be committed. Eban pointed to the non-Zionist Blaustein as one who exemplified extreme care not to deviate from Israeli positions; this, he explained, was why Israel relied on him rather than on the undisciplined Zionist leaders.

with the Soviet bloc. He wanted to see the United States employ the democratic way as a kind of lingua franca capable of drawing diverse cultures and worldviews into an egalitarian dialogue. Within this framework, Silver assigned a particularly important role to Israel's interbloc neutrality. He maintained that such a role would bolster the United Nations's moral stature and serve as a model for dialogue between the United States and the Soviet Union. This vision entailed an approach that reflected the more optimistic and pluralistic Diaspora-Zionist worldview. Silver's opposition to any Israeli commitment to fighting the Soviet Union was, therefore, consistent with his overall effort to base his lobbying activity on an independent Diaspora-Zionist ideology.

In Silver was also aware of the internal debate going on in Israel about the transition from an orientation of neutrality to one of identification with the West.[13] It was clear to the Israeli leadership that Israel's basic interests required it to oppose any expansion of Soviet control into the Middle East and to align itself with the free and democratic world whose values Israel shared and from whom it alone could hope to obtain economic and military aid. However, Israeli policymakers were also aware of the dangers of Israeli involvement in an anti-Soviet security alliance, particularly in light of the concern for Soviet Jewry. Israel thus sought a middle way that would enable it to stand beside the West and rely on its economic and military aid, but without publicly obligating itself to conflict with the Soviet Union.[14]

13. The Israeli position that had coalesced during this period between late 1950 and early 1951 assumed that, in the present state of Cold War tensions resulting from the outbreak of the Korean War, Israel could not afford to remain neutral vis-à-vis the two blocs.

14. This policy was announced by Foreign Minister Sharett, just a few days before the exchange of letters began between Silver and Kenen. In early February 1951, Sharett summoned the military attachés to Israel's diplomatic missions for an explication of the new policy. After setting forth the reasons why Israel had to adopt a Western orientation, as well as the risks entailed by an overt military alliance with the West, he concluded by noting that, as the United Kingdom and the United States had yet to decide on a defense framework for the Middle East, Israel could hope in the meantime to obtain maximal levels of economic and military aid from the West, in return for a minimal military commitment.

This was therefore a rare instance in which Silver's Diaspora-Zionist approach and Israel's practical-diplomacy approach embraced a similar agenda—that of acknowledging the moral-spiritual affinity between Israel and the United States without Israel having to commit to a military alliance with the West. Silver was thus able to express his independent, ideologically informed opinion, and even to subject Kenen to a quasi-reprimand, but from a stance of complete support for what he perceived as a wise Israeli policy orientation. Essentially, he was placing himself in an ideal position, one where his Diaspora-Zionist approach placed his judgment in a positive light compared with the professional American-Jewish lobbyists working on Israel's behalf, and certainly compared with Goldmann, who just two months earlier had been reprimanded by Sharett and Eban for endangering Soviet Jewry.

On the face of it, this would appear to have been a major victory for Silver—an instance in which his ongoing attempt to transform his lobbying activity into a source that expressed ideological identification with Israel, rather than subordination to it, actually bore fruit. This success is hinted at in a letter that Silver received from Eban on February 16, which he quoted in full in his journal. In this letter, the ambassador expressed his agreement with Silver and his opposition to the military issue's inclusion in the bipartisan draft resolution regarding economic aid to Israel. However, this correspondence also underscored the difference between the pragmatic Israeli approach and Silver's ideological approach. On February 27, Kenen telephoned Silver from New York to read him the second draft, which though somewhat different from the original, still described the desired grant-in-aid as a means of promoting joint American and Israeli security interests. Kenen explained that, without this clause, the draft resolution would not pass.[15] Silver, who continued to object to the

15. Silver was not convinced; the next day he telephoned Taft and laid before him the gravity of the case. In an awkward turn of events, however, it emerged that Taft agreed with Kenen; he told Silver that there was no chance for a draft resolution that failed to link American economic aid with an Israeli commitment to safeguard US security interests. Taft noted that similar stipulations had appeared in congressional resolutions regarding

security clause, quickly found out that his ideological stand was overshadowed by other, more practical considerations of Israel's policymakers. Indeed, he had only limited awareness of the extensive Israeli activity that was still taking place behind the scenes. A major instance of this was the emergency trip to the United States by Pinchas Lavon in February. During his visit, Lavon was apprised by the White House of the intention to make economic aid conditional on Israel's explicit military commitment to support global American objectives vis-à-vis the Soviet bloc. This American condition exacerbated a dilemma that had preoccupied the Israeli leadership for several months, namely, how to actualize Israel's Western orientation without endangering its relations with the Soviet Union. Israel, during this period, did its best to reconcile these opposing interests. On the one hand, it strove to please the Americans, as exemplified by the permission granted by Ben-Gurion to the US military attaché to inspect Israeli defense industry installations and the Israeli commitment not to export to the Soviet bloc any products originating in the United States. On the other hand, Israel sought all possible means of doing this without explicitly committing itself to a military alliance. The situation in which these various maneuvers were carried out became even more complex in the face of an American policy stance that placed Israel in an exceedingly uncomfortable position: although the United States pressured Israel to commit itself militarily, it offered no similar assurances to Israel. On the contrary, during this period it emerged that Israel had been excluded from American plans for regional defense, so as not to offend the Arab world (Bialer 1990, 2002; Eytan 1958, 138–39; Kenen 1981, 122–23). Paradoxically, it was precisely Silver's attempt to find a common ground between his ideological position and Israel's practical diplomatic needs that underscored the limits of his awareness of the complex and contradictory considerations by which the Israeli policymakers were guided.

---

economic aid to Western Europe under the Marshall Plan. Letter from Kenen to Silver, February 7, 1951, AHSP I; Telegram from Kenen to Silver, February 27, 1951, AHSP I; Kenen 1981, 71.

Silver's willingness to portray himself as investing all efforts to mobilize unconditionally on the state's behalf became even more pronounced several months later, on June 12, when a new stage in the economic aid campaign got underway. Silver documented in great detail his response to an appeal by Eban, describing in depth how, just two days after he received the request, he moved up his scheduled departure from Cleveland for the ZOA convention in Atlantic City and made a special trip to Washington in order to be updated in person by Eban and Kenen and to conduct an emergency meeting with Taft. By contrast, Silver completely refrained from mentioning in the journal his involvement in disputes between the American Zionists and the Mapai leadership, which were then reaching their peak. With only the journal to go by, one would find evidence of nothing besides Silver's total mobilization on the State of Israel's behalf, and never know that, a few days later, Silver would be leading the ZOA convention to a declaration of support for the General Zionists Party in their campaign against Mapai, just a few weeks prior to the elections for the Second Knesset. In contrast to this self-representation as a disciplined soldier battling on behalf of Israel, Silver often portrayed his rivals as motivated by petty considerations. An early instance of this depiction may be seen in the way that he documented the events of March 1951. In a few short lines he quoted articles in *Ha'aretz* and the *Jewish Morning Journal*, which protested Goldmann's and Hadassah leader Rose Halpern's intrigues aimed at torpedoing any possible reconciliation between Ben-Gurion and himself. Silver portrayed these intrigues as petty political fracas, contrasting it to his own conduct, depicted as maintaining a stance removed from any personal considerations.[16]

16. This depiction of Silver's total and disinterested mobilization on behalf of Israel recurred in the entry immediately following the report on Ben-Gurion's rejection of Eban's reconciliation initiative. In this entry Silver described his response to an appeal by Joseph Schwartz (still in his position with the UJA), who had come to meet with him at a New York Hotel in order to engage his efforts for the UJA campaign. In a matter-of-fact response, which deliberately ignored any conceivable issue of political rivalry or of personal insult regarding Ben-Gurion's recent refusal to invite him to a reconciliatory meeting, Silver immediately agreed to undertake a speaking tour to Kansas City, Indianapolis, and Los

In a similar manner, the only journal entry devoted to the General Zionists seems to have been chosen for its neutrality regarding any political involvement on Silver's part. On December 10, 1952, Silver reported on a congratulatory telegram that he had sent to Yitzhak Ben-Zvi in honor of his election to the Israeli presidency. The entry excluded any mention of the political struggle that had surrounded the election. Ben-Zvi had been chosen as the Mapai candidate after his victory in the Knesset vote two days earlier, on December 8, over the candidate regarded as Silver's ally, General Zionist leader Peretz Bernstein. Ben-Zvi won the election only after three rounds of voting, during the last of which Bernstein finally withdrew his candidacy—a move that enabled an agreement between Mapai and the General Zionists and paved the entry of the latter into the Mapai government.[17] Ten days later, Silver received a telegram from Bernstein and Yosef Serlin in which they notified him of the coalition agreement with Mapai and their anticipated entry into the government. Silver disregarded the entire political background. Once again, as Silver became more aware of the secondary and limited importance of his lobbying and fundraising activity, this selective inclusion approach appears to have reflected his growing tendency to portray his relationship with the State of Israel as one unmarred by any political involvement or personal interest.

Angeles. The impression one receives is that Silver was seeking to contrast the politically and personally disinterested character of his immediate and nonconditional mobilization on Israel's behalf with Ben-Gurion's inability to rise above his narrow political interests.

17. About the connections between the presidential election and the coalition negotiations, see Ben-Gurion's correspondence with N. Goldmann, December 16, 1952, Ben-Gurion Archive.

9

The Attempt to Regain Status in the Wake of Eisenhower's Election

During the early part of 1951, as he was coming to terms with his secondary importance in the eyes of the Israeli political leadership, Silver still tried to maintain his bipartisan strategy of the 1940s in the American political arena and cultivate political connections among the leaders of both the Democratic and Republican parties. However, as the November 1951 elections approached, this effort became impracticable, and Silver was forced to decide whether to support the Democratic presidential candidate, Adlai Stevenson, or the Republican Eisenhower. Two successive entries in his private journal, the first from late March about his relations with the Republican Taft and the second from early April about his interaction with the Democratic leadership testify to this.

In the March 29 entry, Silver described a gala ZOA lunch that he had organized in Taft's honor in Washington. He reported on a donation by the Cleveland Zionist Society, in Taft's name, of five hundred volumes of the *Congressional Record* to the Knesset Library in Jerusalem; he specifically noted the presence of Ambassador Eban and other Israeli Embassy personnel. At this point Taft was considered a frontrunner for the Republican presidential nomination, and it was clear that Silver was positioning himself as Taft's right-hand man before the Israelis.

The second journal entry, dated April 13, was not devoted to Israel-related issues but rather to General Douglas MacArthur's dismissal as commander of the American forces in Korea. Silver, who vehemently opposed the Korean War, supported Truman on this measure against the popular general and, by extension, against his own friend and ally Taft, who sided with MacArthur (whom he was later to seek as his presidential running mate). Silver telephoned the House majority leader, Democrat John McCormack, and asked him to pass on his message of support to the president. He told McCormack that despite his disagreement with the president's policy regarding the Korean crisis, he supported his decision to dismiss MacArthur and viewed it as an important step toward advancing American interests and world peace.

Silver's decision to include his letter of support for Truman in a journal that was devoted to his relations with Israel requires explanation. It stood in contrast to the exclusion from the journal of an earlier letter from mid-December 1950, opposing the president's policy on the Korean War. In the earlier letter, which was sent to the editorial boards of national newspapers, Silver accused Truman of going to war for domestic reasons, as a means of deflecting allegations that he was soft on communism. While the earlier letter had intensified the White House's suspicion of Silver, the second letter was a clear call for reconciliation, one intended not only for Truman but also for the Democratic leadership as a whole. This is why Silver documented the entire answering telegram sent by McCormack three days later, informing him of the degree to which the president had been touched by Silver's gesture. However, by inserting this entry in his journal, Silver also inadvertently underscored the fact that at this stage he had no easy access to the White House, and unlike other American-Jewish figures such as Blaustein, Abraham Feinberg, Eddie Jacobson, and Max Lowenthal, he was obliged to convey his messages indirectly (Segev 2004; Silver 1950c).

Still, a decision to support the Republican candidate was not self-evident. Stevenson, the progressive intellectual, had a track record of friendship with Israel, and was a more natural choice than Eisenhower, the conservative general whose knowledge about Zionism and Israel was minimal. Silver was aware of this discrepancy between the two candidates, especially of the fact that Stevenson was more likely than Eisenhower to attach importance to the commonality of values between Israel and the United States. He was also aware of statements made by Eisenhower during the election year that were intended to improve relations with the Arabs as a means of advancing American interests in the strategically crucial

Middle East. As one who had been involved in the Republican National Convention, he knew firsthand how difficult it was to insert pro-Israeli statements into the Republican platform, along the lines of those featured in the Democratic platform, owing to Eisenhower's refusal to be swayed by "pressure groups" that in his view represented narrow ethnic concerns at the expense of America's vital strategic interests (Alteras 1993, 26–35). Thus, Silver's decision to publicly support Eisenhower was neither easy nor self-evident. Ultimately it reflected no shared ideological outlook, nor even an expectation that Eisenhower's policies as president would be more favorable to Israel; it merely reflected the fact that, of the options available to him for reestablishing his status as a mediator between Israel and the United States, only the Republican option was realistic.

The first event through which Silver documented, in his journal, his support for Eisenhower was a relatively late one, just a month before the elections, despite the fact that his efforts on behalf of the Republican campaign had begun four months earlier. Silver excluded from the journal his public appearance offering the opening prayer at the Republican National Convention in July 1952, as well as his subsequent participation in discussions regarding the convention platform. The failure to mention these activities may have been indicative of his disappointment with the lukewarm tone of the platform's Israel section; this watered-down statement represented a compromise in the face of broad opposition to anything that could be regarded as a perpetuation of Truman administration policies, which Republican foreign-policymakers regarded as biased in Israel's favor. Silver must also have noticed that the calls for a new Middle East policy were coming from the Taft and Dulles camp, which at the time were regarded as closely tied and committed to Silver (Bernstein 1971; Silver 1952c).

Only when Silver felt that his efforts to overcome these difficulties were successful did he report about his involvement in the Eisenhower election campaign. The entry in his journal documents a five-day effort, from October 5 through October 9, to persuade Eisenhower to publicly deliver a pro-Israel statement. Silver began by reporting his contact on October 5 with Senator Taft's secretary, Jack Martin, and the latter's promise to advance a public statement initiative together with Republican Party

National Convention Chair Arthur Summerfield. Both Martin and Summerfield were centrally involved in managing the Republican campaign and were destined to hold important offices in the Eisenhower administration—Martin as an administrative assistant to the president after Taft's death in 1953 and Summerfield as Postmaster General in both Eisenhower cabinets. Silver's interaction with these two Republican politicians indicates the depth of his connections within the party—not just with figures at the top of the pyramid, such as Taft and Dulles, but also with second-tier functionaries whose assistance and cooperation was, on numerous issues, no less crucial than the avowed support of first-rank leaders.

On October 9, once matters had been arranged to his satisfaction, Silver asked the Israeli embassy to suggest the main points to be included in a statement by Eisenhower. Ambassador Eban's place was temporarily being filled by envoy David Goitein, who was to be appointed a justice of Israel's Supreme Court a year later. Goitein, in his role as acting ambassador, emphasized that the most important point from Israel's perspective should be a statement of commitment by Eisenhower with regard to arms supply and economic aid. Goitein's suggestions also included a call for direct negotiations between Israel and the Arabs, resolution of the Arab refugee problem by the Arab countries, and expressions of esteem for the democratic character of Israel's government and society.[1]

During an October 10 telephone conversation with Dewey, Silver proposed an exchange of letters between himself and General Eisenhower.[2] On October 12, he went on to document a telephone conversation with

1. As Silver was well aware of the Republican Party's call for a balanced policy, he suggested that the promise of military and economic aid not be extended to Israel alone, but rather to all pro-Western states in the Middle East.

2. In his journal report on the following day, Silver noted the day's events hour by hour. At 11:00 a.m. he sent drafts of both his letter and the president's response to Dewey, while at 8:00 p.m. Dewey telephoned Silver to arrange the meeting with Eisenhower. Silver's documentation of the events included details apparently meant to call attention to the respect accorded to him by Dewey and, thus, by Eisenhower. He took care to note that Dewey had offered two alternative dates, while he, Silver, had promised to give him an answer only the following day, after he had checked his appointment schedule.

Dewey, in which details were hammered out regarding the meeting with Eisenhower. The meeting was scheduled for the end of that week, on Saturday, October 18 at 11:00 a.m. Initially, Silver proposed that there be no official declaration of support on his part for Eisenhower's candidacy. He explained that such a declaration might be perceived by Jewish voters as part of a political deal, and would thereby compromise their faith in Eisenhower's pro-Israel statement.[3] From this point on, Silver did his best to keep his side of the bargain and to advance Eisenhower's candidacy. His loyalty to Republican interests was particularly evident in the way he cooperated with the public relations effort surrounding his meeting with Eisenhower.

Silver began his day of meetings in New York by breakfasting with Dewey; afterward the two went to Eisenhower's residence in Morningside Heights, on the campus of Columbia University, where Eisenhower then served as president. After a photo session at the entrance to Eisenhower's house and a polite recap of what had already been agreed on regarding Eisenhower's statement, Eisenhower cut to the chase and complained about the recent newspaper reports, according to which President Truman had accused the supporters of the immigration-restricting McCarran-Walter Act of anti-Semitic and anti-Catholic sentiments. Eisenhower, angered by the insinuation that he himself was tainted by anti-Semitic attitudes, noted his involvement in the liberation of the concentration camps and his concern for the Jewish survivors during his tenure as Supreme Commander of the Allied Forces in Europe. He spoke at length about his visits to the liberated camps, his enthusiastic reception by the survivors, and the various measures that he took on their behalf.

It was not by chance that Eisenhower's annoyance became the focus of the meeting; rather, it had been planned in advance as a public relations

3. Dewey, on Eisenhower's behalf, proposed that the section dealing with the American commitment to military and economic aid be revised to discuss economic and political aid that would ensure the security of Israel and of all other peaceable nations in the Middle East. Although this revision touched on the issue that Israel most urgently wished to emphasize, it did not detract from the overall positive pro-Israel spirit of the letter. For Eisenhower's written notes regarding this issue, see Galambos (1989, 1390 n. 5).

operation in the context of the election campaign. Eisenhower had become aware of Truman's allegations a day earlier while campaigning in New Jersey. He had subsequently called a meeting of his advisors, at which it was decided to employ the meeting with Silver on behalf of the election campaign. Silver, who had been let in on the public relations plan during his breakfast meeting with Dewey, acted his part faithfully. On going out to face the press after the meeting, and being asked whether the discussion had touched on Truman's allegations against Eisenhower, he responded that he was shocked by Truman's irresponsible attack.[4]

Silver's seal of approval for Eisenhower was thus part of a planned effort by Eisenhower and his advisors, who enlisted the Roman Catholic Cardinal Francis Spellman of New York for a similar purpose of dismissing allegations of Eisenhower's anti-Catholicism. The incident was reminiscent of Silver's intervention on behalf of Dulles in November 1948, during the race against Lehman for the New York Senate seat. Then as well, Dewey had asked Silver to act on behalf of the Republican candidate, not by directly expressing support, but by attesting to his position regarding anti-Semitism. In the latter case, Silver noted with satisfaction that his defense of Eisenhower had eclipsed the exchange of letters between himself and Eisenhower as a newsworthy item. This remark may indicate that one of the reasons he had agreed to take part in the Eisenhower public relations campaign was to divert attention from the main issue likely to have been raised during the press conference, namely, Eisenhower's lukewarm stand on Israel. Indeed, a few days later, Silver exerted his influence on the American Zionist Council in an attempt to further distract the public from the noticeable difference between the lukewarm stand of that statement and Stevenson's unambiguous pro-Israel stance. On October 24, he contacted Harold Manson, who had been one of his most loyal assistants during the AZEC years, in order to ascertain that the AZC would be issuing a balanced announcement of support for both candidates. He arranged with Manson to have an announcement published, to the effect

4. Eisenhower Mss., White House Central Files, Official File 138-c-4, quoted in Galambos 1989, 1388–90; Letter from Dewey to Silver, October 22, 1952, AHSP I 603.

that there was no significant difference between Eisenhower's declaration and Stevenson's more explicitly pro-Israeli statement (Galambos 1989, 1389 n. 2; Kenen 1981, 91).

How, then, may one explain Silver's unequivocal mobilization for the Republican campaign, to the point of willingness to distort the truth? The answer is probably that Silver regarded his support for the Republican Party as a strategy, one that would position him in a singular status among American-Zionist and Jewish leaders, most of whom supported Stevenson and the Democratic Party. This is probably the reason for the comparison he made in his journal between a Jewish newspaper report on an American-Zionist leadership delegation, headed by Lipsky, Goldstein, and Browdy, that met with Stevenson two days before the elections in order to thank him for his statements on Israel, and an October 20 report devoted to a speech by Eisenhower in New England, in which the presidential candidate stated that he no longer needed to defend himself against Truman's allegations, as his friends Cardinal Spellman, Rabbi Silver, and the Jewish financier Bernard Baruch were doing it for him. In another entry, from October 30, he quoted remarks by Summerfield at a Republican campaign staff meeting, to the effect that the party would be eternally grateful to Silver for supporting Eisenhower.

Such expressions of gratitude received even greater prominence in the journal entries following Eisenhower's victory. In an entry from November 13, he quoted in full Dewey's letter thanking him warmly for his outstanding contribution; in an entry from November 28, he quoted a letter from Secretary of State-elect Dulles, expressing gratitude not only for Silver's efforts during the recent election campaign, but also for his support during the 1949 Senate election. He called Silver a loyal friend who had stood by him during dark times. For Silver, the height of gratification was symbolized by a December 11 letter from Senator Styles Bridges, Chairman of the Joint Congressional Committee on Inaugural Ceremonies, informing Silver that Eisenhower had chosen him to deliver the prayer at his inauguration. In his journal Silver quoted in full the prayer that he delivered on January 20, 1953, Inauguration Day, as well as the January 28 letter of thanks that he received from Eisenhower. As Eisenhower's term of office began, Silver could confidently feel that his Republican strategy had finally proven itself and stood a real chance of benefiting him in his relations with the new administration and, by extension, with the Israeli leadership.[5]

Following this success, Silver considered it necessary to display in practice an approach that was suited to his new leadership status. Two salient actions demonstrated this self-image well; the first case referred to a letter that he wrote to Eisenhower on December 26, 1952. A day earlier, *The New York Times* had published Stalin's response to the newspaper's correspondent James Reston, in which the Soviet leader voiced his willingness to meet with the president-elect and engage him in dialogue about the Cold War. Silver hurried to send Eisenhower his opinion on how to address Stalin's proposals. He urged the president-elect to meet with the Soviet leader, and promised him that if he should do so, he would receive broad public support. He called on Eisenhower not to be afraid to take calculated risks for peace, just as he was not afraid to do so during the war. In the past, Silver had issued calls for peace and ending the Cold War; the difference in this case lay in his presumption of assuring the president-elect of public backing, perceiving himself as a leader whose position within the Jewish public gave him the authority to voice his moral and ethical opinion to the president on broad issues of peace and social justice pertaining to the American nation as a whole, not only on the matter of Middle East policy. In a similar way, Silver felt that his new leadership status was also supposed to position him differently with the Israeli leadership—not as merely a lobbyist in the service of Israeli interests, but as someone who could push toward a comprehensive Jewish agenda, in which Israel was only one component. This proactive approach received prominent expression in a letter dated January 30, 1953. In this letter, Silver turned to the Soviet ambassador to Washington, Georgy Zarubin, and warned of displays of Soviet anti-Semitic and anti-Zionist propaganda. He presented himself as representing an influential position within the non-Communist American public that wished to show goodwill and establish

5. Letter from Dewey to Silver, November 10, 1952, AHSP I 603; Silver's Diary, 1949–1963, October 1951 and January 1952, AHSP V.

peaceful relations between East and West; he made it clear that his supporters expected explanations from the Soviet leadership regarding its dangerous display of anti-Jewish and anti-Israeli policies. Instead of trying to determine his position in such a way that would suit the considerations of Israel's foreign and domestic policy, this time Silver believed that he was in a position to initiate a Jewish agenda of his own, and to do so whether this pertained to defending Soviet Jewry against anti-Semitism or to defending Israel against hostile Soviet policy. Clearly he felt that he had finally found the formula for establishing a Zionist leadership position that while committed to Israel was not subordinate to it, and neither drew its prestige nor authority from it (Silver 1953c).[6]

How realistic was Silver's leadership presumption? To what extent did he have a real chance of positioning himself as having a status similar to that of the Catholic Cardinal Spellman in the eyes of the Republican administration and the Jewish community? There is no doubt that Silver overrated the way he was perceived by the Republican administration, as it soon became clear that his electoral importance to the Republicans was mainly symbolic, and the overwhelming majority of Jewish voters remained loyal to the Democratic Party. In this situation, Silver had no real public leverage to use on the government. Silver tried to represent to Eisenhower and Dulles a moral and ethical stance of global scope, as was expected from a leader of high religious standing; however, unlike Cardinal Spellman, Silver was compelled to do so without the backing of tens of millions of Catholic voters who were subject to his influence and religious authority. To have a chance of real political influence even without the backing of the Jewish electorate, Silver had to shake off the image of a sectorial leader. He had to appear before the administration in the name of an ideology that had a broad common denominator with the views of the president and the circle of decisionmakers surrounding him—an ideology in which the Israeli-Zionist issue was only one aspect. It is doubtful whether he was perceived this way by the Republican leadership. As mentioned earlier, Silver's views regarding key social and economic issues

6. Silver's Diary 1949–1963, December 1951 and January 1952, AHSP V.

were usually closer to the liberal and progressive views espoused by the Democratic Party. This being the case, Silver never had a real chance for a diverse common discourse that was not limited to the Israeli issue, such as the discourse conducted by other Jewish leaders who were rooted in the heart of the social and political circle of the Democratic leadership. Given this situation, Silver was consigned, to his detriment, to the position of a lobbyist for an issue that was of marginal interest to most of the Republican voters and elected representatives.

Silver's difficulty in breaking free from his position as a sectorial leader was to become a central obstacle in his activity vis-à-vis the new administration. The new administration was eager to differentiate itself from the policies of the Truman administration, which was now being portrayed as tainted with irrelevant domestic considerations. This criticism pertained to all areas of foreign policy, but received special emphasis on the Middle Eastern issue. In the first six months of its term, the new administration announced a "New Look" toward its Middle East policy, which was supposed to measure the relations with Israel according to the overall strategic interests of the United States and the free world in the Middle East rather than through what was portrayed as the narrow prism of domestic considerations with regard to Jewish pressure groups. The Middle East was perceived as a key point for implementing the strategy of containment; the assumption that was formulated by the US National Security Council was that if the Soviet Union should succeed in taking over the Middle East, the ability of Western European states to resist communism would be significantly reduced. Therefore, US foreign policy placed major emphasis on the attempt to prevent Soviet influence from infiltrating into the region, and sought to do this by means of economic and military aid to the Arab states, and by establishing with them a Middle Eastern security pact—the Middle East Defense Organization, or MEDO. The idea of basing Middle Eastern policy on this strategic doctrine did not bode well for Israel. From this perspective, the attitude toward Israel would have to be determined according to its influence on the ability of the United States to mobilize the support of the Arab states against the Soviet Union.

It should also be added that the focus on Middle East policy was a convenient way of presenting a new diplomatic tone without paying political price within the Jewish electorate, the overwhelming majority of which was inclined to support the Democratic Party. From an early stage in the new administration's term, reports were leaked about the intention to adopt a balanced policy that would not yield to American-Jewish pressure groups. At the beginning of February, in a *New York Times* article by James Reston about the "New Look" strategy in the Middle East, and on March 1, on the eve of Eisenhower's meeting with the Saudi foreign minister, Prince Faisal Al Saud, senior State Department sources were quoted as saying that Israel had received more economic aid in the previous four years than all the Arab states combined. Eisenhower himself spoke in the same vein during a meeting with the Egyptian ambassador on June 1. He told the ambassador that he was aware of statements to the effect that there were five million Jewish voters in the United States and very few Muslim voters, but said that he was immune to this influence, and that no one would be able to force him to act against the principles in which he believed (Alteras 1993, 37–40; Ganin 2005, 186; Kenen 1981, 92). About a month later, Secretary of State Dulles went on a twenty-day, twelve-country fact-finding mission to the Middle East, during which Israel was the second stop after Egypt. During his visit to Egypt, he took pains to make it clear that US policy would be balanced and, unlike the policy of the Truman administration, would not be influenced by pressure groups within the United States. A few days later, while in Lebanon, he explained to his hosts that the Jewish influence that was dominant in the days of the previous administration did not exist in the current administration. During his visit to Israel, Dulles raised the issue of the harmful intervention of American-Jewish leaders in US foreign policy. He warned that many American Jews working on Israel's behalf were not capable of grasping the strategic importance of friendship with the Arabs to the interests of the free world. He asked Ben-Gurion to restrain this harmful lobbying activity and to explain to the American Jews acting on behalf of Israel the broad contexts of the American policy of "friendly neutrality" and its long-term benefit to Israel (Alteras 1993, 68–73).

Clearly, this situation was not conducive to Silver's aspirations of building a position of influence within the administration on the Israeli issue. Silver became one of the most prominent American Jews who were close to the administration at a time when the State Department was eager to prove that it was not influenced by Jewish pressure groups. Paradoxically there was a concurrent Israeli approach, which looked unfavorably on the possibility that Silver would accrue power and influence. This slightly peculiar convergence of interests between the American and Israeli approaches already found expression in the immediate period after Eisenhower's victory. At that time, Eban was engaged in rebuilding the entire network of relationships that existed with the Truman administration. Still, in the first days after the elections, he sent a telegram to Ben-Gurion and Sharett, stating his evaluation that Silver must not by any means be made the intermediary between Israel and the United States. In this message, Eban expressed the traditional opposition of the professional echelons in the embassy to the activity of American-Zionist leaders, who by virtue of their Zionist record believed that they had a right to independent discretion regarding the nature of their lobbying activity for Israel. In this case, Silver's authoritative pattern of action—a pattern with which Eban was familiar from the period of the struggle in the United Nations for the establishment of the state—seemed to ensure that if Silver were to become Israel's main liaison with the administration, he would not settle for the status of someone who merely received instructions from the embassy. Against this backdrop, it comes as no surprise that Eban was opposed to relying on Silver's mediation services, and from an early stage took care to build up alternative ties with the administration.

Opposition to Silver was also expressed in talks held by the Israeli leadership with Dulles during his visit to Jerusalem. After Dulles requested to rein in the harmful activity of American-Zionist leaders, Eban replied with his own contention, warning of the secretary of state's willingness to hold frequent meetings and telephone conversations with certain American-Zionist leaders, saying that the administration should give preference to official Israeli representatives in presenting the Israeli issue. Although Silver's name was not specifically mentioned, it was clear that his accessibility and potential ability to influence matters were perceived as an obstacle that the United States and Israel had a common interest in neutralizing (Eban 1977, 172–78; Ganin 2005, 182–84).[7]

Against this backdrop, one should evaluate Silver's first meeting with Secretary of State Dulles. The meeting occurred on March 17, 1953—nearly five months after the elections. Eban conducted a briefing with Silver only an hour before the meeting simply as a means of containing the damage liable to ensue from Silver's unfamiliarity with the nuances of Israeli foreign policy. By this time Eban had already established a relationship of his own with Dulles and other State Department personnel, and felt that he had no need of Silver for this purpose. As of this date in mid-March, he had already held meetings with Under Secretary of State Walter Bedell Smith and Assistant Secretary of State for Near Eastern Affairs Henry Byroade, as well as two meetings with Dulles. Eban also preferred not to turn to Silver for lobbying purposes, calling instead on American Jews whom he viewed as less problematic, among them Blaustein, who had met with the president a month earlier. If Silver had been hoping for different treatment at Dulles's hands, here as well disappointment awaited him. At the beginning of his meeting with Dulles, he promised the latter that the details of their discussion would remain confidential and urged him to speak frankly about the real meaning of the administration's "New Look" policy for the Middle East. Essentially, he was offering Dulles a discrete message-bearing channel to Israel. Dulles, however, did not take up the offer. Even when subjecting documentation of the meeting to meticulous analysis, one finds nothing but general statements by Dulles about America's commitment to peacemaking efforts between Israel and the Arab states. In response to Silver's expression of dismay over anti-Israeli statements that had been leaked to the press by senior State Department officials, Dulles merely made a vague promise to clarify matters at an upcoming press conference. Having no meaningful discussion to report on, Silver documented in his journal the secretary of state's gratification when complimented on having included Israel in the itinerary for his

7. Letters from Eban to Ben-Gurion and Sharett, November 8, 1952, Israel State Archive 93.01/2208/15.

scheduled trip to the Middle East in May. This compliment by Silver stood in stark contrast to public statements made by the secretary of state, who had noted several times that most of his trip would be devoted to the Arab states, whereas Israel had been included only because it happened to be in the region as well.

The discrepancy between wish and reality regarding his special relations with high-ranking figures in the Eisenhower administration became even more pronounced as the day went on. At about the same time that he reported to Eban on his meeting with Dulles, he had to contend with an embarrassing situation of implicit competition with the AZC, whose leaders notified him that they had succeeded in arranging a meeting with Eisenhower without his mediation. This new initiative made it clear to Silver that he had no monopoly on interaction with the new administration and that he was competing this time with his own camp of loyal followers. Immediately after his meeting with Dulles ended, he received a phone call from AZC President Rabbi Irving Miller, a loyal and long-time ally, in which the latter informed him that an AZC request for an interview with Eisenhower, submitted ten days earlier, had been granted. Silver led Miller to understand that this development was not to his liking; Miller therefore called an emergency meeting of the AZC leadership with the clear intention of placating Silver. Two days later, on March 19, Silver received a telegram from Lipsky, as AZC chairman, informing him of the AZC leadership's unanimous decision to invite Silver to serve as honorary chairman of the delegation scheduled to meet with Eisenhower on the twenty-third of that month. Even before the telegram arrived, Silver received a phone call from AZC Director Unger notifying him of the decision. During the course of this conversation, Silver told Unger that he had no intention of attending the meeting; the next day he reiterated his refusal in a telegram to Lipsky. Silver's wording of the response to Lipsky indicates that he was seeking a means of adjusting to what was, for him, a new situation. He was aware that, a week after the AZC's scheduled meeting, on the twenty-eighth of the month, Eisenhower would be meeting with Israel Goldstein, president of the American Jewish Congress. He also knew that, over the past few weeks, there had already been several meetings between the president and such senior American-Jewish leaders as Blaustein and Simon Sobeloff. Silver sought a means of distinguishing himself from the other lobbyists knocking on the president's door; he formulated the telegram to Lipsky in such a way as to insinuate that the scheduled AZC meeting was merely one of protocol. He advised Lipsky to stick to common expressions of politeness and guided him in the composition of a general concluding statement that would express confidence in the administration.[8]

As part of this attempt to differentiate himself from other lobbyists, Silver sought to depict his own scheduled July 8 meeting with the president as evidence of a relationship of an entirely different order. These efforts, and the disillusionment that followed, are clearly reflected in the documentation of the events as they unrolled over the course of a month. However, despite conscientious and discrete preparatory activity,[9] Silver quickly became aware that neither Israel's official representatives nor Eisenhower viewed him as the discrete leader on whom they could depend for mediation purposes. Silver could, indeed, have inferred the marginal importance attached by Israel to his meeting with Eisenhower when he met with David Goitein, the Israeli Embassy's envoy, only two hours prior to his meeting with the president while Eban was on vacation. The shunning of Silver's services was manifested quite blatantly in Goitein's refusal to share with him the Israeli concerns regarding Eisenhower's "New Look" policy. When asked by Silver whether there was a message that Israel wished him to convey, Goitein replied that no crisis

8. Silver suggested his help only in editing the statement draft before its submission to Eisenhower and the press.

9. The beginning of Silver's preparations for the meeting with Eisenhower was noted in a letter sent to Eban on June 2, for the purpose of ascertaining Eban's reaction to Dulles's concluding statement on the completion of his trip to the Middle East. The statement had been broadcast on television the previous day and had attracted considerable criticism from the Jewish and Israeli leadership. Particularly worrisome was the understanding expressed by Dulles for Arab fears of Israeli expansionism. The next stage of preparation was a dinner meeting on July 7—the day before the meeting with Eisenhower—with Maxwell Rabb, one of the few Jews serving in a senior position in the Eisenhower administration as cabinet secretary and the official responsible for relations with the Jewish community.

was underway between Israel and the United States. This was essentially a polite way of telling Silver that Israel had no need of his services. Goitein's only advice to Silver was to stick to protocol with the president and not to touch on concrete issues such as Israel's requests for economic aid.

In the absence of Israeli willingness to make use of his connections in the White House, Silver sought to conduct his meeting with the president in the framework of an exchange of opinions between two prominent leaders who periodically met to discuss international and domestic social problems, among them major issues pertaining to Israel. However, what actually comes across was Silver's inability during his half-hour interview with Eisenhower to go beyond generalities or to elicit from the president anything other than his usual public assurances. Silver began the meeting with words of praise for American foreign policy and its aspiration to global peace and democracy, referring in particular to Eisenhower's speech on that very topic before an audience of major newspaper editors on April 16 of that year.[10] The time that remained was devoted to Israel; but here as well, only noncommittal generalities were uttered. The president spoke about the severe sense of injustice then prevailing in the Arab world, noting that, although he himself did not believe that feeling to be justified, it was nevertheless necessary for Israel to neutralize it; he proposed that some of the funds donated by American Jewry be diverted to the Palestinian refugees. Finally, Eisenhower affirmed that the Jews need not view the administration's economic or military aid initiatives toward the Arab world as hostile to Israel; one should not expect US policy to dictate a tank-for-tank balance.

10. He went on to express satisfaction with the president's celebrated Dartmouth College commencement address, in which he had opposed Senator McCarthy's call to ban and burn subversive books. Finally he praised the president's efforts to amend the McCarran-Walter Act, which, as noted above, bore racist overtones, had been passed by the previous administration, and whose terms Eisenhower was now seeking change so as to enable the immigration of an additional 240,000 people to the United States over the course of 1954. All of these things delineated a liberal agenda that Eisenhower certainly did embrace, though its dominance in shaping the administration's policies was probably less than Silver made it out to be.

Although Silver tried to stress the positive aspects of the meeting, the summary that he wrote for himself in his journal testifies to the disappointment he felt at its conclusion. He wrote that Eisenhower's understanding of Israel was limited, both in terms of historical background and current affairs. He also expressed anxiety over the president's exposure to elements hostile to Israel, though his overall impression was that Eisenhower was a fair-minded person who would not willingly act against the Jewish state (Alteras 1993, 68–73).[11] Compared with the dubious tone of the summary that he composed for his private journal, Silver's statement to the press was worded more diplomatically; it emphasized the deep commitment to peace and democracy that Silver had discerned in the president, as well as his strong friendship with both Israel and the Arab countries. In Silver's words, the meeting, as represented in the statement, had not been intended to advance any immediate practical issues; rather, it had been a forum for the exchange of opinions between two leaders, along the lines of their previous meeting in October, just prior to the presidential elections. How accurate was Silver's depiction of the meeting? Although there was a grain of truth to his description, the meeting had not been an ideological exchange on justice and democracy between the leader of the free world and the preeminent spiritual leader of American Jewry; rather, it had been a protocol-driven meeting that sidestepped the major issues of US Middle East policy. The president had refrained from mentioning to Silver that he was about to approve, just three days after the meeting, a National Security Council decision to promulgate a new Middle East policy, which, in the spirit of Dulles's televised speech, was intended to "correct" the Truman administration's pro-Israel bias. Silver was not informed by the Israeli Embassy that, just two days after his meeting with the president, Israel was planning to transfer its Foreign Ministry offices to Jerusalem—an event that led to a major crisis in its relations with the Eisenhower administration.

11. On other Jewish and Israeli leaders who were disappointed by the president's knowledge and understanding of Zionism, see Alteras (1993, 46–49); Ganin (2005, 184); Israel State Archive, April 17, 1953, 142479/11.

Silver was deeply hurt by this lack of communication from both sides; over the following four months he strove to avoid any involvement in US-Israel relations.[12] Only on October 24, 1953, against the background of a major crisis in US-Israel relations, did he telephone Dulles and request a meeting. The two months that had preceded the crisis had witnessed two major incidents that cast a dark shadow over relations between the two countries. The first of these was that of the diversion of Jordan River waters in the demilitarized area of the Bnot Ya'akov Bridge, on the Israeli-Syrian border about 10 kilometers north of the Sea of Galilee. The affair came to light in early September,[13] when Israel began work in the area despite a September 23 ruling by the chief of staff of the United Nations Truce Supervision Organization, General Vagne Bennike.[14] The United States, for its part, demanded that Israel act in accordance with UNTSO decisions, threatening to freeze economic aid if it did not cease the construction work. The depth of the crisis was underscored during a meeting between Eban, Reuven Shiloah, the embassy minister in Washington, and Dulles on September 25, and in a report prepared by the assistant secretary of state for Near Eastern affairs, Henry Byroade, prior to a subsequent meeting with Eban. In addition to the unequivocal demand that the work be halted, Byroade insisted that Israel reconsider its policy of unrestricted immigration, which raised Arab fears regarding Israeli expansionism,

12. This could be seen in Silver's refusal to respond to the urgent telegram that he received from Dulles on July 13, a week after his meeting with the president. The telegram was sent after Silver failed to take a phone call from the secretary of state, who wanted to speak with him about the Israel Foreign Ministry's move to Jerusalem. Silver understood that Dulles's appeal did not reflect a desire on the part of the administration to employ him as mediator, but rather to use him as yet another means of pressuring Israel.

13. In early May 1951, during a visit with Sharett in the Israeli-Syrian border, Silver was a witness to an earlier stage of this version—the Tel-Mutivla incident between Israeli and Syrian forces (see Drory 2005, 95–99).

14. The Israeli plan was to take advantage of the area's higher altitude and build a power station to enable water to be pumped from the Sea of Galilee into the National Water Carrier system. Syria opposed this plan, calling it a violation of the armistice agreements and an infringement on the rights of local Syrian farmers, whereas Israel maintained that it was exercising its rights as set forth in the armistice agreements.

and make territorial gestures aimed at resolving the refugee problem (Alteras 1993, 88–91; Kenen 1981, 96, 99).[15]

The second incident that arose to jeopardize Israel's relations with the United States was that of the Israel Defense Forces' (IDF) retaliatory action on October 14–15, 1953 at Qibya, in response to an attack by infiltrators from Jordan who had thrown a grenade into a home in the town of Yehud and killed a woman and her two children. In an attempt to force the Jordanians to subdue the infiltration activity, Israel strove to inflict maximal human and property damage upon the village of Qibya. Unit 101, under the leadership of Ariel Sharon, killed sixty-six civilians—including women and children—and bombed forty-two dwellings, a school, and a mosque in the highest-casualty military action to have been carried out since 1948. The raid drew overwhelming worldwide condemnation; the State Department described it as "shocking" and demanded that those responsible be called to justice. The discussion and harsh denunciation by the UN Security Council were to take place only a month later, on November 18, but in the meantime Israel's standing in American public opinion had already eroded severely. This was evidenced by an official announcement by Dulles on October 20 that the threat to freeze American economic aid to Israel would be acted on because of Israel's refusal to cease its work in the Bnot Ya'akov Bridge area.

In the context of this crisis, the Israeli Embassy turned to Silver on several occasions. At first Silver chose not to respond, probably because he was still offended by Israel's behavior toward him four months earlier. On September 29, Eban sent another letter in which he asked Silver to come to Israel for an emergency meeting with Ben-Gurion; when Silver did not respond, Esther Herlitz, then serving as the Embassy's first secretary, sent him a telegram conveying Eban's urgent request to speak with him by telephone. Immediately after this phone conversation, Eban sent Silver a memorandum that he had composed for the Foreign Ministry on his and Shiloah's September 25 meeting with Dulles; a few days later this was

15. Minutes of Meeting of Eban and Reuben Shiloah with the Secretary of State, Mr. John Foster Dulles, September 25, 1953, at the State Department, AHSP I.

followed by another memorandum on tensions at the Israeli-Jordanian border, and on the dispute regarding work in the Bnot Ya'akov Bridge area. To this latter memorandum, Shiloah appended a valuable gift—an antique map from 1584 of Palestine that he had purchased in a secondhand bookstore in New Orleans, intended for Silver's personal Judaica collection. These various gestures were unquestionably attempts by the Israeli official echelon to court Silver. However, the fact that this time, precisely when he was ostensibly being wooed by the Israeli Embassy, he chose not to make note of it in his journal indicates that he was having second thoughts regarding his ability to serve as a mediator between the Eisenhower administration and the Israeli government without getting caught repeatedly in embarrassing situations—disregarded and uninformed by both the Israeli government and the administration. Thus, although the phone conversations and follow-up memoranda ultimately persuaded Silver to contact Dulles on June 24 with a request for an urgent meeting, it is clear that he did this in a spirit of suspicion toward both Israel and the American government. In this context, it should be noted that, because of the seriousness of the crisis, Eban decided to appeal not only to Silver but also to other possible sources of assistance. He was able to secure a meeting between Proskauer, of the American Jewish Committee, and Dulles on October 22. He was also in contact with Congressman Jacob Javits, who organized a delegation that included a number of American Jewry's most distinguished leaders. Finally, he received backing from Jerusalem in the form of Foreign Ministry officials Gideon Rafael and Yosef Tekoa, as well as General Moshe Dayan, who, on his return to Israel, was to be appointed the IDF Chief of Staff. The appeal to Silver was, therefore, just one element of the Embassy's intensive effort to address the most serious crisis yet to emerge in Israel's relations with the United States, and to prepare for the no less problematic UN deliberations that would be taking place with regard to the Bnot Ya'akov Bridge and Qibya affairs (Kenen 1981, 67–69; Sheffer 1996, 690–69).[16]

16. Letters from Eban to Silver, September 29, 1953, and from Ester Herlitz, First Secretary, to Silver, October 2, 1953; Minutes of Meeting with the Secretary of State, Mr. John

What ultimately eased matters from an Israeli perspective was the New York City mayoral campaign then underway, in which the Jewish Republican Harold Riegelman was running. Riegelman had to go to great lengths to prove his friendship with Israel, inasmuch as his opponent, Robert Wagner, Jr., benefited from the reputation that his father, Senator Robert Wagner, had earned as one of the Senate's staunchest supporters of Israeli statehood. The struggle for the Jewish vote in New York caused Riegelman to pressure Dulles to rescind the suspension of economic aid to Israel. Although Dulles repeatedly noted his opposition to any mingling of domestic concerns with foreign policy issues, he nevertheless pursued all possible means of aiding Riegelman and the Republican Party in New York, which happened to constitute his own political power base. As Eban was to relate in his memoirs, the threat of economic sanctions was removed after Byroade, on Dulles's behalf, came to him in New York and urgently pressed him to agree to a formula that would enable aid to Israel to be resumed, so that an end to the affair could be declared in advance of the mayoral elections scheduled for November 3 (Eban 1992, 234; *Time* 1953).

Silver, in his journal, presented the progression of events in an entirely different manner. Based only on Silver's account, one would conclude that it was solely Silver's intervention that ensured the resumption of aid. In his journal Silver reported a phone call received on the afternoon of October 26 from Riegelman, asking his opinion of a message from Dulles to the effect that the economic aid to Israel would resume immediately after the Bnot Ya'akov Bridge affair was resolved. Silver told him that Dulles had not appreciably altered the stance expressed in his ultimatum to Israel, and that the message was therefore insufficient. Javits telephoned Silver the next day and updated him on his own meeting with Dulles and Byroade: the secretary of state and the assistant secretary had once again contended that, in order for a comprehensive solution to be reached, the United States had to regain Arab trust, and American Jewry had to refrain from placing obstacles in the government's way (Alteras 1993, 98; Kenen

---

Foster Dulles, September 25, 1953, at the State Department; Letter from Reuben Shiloah to Silver, Minister Plenipotentiary, October 27, 1953, AHSP I.

1981, 102–3). Silver noted that in contrast to the failures of Riegelman and Javits, his own lunch meeting with Dulles on Wednesday, October 28 ended with an apparently pleasant surprise. Silver made a point of noting in his journal that the conversation lasted for an hour and a quarter, and that he preached to Dulles about the need for an exhibition of friendliness toward Israel on the part of the State Department. Dulles, according to Silver, declared his commitment to Israeli security, while also denouncing the failure of Arab states to use their oil revenues for their citizens' benefit. At the end of the meeting he called a press conference, affirmed his debt of gratitude to Silver, and announced the immediate renewal of economic aid to Israel.

Thus, the impression one gains from the journal is that it was Silver who succeeded where Riegelman and Javits had failed. However, in actuality, over the two days prior to Silver's meeting with Dulles, the latter had conducted a series of phone consultations with the US ambassador to the United Nations, Henry Cabot Lodge, Jr., during which they agreed on the compromise formula that Byroade had proposed to Eban at their meeting in New York. In accordance with this agreement, the UN Security Council adopted on October 27, the day before the Silver-Dulles meeting, a French proposal (S/3128) calling for a halt to the work in the demilitarized zone while UN deliberations were ongoing. Subsequent to this resolution, Eban announced Israel's agreement to suspend its work for the period of the Security Council deliberations, and the next day, that on which Silver met with Dulles, Eisenhower announced at a press conference that economic aid to Israel totaling some $26 million would be renewed (Alteras 1993, 98–99).[17] Silver doubtlessly had heard of the UN resolution that had been passed with Israel's concurrence the day before the meeting; he also fully understood that this was no great Israeli achievement but rather subordination to American dictates put forward by Dulles, precisely in accordance with Dulles's proposal to the delegation headed by Riegelman and Javits. It was also clear to Silver that Dulles's actions took place against

17. Conversations between Dulles and Lodge, October 26, 1953, 4:00 p.m., October 27, 1953, 2:50 p.m. and 6:20 p.m., Telephone Call series, Box 1, Dulles Papers.

the background of the upcoming New York elections, and that Dulles was trying to make the Republican candidate look good in the eyes of Jewish voters. As Silver had already proven several times in the past, he was prepared to swerve from the path of the Jewish lobbying organizations and openly support Republican candidates in return for their support for Israel. He agreed to meet with Dulles after the secretary of state promised him that the goal of the meeting would be a public announcement of the resumption of economic aid. Only then did Silver agree to fulfill his part of the "deal"—to participate in an effort aimed at assisting the Republican candidate for mayor of New York. Thus, the achievement from Silver's point of view was not the withdrawal of the threat to freeze aid, but rather his return to the status of prime Jewish contact on behalf of the Republican leadership, with concomitant Israeli recognition of his usefulness as a mediator with the Eisenhower administration.

From Silver's perspective, in order for the affair to be considered a success, he would have had to reestablish himself as a senior American-Jewish leader, one whose services were needed by both the Israeli and the American governments. However, as may readily be imagined, this hope of Silver's was unfounded in terms of his actual political power at the time. It should be noted that Silver was unable to secure the "Jewish vote" for the Republican Party, and the Democratic candidate, Wagner, ultimately won the New York mayoral campaign. As had already happened twice in the past, in the November 1949 New York Senate-seat election and in the 1952 presidential campaign, most Jewish voters remained loyal to the Democratic candidates, regardless of Silver's pro-Republican efforts. That Silver was one of many players to whom Israel turned for help at this critical juncture is also worthy of attention; the appeals by the Israeli Embassy notwithstanding, there was no chance that the Embassy would willingly confer on him the status of exclusive mediator with the administration. As Silver had found out before and was destined to discover again, without full and unambiguous Israeli acceptance of his leadership, he had no chance of attaining the kind of authority and power that he had enjoyed during the 1940s.

Finally, it appears that the place of Israel and the American-Jewish community within the agenda of the Republican administration were additional factors working against Silver. The small chance of a victory in Jewish New York was not enough to sway the administration from its "friendly neutrality" policy. The resumption of economic aid took place only after Israel had committed to cease its activity in the Bnot Ya'akov Bridge area; except for a few cosmetic changes, Israel complied with the American demands as presented to Eban and Shiloah on September 25 and to the Riegelman and Javits delegations on October 26.[18] Moreover, Israeli capitulation regarding the Bnot Ya'akov Bridge activity did not prevent American support for the UN's resolution condemning the Qibya raid; Silver's lobbying efforts in this instance proved futile. Nor did the administration change its position regarding the need to regain Arab trust by taking a hard line toward Israel. On October 26, at the height of Dulles's effort to aid Riegelman in his mayoral campaign, Eisenhower met with the secretary of the Arab League, who praised the decision to suspend economic aid to Israel. Two days later, immediately after announcing the renewal of economic aid, Eisenhower sent a note to Dulles in which he decried Zionist efforts to influence American foreign policy. Thus, at least in retrospect, Silver would have had to acknowledge to himself that he had sanctioned the hostile policy practiced by the State Department toward Israel—a policy that, despite Silver's connections, meetings, and joint press conferences with Eisenhower and Dulles, only became harsher with time.

Indeed, the day after his press conference with Dulles, on October 29, a coordinating meeting was held without Silver's knowledge between the various arms of the administration, within the framework of the advisory body to the National Security Council (the Operation Control Board, OCB), in which policy recommendations were formulated with grave ramifications for Israel. For the first time, recommendations issued by an official organization within the administration called into question the State of Israel's Jewish character. First and foremost, they called for pressure on Israel, through cuts in economic aid, as a means of limiting unselective

18. Kenen's (1981, 104) memoir characterized Eban's agreement as a total surrender on Israel's part to an American ultimatum.

Jewish immigration to the country. These anti-Israeli recommendations were made public in two speeches by Byroade, who expressed his criticism of Israel in exceedingly strong terms. The first and more moderate of these addresses was delivered on April 19, 1954, while the second, more critical speech took place on May 1 in Philadelphia, before the anti-Zionist American Council for Judaism. In the second speech, entitled "Facing Realities in the Arab-Israel Dispute," Byroade described the Law of Return as the main impetus for the ongoing conflict between Israel and the Arab countries, and called on Israel to change its immigration policy in a way that would calm Arab fears regarding its expansionist intentions. Essentially he was demanding that Israel divest itself of its Zionist ideology and Jewish identity (Alteras 1993, 104–5).

As may have been expected, these speeches generated considerable uproar within American Jewry. They were decried as an attempt to drive a wedge between Israel and Diaspora Jewry. The voices of protest grew louder as it emerged that the United States was planning to supply weapons to Iraq as part of an effort to create a pro-Western regional military alliance, known as the "Baghdad Pact." The pact was to take effect just a year and a half later in February 1955, but even in March–April 1954, the State Department was already issuing statements regarding its intentions to supply arms to Iraq within the framework of the planned security alliance (Alteras 1993, 108–12, 126–56; Kenen 1981, 122–30). These two issues—the Byroade speeches and the provision of arms to Iraq—formed the background for Silver's decision to try once again to influence the Eisenhower administration's Middle East policy. The first meeting was scheduled for April 20, the day after Byroade's first speech, and was held with White House Chief of Staff Sherman Adams. The second meeting took place three weeks later, on May 11, 1954, ten days after Byroade's second speech, with Secretary of State Dulles. By this point Silver had already lowered his expectations regarding his ability to influence the administration's policies. Although he took pains to unfold before Adams and Dulles his critique of Byroade and of the intention to supply arms to Iraq, he ultimately settled for a vague promise from Dulles to seek an opportunity to deliver an Israel-friendly speech that would counterbalance the anti-Israel tone of Byroade's addresses.

The main remedy proposed by Silver for easing tensions between the United States and Israel amounted merely to a request that Under Secretary of State Robert Murphy deliver a pro-Israel speech at the ZOA convention held in New York on June 21. His correspondence with Dulles on the topic reveals a problematic development from the perspective of his relations with the Eisenhower administration.[19] On the face of it, the correspondence was polite; however, a growing sense of disappointment on Silver's part could be detected between the lines. Silver's first two letters to Dulles maintained a high degree of courteousness; he strove to clarify that he was not seeking to exert political pressure on Dulles or cause him embarrassment. He also reiterated that he was not expecting a speech that would extend concrete political promises, but rather a general statement of goodwill. Yet in response to Silver's cautious appeal, Dulles wrote on June 4 that he was having second thoughts about the matter. Essentially, he responded that at this juncture—when the United States was seeking to win Arab trust—any statement of support for Israel, however general or lukewarm, risked undermining American foreign policy.

Silver could not reconcile himself to such a state of affairs. In his letters to Dulles he referred to the cancellation of the speech as a gross violation of the political alliance between the Republican administration and himself. On June 11, 1954, he noted, in what could be interpreted as a veiled threat, that a major embarrassment to the State Department could be avoided, as he was scheduled to speak at the convention and hoped to cast the administration's policy toward Israel in a positive light. Dulles answered this letter on the fifteenth of the month with what was, essentially, a commitment to comply with Silver's demand. However, he also responded to Silver's implied threat by noting that, although he appreciated Silver's frankness, he feared that Murphy's noncommittal assurances would disappoint the Israeli and Zionist leaderships. As though in

19. Letters between Silver and Dulles, May 24, 1954, June 3, 1954, June 4, 1954, June 11, 1954, June 15, 1954, June 21, 1954, June 25, 1954; Letter from David Linebaugh (special assistant to Murphy) to Irving Miller, June 8, 1954; Letter from Roderic L. O'Connor (special assistant to the secretary of state) to Silver, June 9, 1954.

answer to this, on the very day that the convention began, June 21, Silver sent yet another letter to Dulles, in which he recommended that the tone of Murphy's speech be warm and positive. Specifically, he warned against any mention of Byroade's speeches, which, he maintained, had roused much anger and necessitated many superfluous explanations. At least superficially, the affair concluded on a positive note, with Silver sending Dulles a letter of gratitude immediately after the ZOA convention ended. He assured Dulles that Murphy's address had been excellent and had enjoyed a positive reception. He added that Murphy's humor and warmth, as well as the message that had been read aloud on Eisenhower's behalf, had helped to soften the impression made by Byroade's hostile statements. At the same time, Silver neglected to mention his own speech at the convention. Despite Murphy's friendly address, Silver made good on the threat hinted at in his previous letter to Dulles and openly denounced the State Department and its Middle East policy. He treated with sarcasm the rationale for supplying arms to Iraq, asking how the weapons meant to enable Iraq to deter Russian aggression could—as the administration maintained—pose no danger to Israel. It was clear that Silver had not only openly disagreed with the administration's policy, but, for the first time, had expressed a lack of faith in the sincerity of its assurances.[20]

This critical tone toward the administration indicates that Silver had become increasingly doubtful of the usefulness of his decade-long identification with the Republican Party. Silver was able to acquiesce in this only for so long as he believed the differences between Israel and the Eisenhower administration to be bridgeable through the offices of an experienced leader such as himself—one who knew how to employ "cosmetic" means, as in Murphy's conciliatory speech, to smooth over misunderstandings. However, Dulles's reluctance to grant even so noncommittal a gesture as the Murphy speech had shown Silver that the affair at hand was no mere misunderstanding; rather, the basic assumption of shared

20. Kenen described this speech as a turning point—an indication that even the most staunch supporter of the Republican administration harshly criticized the US policy on the Middle East (Kenen 1981, 122).

values and interests between Israel and the United States was being called into question by the administration. If this situation were to continue, it was bound to force Silver to choose sides and give up his hope of being an impartial mediator between Israel and the United States. It seems that Silver was as yet unable to acknowledge the full implications of this state of affairs. Time would have to pass before he could come to terms with the situation and formulate a new approach to his position regarding Israel and the American policymaking echelon.

10

A Recurrent Existential Threat to the Jews

A KEY ISSUE that contributed to the critical turn in Silver's attitude toward the Republican administration was the debate regarding American policy on supplying weapons to Israel and the Arab states. Although this issue had previously come up during the Truman administration, it became more pronounced within the "New Look" and containment policies adopted by Dulles. The debate now focused on the disparity between the American willingness to supply arms to the Arab states and forge a regional anti-Communist military alliance with them versus an adamant refusal to act the same way toward Israel. An examination of Silver's speeches demonstrates that he began to perceive this disparity as evidence of America's willingness to sacrifice vital Israeli interests for the sake of broader strategic American needs. In retrospect, it can be doubted whether this fear indeed reflected reality in terms of the balance of power between Israel and the Arab states, and whether Dulles and the administration were indeed willing to ignore the State of Israel's existential needs in order to gain the friendship of the Arab states (Alteras 1993, 126–56; Laron 2009). Yet this is how the situation was characterized by a major part of the Israeli leadership; from the distant perspective of Diaspora Jewry, the existential threat to Israel was perceived as even stronger. The sense of threat peaked in the course of 1955–1956, against the backdrop of Russia supplying arms, through Czechoslovakia, to Egypt, while the West provided arms to other Arab countries. This sparked the fear that, as in the Holocaust period, it would once again be legitimate for the free world to sacrifice the Jews, and that Israel might find itself in a position of military inferiority, standing alone and lacking any commitment for support by the world powers.

The heightened sense of existential danger to Israel had far-reaching implications for Silver's Jewish-Zionist agenda. In the years immediately following the founding of the state, he believed that a new era had arrived in which the exclusive Jewish focus on the existential struggle would finally end and Zionist efforts would be directed toward universal goals of world peace and lowering interbloc tensions. Now he found himself compelled to take a step backward and, as in the 1930s and 1940s, to mobilize once again for a renewed struggle over national Jewish existence. Gradually he changed the tenor of his Zionist activity. Instead of focusing on an internal-Zionist struggle against the Israeli leadership regarding the legitimacy of a separate universalistic Diaspora-Zionist agenda, it now appeared that he had accepted the Ben-Gurion approach, according to which the sole Zionist responsibility of Diaspora Jews was to focus on total mobilization in defense of the State of Israel in order that it would not remain exposed to the mounting military threats by Arab states without the protective defense umbrella of the United States. And so, as opposed to early 1951, when Silver objected to linking the American economic grant to Israel and Israel's military commitment to the United States, thereby dragging it into the interbloc struggle, he now regarded with growing criticism the US refusal to extend an unequivocal military commitment to Israel's existence by means of signing defense treaties with it.

All of these concerns contributed to an acute need for Silver to reevaluate how to fulfill the separate Diaspora-Zionist ideology. On the one hand, the struggle on behalf of a separate Diaspora-Zionist agenda was perceived as almost illegitimate at a time when the main thrust of attention was directed at the State of Israel's existential struggle. On the other hand, since the start of his Zionist career he had been opposed to making the existential struggle the focus of the sense of Jewish identification and viewed Diaspora-Zionist solidarity as a way of breaking free of this "negative" pattern of identification. A gap arose, therefore, between the rising need for unconditional mobilization for Israel and the Diaspora-Zionist ideology; this gap would only widen as the security threats against Israel increased. In this context a key issue for Silver was whether US support for Israel could still be taken for granted. An expression of this troublesome concern could be seen in a speech that Silver gave in February 1955 at a conference marking three hundred years of Jewish life in America (Silver 1955k). In effect, he turned this anniversary speech into an essay on the historical continuity of American commitment to collective Jewish existence. This type of rhetoric was characteristic of his style during the 1940s; the fact that Silver now elected to reemphasize it demonstrates that once again, as in the time of the Holocaust, he perceived a rising tension between the definition of the broad strategic American goals and Jewish existential interests. The need to argue repeatedly that the commitment to collective Jewish existence was necessarily derived from the American democratic way shows that he was unable, once again, to take this argument for granted.

In this anniversary speech, Silver identified the start of the American commitment to collective Jewish existence as early as Columbus's journey to America, as if it was predestined that America would play a vital role in ensuring Jewish existence. He subsequently reviewed several attempts to set up Jewish colonies in America, and here too emphasized the fundamental American commitment to supporting collective Jewish existence, a salient example being Mordecai Emanuel Noah's Ararat initiative. The lesson that should be learned from these historical examples, according to Silver, was that American support for the Zionist project was not the outcome of an incidental political situation, but rather reflected deep-seated trends in American tradition. He therefore stated that in the mid-1950s as well, support for the State of Israel was the articulation of a mainstream American tradition. Again and again, he expressed confidence that despite the ongoing attempts of a small group in the State Department to undermine the Zionist enterprise, basic American support for Israel remained intact, and just as had happened in the past, it was this basic support that would ultimately prevail.

An example of Silver's criticism toward American foreign policy could be seen in his speeches that compared the dangers that were posed by the rearmament of West Germany and its acceptance into the NATO defense pact and the armament of the Arab states for the purpose of establishing anti-Communist regional military alliances with them (Silver 1954b,

1954g, 1955d, 1955g, 1955h). He pointed out that during Hitler's time as well, Western state leaders had hoped that Germany would serve as a bulwark against the spread of communism, which became the rationale for their consent to German rearmament despite its acts of oppression and murder. Silver was not convinced by the prevalent talk about the "new Germany" and feared that militarism and Nazi nationalism would regain control of Germany as soon as its army was rebuilt. An American foreign policy that truly strove to defend the democratic way of life should have reunited Germany, leaving it permanently neutral and demilitarized. In a similar vein, Silver also criticized the intention to arm the Arab states with the hope that they would block the danger of Communist expansion. He argued that the antidemocratic rulers of the Arab states could not be expected to become defenders of the democratic world against the Russians. It was more reasonable to expect that they would use the weapons received from the West to suppress any political protest in their own countries, and would ultimately turn these weapons against the only democracy in the Middle East—Israel. In this context, he mentioned a declaration by the Saudi king that he would be willing to sacrifice a million soldiers for the purpose of destroying Israel.

Despite the great similarity in Silver's criticism of US foreign policy toward Germany and the Arab states, one could distinguish a difference in his attitude toward the two issues. In the German case, Silver was opposed to including Germany in NATO and advocated a united, demilitarized state that would serve as a model of dialogue between the two blocs. He did not, however, take the same direction in his speeches dealing with the Israeli-Arab conflict. In these speeches, he did not focus on plans for regional or interbloc cooperation, but, on the contrary, as reports of the provision of arms to the Arab states increased and his concern for Israel's existence mounted, he increasingly emphasized the need to strengthen Israel's military power and include it in Western defense alliances. An example of this can be seen in a speech given in March 1955 (Silver 1955h), which focused on the reprisal raid in Gaza that was conducted about two weeks earlier on the night between February 28 and March 1. Thirty-seven Egyptian soldiers were killed in the raid, and this harsh outcome was met with sharp criticism by US policymakers, who described it as a manifestation of a belligerent and disproportionate Israeli policy that was liable to send the entire region into an arms race that the Soviets would exploit (Alteras 1993, 136–37). Silver was aware of the severe criticism voiced not only within the administration but also within Israel.[1] Although Silver personally shared this criticism, he was careful not to give it any public expression. In response to the American condemnations of the raid, Silver asserted that it would not be correct to examine whether the scope of the Gaza raid conformed to the local incidents that preceded it; rather, the raid should be seen within the context of the ongoing Egyptian rejection of peace talks versus the calls on Israel's part for negotiations without prior conditions. In his opinion, US foreign policy had to support measures that would persuade the Arab states that there was no chance of defeating Israel, and certainly it must not arm the Arab states or forge regional alliances with them. In the same spirit, he attacked the rationale behind the New Look policy. Silver explained that Israel was the most stable and reliable country in the region in its support for the West and its democratic values, and therefore any Western policy that sought to ensure democracy in the Middle East would have to be based on unequivocal support for Israel. Silver did not abandon the vision of turning Israel into a hub of regional cooperation and democratization, but at this point he viewed such a vision as contingent on a Western policy that would unequivocally support bolstering the State of Israel's military strength so that it would not be possible to call into question its right to exist.

A clear indication of this emphasis shift can be seen in Silver's refusal to support the American peace initiatives of that period. On the face of it, this refusal (as well as the lack of independent peace initiatives on Silver's part) is surprising. Ostensibly, turning the peace negotiations between Israel and the Arab states into the main objective of US foreign policy in the region should have been a central theme in his actions. A peace accord between Israel and its neighbors could have removed from the

1. The "moderate camp" was headed by Prime Minister Sharett and included the General Zionists and Progressive parties. It was fighting a rearguard battle against the activist camp headed by Ben-Gurion.

agenda the dual loyalty dilemma of many American Jews between support for the strategic interests of the United States and mobilization on behalf of the State of Israel's existential needs. A peace accord between Israel and the Arab states could make Israel a legitimate member of Western regional alliances, thereby transforming American support for the Jewish state from an obstacle to the overall management of US foreign policy into one of the most effective tools of this policy. It should also be said that the administration shared this hope; it appeared that Dulles truly believed that an accord between Israel and its neighbors could prevent Russian penetration of the region, and therefore he did not only issue general declarations about the need for peace, but also launched a number of mediation initiatives between Israel and its neighbors. If Silver had promoted the American mediation plans, this could have restored the trust between him and Dulles, who viewed the mediation initiatives as an important component of his Middle East policy. No less important, Silver's mobilization on behalf of these plans could have served as an excellent opportunity to emphasize the unique alternative to the Israeli agenda offered by the pluralist-universalistic agenda of Diaspora Zionism. But as stated above, in this period of rising tensions between Israel and the Arab states, Silver chose not to pursue this course.

One initiative that did not reach fruition was the idea of assigning an under secretary of state, General Walter Bedell Smith, the task of mediating between Israel and Egypt. Silver received copies of the correspondence on the matter, including messages that were classified and therefore had to be sent to him with the knowledge of Dulles and Smith, the main addressees of the initiative.[2] Although this was a high-ranking mediation initiative, which if implemented would have been sympathetic to Israel's demands (Bedell Smith was known for his friendly attitude toward Israel), Silver chose not to address the initiative, even privately, by documenting it in his journal. Silver also gave scant mention to the mission of

2. Letters between Major General Julius Klein and Dulles, October 3 and October 8, 1955; Letters between Klein and Walter Bedell Smith, October 11, 1955; Letter from Klein to Silver, October 19, 1955, AHSP I.

Eric Johnston, a much more serious and tangible mediation initiative on the part of the administration. The plan sought to turn the proposal of dividing the Jordan River's water between Israel and its neighbors into the basis of a regional development program to set up the "Jordan Valley Authority," which would also enable resolution of the Palestinian refugee problem. This project, known as the "Main Plan" after the American engineer Charles Main who prepared it, was reminiscent of the regional cooperation plans that Neumann and Silver had tried to promote back in the 1940s, and which, like the Main Plan, were based on the regional development programs of the Tennessee Valley Authority (Medoff 1997, 126–27; Segev 2004, 99–100). Despite the great importance attached by the administration and part of the Israeli leadership—mainly Sharett—to Johnston's mission, the few occasions Silver mentioned it he did so only to stress the need for strengthening Israel's security situation as a vital precondition for the initiative's success.

Another peace plan, perhaps the most important one from the administration's perspective, was known by the code name "Project Alpha." In this case, it was a joint American-British plan, and although Silver was not personally informed about it, he certainly knew about the initiative, at least after August 26, 1955, when Dulles made it public in a speech in New York. This peace plan significantly furthered Israeli positions. The head of the American team, Francis Russell, was a diplomat who had served in Israel and was considered sympathetic toward the Israeli point of view. The plan accepted, to a large degree, Israeli positions on the matter of the Palestinian refugees, the issue of Jerusalem, and the matter of removing the anti-Israel economic boycott and blockade. Even on the issue of borders (i.e., the gap between the partition and armistice borders), the plan closely adhered to the Israeli position. It demanded that Jordan give up part of the Latrun area in order to enable reconnection of the main road between Tel Aviv and Jerusalem; in return, Israel was called on to make concessions in the Negev that would enable territorial continuity between Egypt and Jordan, but without impairing the Israeli territorial continuity of the route to Eilat. However, Israel rejected the initiative, and here too Silver's voice was not heard. It would appear that a key reason for Silver's silence was his growing sense of suspicion toward any peace initiative that was not based on preliminary, unequivocal support for ensuring Israel's military superiority. On this matter, Silver identified completely with the Israeli position. In the face of American efforts to promote the Johnston initiative and Project Alpha, the main Israeli response lay in the demand to ensure its military superiority over the Arab states, as a precondition for any peace plan or negotiations.[3] Whether or not the Israeli reaction was justified, there is no doubt that it gained growing dominance, particularly after September 1955, following the Czechoslovakian-Egyptian arms deal and the large number of hostile statements made by Gamal Abdel Nasser against Israel and the West.

The sense of urgency and peril that stood behind the Israeli position became even stronger at the beginning of 1956, following the failed shuttle diplomacy between Israel and Egypt carried out by the president's personal emissary, Robert Anderson, who arrived in the region after the Czechoslovakian-Egyptian arms deal was signed. Anderson sought to revive Project Alpha as a means of distancing Egypt from its ties with the Communist bloc. After two rounds of shuttles in January and March 1956, which were codenamed "Project Gamma," Nasser rejected the main points of the plan. He demanded that Israel give up all territory in the Negev and allow the return of Palestinian refugees to their territories. He declared that even if Israel should accept his terms, the entire matter would still have to be brought before all the Arab states for approval. At least as the situation was perceived from the perspective of the Israeli leadership, Nasser appeared to be headed for war; the arms deal with Czechoslovakia and his success in spreading his pan-Arab ideas strengthened his confidence in his ability to fulfill his public threats against Israel. It would appear that in the period prior to the Sinai Campaign, the Israeli leadership became increasingly convinced that war with the Arab states was

3. The Israeli concern focused on the possibility that in Nasser's acceptance of various kinds of contacts and discussions with Israel, his sole intention was to buy time in order to enable Egypt to train its army in the use of the advanced Russian weapons it had purchased, in advance of an all-out war that it was planning against Israel (Sheffer 1996, 845).

inevitable, and therefore it would be best for Israel to launch a preemptive war that would ensure the preservation of Israel's military superiority.[4]

On this matter Silver shared the Israeli perspective. When he mentioned the issue of peace, he only referred to this as evidence of Israel's urgent need for security and defense measures. Like the Israeli leaders, he asserted that the path to a future peace required an unequivocal clarification of Israeli military superiority over any offensive coalition of Arab states. He stated that only American guarantees and unequivocal Israeli military superiority, which would persuade Arab rulers that they could not expect any military or diplomatic gain from war, could lead them to engage in peace negotiations with Israel. He also warned that as long as the Arab leaders believed that there was a chance of destroying Israel, any peace initiative could be expected to turn into a guarantee of renewed Arab aggression and violence.

It should be noted that despite the fact that the Israeli sense of an impending siege was widely shared in the Israeli government, there was still a power struggle within the Israeli leadership between the security-oriented camp headed by Ben-Gurion and the moderate camp headed by Sharett, who on the diplomatic issue was in a coalition with the General Zionists Party.[5] The former believed that the conclusion from the failure of UN forces and the world powers to uphold the armistice regime demonstrated that Israel's future was dependent first and foremost on Israeli military initiatives. The Sharett camp, conversely, considered the solution to Israel's security problems to lie in dialogue and constant aspiration toward diplomatic initiatives; even if these were not likely to bring peace in the immediate term, they would at least reduce security tensions and prevent war (Sheffer 1996, 731–32).

4. For a different perspective, according to which the Israeli intelligence estimated that Egypt was not capable of weighing war against Israel, see Laron (2009).

5. The struggle between the two camps heightened following Ben-Gurion's announcement in May 1953 that he intended to resign, and following Sharett's appointment as acting prime minister starting in July 1953 and his tenure as Israel's second prime minister from January 26, 1954 to November 3, 1955.

Judging by his views on the Korean War and the Cold War, Silver could have been expected to mobilize publicly on behalf of a diplomatic approach—yet he did not do so. He neither publicly supported the diplomatic engagement efforts made by Sharett, lauded his efforts to improve the situation of the Palestinian minority in the State of Israel, nor publicly attacked the approach that placed an excessive emphasis on solutions based on military force. The genuine sense of anxiety that Silver felt for Israel's existence took precedence over his long-term concerns about Israel's character and the desired universalist-Zionist agenda. One indication of Silver's intense and urgent existential concern at that time can be found in the repeated mention of the Holocaust in his articles and lectures, and his recurring comparison of the threat in the 1930s posed by Nazi Germany with the current threat on the part of Arab dictatorial regimes. In these references, Silver represented a typical sensitivity of Diaspora Jews to the possibility of a renewed threat to collective Jewish existence, of which the State of Israel was now the most distinct symbol.

Yet in contrast to the all-encompassing sense of suspicion that many Israelis, including his allies in the General Zionists Party, exhibited toward the American Middle East policy of Dulles and Eisenhower, Silver was careful to accompany his criticism of US foreign policy with repeated statements about his belief in the administration's basic goodwill. For example, in an article published on Erev Rosh Hashanah (the eve before the Jewish New Year) in September 1955 in *Haboker*, the newspaper of the General Zionists Party, Silver was quoted as saying that even if at times the State Department acted in a manner that elicited criticism among Israel's friends, he had no doubt as to the friendly and sincere intentions that stood behind the long-term idealistic goals of its Middle East policy. He mentioned Eisenhower's request from Congress to continue the American support for friendly states in the Middle East, and cited this as an indication of the American commitment to work with peoples and governments on both sides in order to improve their economic status and promote permanent peace in the region. The article, which was based on quotes from his lecture at the June 1955 ZOA convention, sparked great criticism in Israel, as it was perceived as an expression of support for the administration's policy and, implicitly, for the pressure it placed on Israel.

The criticism was so sharp that Harold Manson, one of Silver's most loyal supporters, urged him to clarify that the *Haboker* article did not represent his opinion. And indeed, despite the fact that the statements did not go beyond the usual distinction that Silver made between the desirable idealistic intentions of the administration and its concrete actions, at Manson's request he issued a clarification claiming that the statements made in *Haboker* were taken out of context. It would appear that at this time of mounting threats to Israel following the Czechoslovakian arms deal, Silver was averse to any public statement that could have been interpreted as deviating from Israel's diplomatic line and as support for an American policy that did not explicitly align itself with Israel's positions.

The eventful months of November and December 1955 underscored Silver's uncritical stance on behalf of Israel even further. During this period, Sharett made a trip to the United States as foreign minister rather than prime minister. Despite his waning influence, Sharett, in addition to presenting arms supply requests, persisted in raising proposals for dialogue between Israel and the Arab countries.[6] Just as his strategy appeared to have paid off in the form of plans for a meeting between Nasser and Ben-Gurion, as well as an American commitment to supply arms to Israel, Ben-Gurion authorized Operation Olive Leaves—a retribution operation carried out on the night of December 11–12 on the eastern coast of the Sea of Galilee in which forty-six Syrians were killed and thirty captured. This operation was widely perceived as a disproportionate reaction to Syrian attacks on Israeli fishing boats. Whether justified or not, the action unquestionably undermined Sharett's efforts. In his personal correspondence, Silver raised doubts regarding the operation's necessity. He was aware of Sharett's concern that Israel was exaggerating existing border tensions in order to justify its arms demands; in his view, the tactic was a dangerous one that could ultimately become a self-fulfilling prophecy and draw the entire region into war (Eban 1992, 349–50; Sheffer 1996,

6. Sharett suggested a seven-point peace plan, among which were a rite of passage to the Arab countries through Israel, access to Jordan in Haifa Port, and an agreement for a return of a small number of Palestinian refugees (Caplan 1997, 195–96).

845–49, 861). Still, he refrained from expressing his reservations beyond the private sphere; these concerns did not keep him from accepting the Israel Bonds chairmanship or from launching an ambitious fundraising campaign aimed at addressing Israel's security needs.

Toward the end of January, six weeks after Operation Olive Leaves, Silver commenced a new round of lobbying for America to provide arms to Israel. On January 25, 1956, Silver met with the White House Chief of Staff Sherman Adams. Silver focused on the Israeli concerns regarding the upcoming summit between Eisenhower and British Prime Minister Anthony Eden.[7] These concerns were rooted in suspicions that dated back to the British Mandate period and had been rekindled by Eden's November 9, 1955 parliamentary speech, in which he stressed the territorial concessions that Israel would be expected to make within the framework of an Anglo-American Alpha Project initiative. This speech was perceived in Israel as reflecting a dangerous policy line; it had been decided, in response, to publicly condemn the Alpha Project, and to represent arms provision to Israel and the establishment of Israeli military agreements with the United States as necessary preconditions to any mediation endeavor. Now that the Eisenhower-Eden summit was approaching, Israel intensified its efforts in this direction. Ben-Gurion sent a memorandum to Eisenhower in which he set forth the Israeli weapons requests in detail; at the same time, Israel organized a broad-based lobbying campaign. Thus, in a January 28, 1956 press release, a group of senior figures in the Democratic Party, headed by Eleanor Roosevelt with the backing of former President Truman, called for American arms provision to Israel as a means of reestablishing the balance of power between Israel and Egypt, and on February 3, forty congressmen issued a similar appeal. Even before that, on January 30, Eban, speaking in Washington, had called for American arms to be supplied to Israel without delay. Silver's White House meeting in January was, therefore, part of a broader campaign orchestrated by Israel for the purpose of persuading the Eisenhower administration to provide

7. Letters from Eban to Silver, December 19, 1955, and from Silver to Eban, December 29, 1955, AHSP I.

Israel with weapons as a precondition for any mediation initiative (Alteras 1993, 174–75; Sheffer 1996, 855).

It should be noted that Dulles rejected the Israeli position. Indeed, he warned Israel against an approach that was based exclusively on maintaining military supremacy; he also counseled against "retribution" and preemptive war policies. Although Dulles was prepared to consider arms provision,[8] he nevertheless insisted that Israel's main security problems would have to be solved via agreements based on territorial concessions, as proposed by the Alpha Project (Eban 1992, 234). In accordance with Dulles's views, the State Department responded to the Czechoslovakian-Egyptian arms deal not by a counterprovision of arms to Israel, but rather with renewed efforts to revive the Alpha Project. As noted earlier, since January 19, the president's personal envoy, Robert Anderson, deputy secretary of defense and future secretary of the treasury, had been shuttling between Israel and Egypt, primarily for the purpose of renewing the initiative that had been halted in the wake of Operation Olive Leaves and arranging a personal meeting between Nasser and Ben-Gurion.[9] The main thrust of this initiative was the administration's promise of security guarantees for Egypt and Israel, as well as economic aid for both countries—the Aswan Dam Project for Egypt and, for Israel, the funding of compensation programs for Palestinian refugees. On the face of it, the Eisenhower administration's promises of support for refugee settlement projects and the construction of the Aswan Dam were entirely compatible with Silver's views. In the case of the Aswan Dam, the project was expected to increase Egypt's arable land area by a third and to meet half of the country's energy needs. The project's astronomical cost—$1.3 billion—would have ensured that, even after the United States, the United

8. In early February, following the Eisenhower-Eden summit, the United States did, in fact, permit France to provide Israel with jets equipped with American engines, whose provision had been prohibited in the aftermath of Operation Olive Leaves.

9. The mission was one to which the administration attached great importance, as evidenced by the complex logistical system that Allen Dulles, the head of the CIA and the secretary of state's brother, was personally involved in establishing—a system intended to ensure personal contact between Anderson, Dulles, and the president.

Kingdom, and the World Bank had put up half of the money required,[10] the need for local investment would have prevented Egypt from tying up additional funds in arms deals. This, the administration hoped, would keep the Soviet Union from taking advantage of a looming conflict in order to extend its regional influence.

In its effort to promote this plan, the administration had to contend with a rare congressional coalition that included representatives of the southern states concerned for cotton growers' interests, right-wing conservatives favoring American insularity, and supporters of Israel who viewed any strengthening of Egypt as automatically endangering Israel. In his lobbying efforts, Silver's position was completely consistent with the security and military emphasis of Israeli policy. Silver represented this Israeli strategy at his meeting with Adams on January 25, 1956, and expressed it even more strongly in his February 20 meeting with Assistant Secretary of State Herbert Hoover, Jr. A son of the former president, Hoover was an engineer by training with expertise in oil prospecting; in 1953, he joined the State Department and gradually took on the role of Dulles's stand-in and right-hand man, and was personally involved in all stages of the Alpha and Gamma projects. In his talk with Silver, he indicated his hope that, within ten days to two weeks, the Gamma initiative, which at that stage was still a secret mission, would produce developments of a most important nature. In a manner characteristically consistent with Israeli policy, Silver expressed concern over the mediation initiative's disclosure, and rather than addressing its prospects of success, he focused on the dispute then raging over the provision of eighteen tanks to the Saudis.

Two weeks later, on March 8, in yet another White House meeting between Silver, Adams, and Hoover, Silver displayed the same quasi-automatic pattern of response to the American mediation initiatives. Hoover, then acting secretary of state, was still entirely preoccupied by

10. Dulles announced, on December 16, 1955, a tentative agreement in which the United States, the United Kingdom, and the World Bank would cover half of the project cost, with Egypt funding the other half.

the Anderson effort, whose ultimate failure he would report to Eisenhower two days later. If Hoover was hoping to find in Silver an ally supportive of his last-ditch effort to save the initiative, he was undoubtedly disappointed. Silver devoted his hour-long discussion with Hoover and Adams, held in the latter's office in the White House, to the Saudi arms deal affair. Silver focused on Dulles's allegations before the Senate Foreign Relations Committee regarding the extraordinary alliance between pro-Israeli Senator (and future vice president) Hubert Humphrey, and the committee chairman, Senator William Fulbright, generally known as a critic of Israel. This coalition had emerged on the basis of a shared opposition to US funding of the Aswan Dam project; in Dulles's eyes, it clearly exemplified the way in which the narrow interests of pressure groups could undermine America's long-term strategic foreign-policy interests. Had the issue under discussion by the Senate Foreign Relations Committee been a regional conflict between India and China, or between the two Germanys, Silver probably would have staunchly supported Dulles's effort to halt the arms race and called on him to stand firm against the pressure groups concerned. He would certainly have voiced his support for mediation initiatives and economic projects aimed at calming the region and preventing a slide into war. However, in this instance, Silver was unwilling to give credence to the argument that supplying fighter jets to Israel was not the appropriate long-term solution to Mideast regional difficulties, or that efforts should be devoted primarily to economic projects such as the Aswan Dam.

Silver's unequivocal identification with the Israeli position was manifested even more clearly during his April 26 meeting with Eisenhower and Dulles. In their reports on this meeting (Alteras 1993, 177; Ganin 2005, 211–12; Raphael 1989, 200),[11] the president and the secretary of state

11. *The Papers of Dwight David Eisenhower*, vol. 16, 2123–24, note 4, based on Dulles Papers, telephone conversation between Eisenhower and Dulles; Memo from Dulles to Eisenhower, April 24 1956, 611/84A/4-1056, Department of State Records, National Archives, Washington, DC; Memo of Conversation between Eisenhower, Dulles, and Silver, April 26, 1956, Dulles Papers, Box 4, Dwight D. Eisenhower Library, Abilene, Kansas; Silver to Dulles, April 27, 1956, Dulles Papers, Box 104, Princeton University Library.

indicated their perception of Silver not as an American-Jewish leader with an agenda of his own, but as a kind of lobbyist on behalf of Israeli arms demands. Dulles clearly expressed this perception in a concluding memorandum that he drafted for the president. He noted that Silver, in emphasizing the urgent Israeli need for American weapons, had repeated, nearly word for word, arguments employed earlier by Eban. Dulles's impression was that Silver had been briefed by Israeli officials (Silver had indeed met with Eban and Shiloah on April 25) and that he had essentially become a full partner in the Israeli lobbying effort.[12] From the perspective of Eisenhower and Dulles, Silver's position constituted an illegitimate attempt by the pro-Israel lobby to keep them from implementing American foreign policy as they understood it. When during the course of the meeting Silver persisted in arguing for the necessity of supplying weapons to Israel, Dulles lost his patience and railed against the Zionist lobby, while Eisenhower affirmed that he would do the right thing, even if it meant defeat in the upcoming presidential election. Silver, for his part, responded in a belligerent manner similar to that which he had employed vis-à-vis the Roosevelt and Truman administrations of the 1940s. He pointed out that any talk of risking the election by standing up to the Jewish lobby was baseless, since Eisenhower could clearly be reelected without the vote of even a single Jew. He accused them of employing a smoke screen in their attempt to portray their defiance of Jewish pressure as a principled and courageous stance. On the contrary, this was a tactic aimed at delegitimizing a position strongly rooted in American tradition, rather than one based on parochial interests. Not only did this tactic have nothing to do with political courage, but it also, in Silver's view, constituted an act of cowardice on the part of the president and the secretary of state, and reflected an unwillingness to address the real arguments for fear of appearing to capitulate under pressure.[13]

12. In a private telephone conversation between Eisenhower and Dulles five days before the meeting, they had already expressed an expectation that Silver would focus on the Israeli arms demands and agreed that no acquiescence should be forthcoming.

13. Silver to Dulles, April 27, 1956, Dulles Papers, Box 104, Princeton University Library.

This was, without a doubt, an uncommonly bold manner in which to address the president, especially to his face, and particularly on the part of one generally regarded as a supporter of the administration. Unlike the 1940s, the tension that prevailed at this later meeting led to no open falling-out between Silver and the White House. In this instance, Silver's political weakness appears to have worked in his favor. Eisenhower and Dulles did not need Silver to remind them of their lack of dependence on the Jewish vote; they could, therefore, afford the luxury of humoring him as a man of principle who always spoke his mind. Dulles ended the quarrel by telling the president that Silver had taken a similarly resolute tone while defending him in his 1949 senatorial bid; the president acknowledged this, adding that Silver always said what he thought out of a sense of deep conviction.

Silver soon realized that this attitude of forbearance toward him as a man of principle ultimately translated into his exclusion from the pragmatic political sphere in which the Israeli cause needed to be pursued. One may say that, rather than severing ties with Silver, Dulles elevated him to the rank of a "man of conscience" whose adherence to principle, however pure the intentions that motivated it, nevertheless disqualified him from participating in the complex political reality of contradictory goals and principles. It is also clear that there was a very thin line between this attitude and one that would have dismissed Silver as an "extremist" unskilled in the art of statesmanship.[14]

This was the background of Silver's continuous unequivocal support for Israel's belligerent policy during the six months that passed between his meeting with Eisenhower and Dulles and October 29, the first day of the Suez Crisis and Sinai War. This half-year period was characterized by deteriorating relations between Egypt and the Western powers, and by a concomitant rise in tensions between Israel and its neighbors. On

14. As opposed to previous periods, when Dulles responded personally to Silver's appeals, now he received responses only from Dulles's administrative staff. Letter from Hames to Silver, May 2, 1956, AHSP I; Letter from John P. Meagher to Silver, September 27, 1956, AHSP I.

May 16, 1956, Nasser recognized Communist China, a move that drove the United States and Great Britain, on July 19, to withdraw their offer of a loan for the construction of the Aswan Dam. In response, on July 26, Nasser announced the nationalization of the Suez Canal Company and the intention of using its profits to fund the Aswan Dam. The blow to British economic and military interests—and, no less important, to British prestige—was devastating;[15] it is not, therefore, surprising, that Nasser came to be regarded during this period as the "Hitler of the Nile," not only by the British, but also by the French, who were concerned by the aid that Egypt was then supplying to the rebel forces in Algeria.

On October 14, after the Soviets vetoed an Anglo-French proposal to resolve the crisis, the secret talks that had been taking place for some time between Great Britain, France, and Israel gained momentum; about ten days later a secret Israeli-French-British agreement was reached. Silver, of course, was unaware of these secret talks, but the newspaper clippings in his private archive show that he monitored continuously the signs of impending war. Like many others—including high-ranking officials in the Eisenhower administration as well as Ambassador Eban—he fell into the trap set by the Israelis and adopted the erroneous view that the main danger facing Israel was the eruption of hostilities along the Jordanian border. He tended toward this view particularly in the wake of the Qalqiliya retribution operation of October 10–11, when Jordanians demanded that the British make good on their defense agreement with them. His fear of war intensified when, on October 22, supporters of Nasser won the Jordanian elections and the new Jordanian prime minister announced his intention of annulling the defense treaty with the British and joining the Egyptian-Syrian military alliance.

The American reaction to this state of affairs differed not only from that of the Israelis, but also from those of the British and the French. While the latter were preparing for a military operation aimed at deposing Nasser and restoring the status quo ante in the Suez, the Americans

15. Great Britain owned a 44 percent share in the canal, and a third of whose imports passed through it, as well as supplies for its military forces stationed in the Middle East.

took all possible diplomatic measures to calm the situation and prevent war. As the Americans saw it, a war might only confirm prevailing Arab perceptions of Western and American imperialism, thereby helping the Soviets expand their influence in the region. In accordance with this view, the United States declared its recognition of the legitimacy of nationalizing the Suez Canal and its profits, focusing their efforts on the assurances of international shipping rights and safety in the canal. In doing so, the Americans sought to distance themselves from the exploitative, colonialist image of Britain and France, and to portray themselves as impartial actors in the world arena, motivated by the ideal of global justice in the spirit of the UN Charter.

As part of this effort to occupy the moral high ground, the United States persisted in its refusal to supply weapons to Israel despite its willingness to allow France, Britain, and Canada to do so. Moreover, at the Republican National Convention, the Republican National Committee refused to include arms provision to Israel in the GOP platform, limiting itself to general assurances of the American commitment to Israeli security. This was an embarrassing situation from Silver's point of view, particularly in light of the Democratic platform's clear commitment to supplying Israel with weapons and establishing a defense treaty with Israel. He also had to contend with the American focus on Israel's aggression and dissuading it from taking any action on its own. On October 27, two days before the war erupted, Eisenhower warned Ben-Gurion not to start a preemptive war against Jordan; Dulles extended similar counsel in a meeting with Eban on the same day. On the twenty-eighth, Eisenhower again cautioned the Israelis against attacking, and even as Operation Kadesh was taking shape, the American ambassador to Israel demanded guarantees from Ben-Gurion that there would be no Israeli attack.

It is important to note that Silver's public endorsement of Israeli arms requests, and his condemnation of what he viewed as American appeasement of the Arabs, did not indicate personal concurrence with Israeli policy insofar as that policy embodied a belligerent, militaristic approach. In contrast to Eisenhower's and Dulles's perception of him as one-dimensional idealist, Silver was actually well aware of the dangerous implications of Israel's belligerent approach. He therefore continued in private to express reservations about the retribution operation policy and the idea of an Israeli preemptive war; in this respect he was no different from other moderate American-Jewish leaders such as Jacob Blaustein and Nachum Goldmann. These figures supported the line taken by Sharett before his resignation, namely, that strengthening the Israeli military was the best means of preventing war and, ultimately, of reaching a peace agreement. Blaustein, Goldmann, and Silver were similarly concerned that Sharett's resignation from the government on June 22 heralded either a change in Israeli policy or represented failure on Sharett's part to keep Ben-Gurion from undertaking preemptive action.

However, unlike Blaustein, who aired his concerns before Dulles and warned him that Sharett's resignation pointed to a strengthening of militaristic tendencies in the Israeli political arena (Ganin 2005, 212), Silver was careful to project an image of unreserved support for the Israeli government in its current configuration. He expressed his concerns only in private, as may be seen in his correspondence with Yosef Sapir of the General Zionists. Examining this correspondence, one can see that both men opposed the idea of a preemptive war and both misread the political map, failing to see that it was the Mapai leadership's growing hawkishness that had in fact led to Sharett's resignation. Sapir was sufficiently misinformed to believe that Sharett's resignation was motivated mainly by interpersonal conflicts and that Ben-Gurion's approach to foreign and security policy had not significantly changed since his return to the premiership. Sapir went so far as to assure Silver that Ben-Gurion was not planning any major military operations; he concluded by insisting, with satisfaction, that his and Silver's fears of growing Israeli belligerence were exaggerated and premature.[16]

The contrast between public support for Israel and private criticism of Israel's growing militarism reached its peak during the first days of the Sinai Campaign. Silver spoke with Eban by telephone on October 29, the night that the Israeli actions began. During this conversation, Silver promised to display solidarity with Israel and work on its behalf, but at the

16. Letter from J. Saphir to Silver, July 31, 1956, AHSP I.

same time he voiced his opinion that Ben-Gurion had displayed exceedingly poor judgment. That Silver's views were shared by many American Jews became all too obvious the next day, October 30, during an emergency meeting of the Conference of Presidents of Major Jewish Organizations, held in New York with the participation of the Israeli envoy Reuven Shiloah. Silver, though invited,[17] did not attend the meeting, but many of the Jewish leaders present expressed similar dissatisfaction with the Israeli operation. Up until the eruption of war, they had taken seriously the Israeli line, according to which Israel's effort to strengthen its army was aimed at preventing war. During the aggressive fundraising campaign that Israel had conducted in order to fund arms purchases from France—a campaign in which Silver, as head of Israel Bonds, had been deeply involved—these leaders had received reassuring messages to the effect that the French arms shipments were indeed enhancing Israel's military status. They therefore had good reason to believe that the goal had been attained and that the danger of war had passed. Now they felt betrayed; some contemplated publicly expressing their opposition to Israeli policy or even organizing a demonstration before the Israeli Consulate in New York. Ultimately, however, they, like Silver, preferred to keep their criticism private, while presenting a public face of solidarity with Israel.

This public/private discrepancy could also be seen in the behavior of Nahum Goldmann, who had long regarded the Israeli emphasis on military supremacy and deterrence as misguided. In his view, this policy was leading to Israeli isolation within a hostile Arab and Muslim sea, and would, in the long run, endanger the state's survival. Like Silver, he regarded the Israeli Sinai initiative as a grave lapse of judgment and predicted that, even should the conflict end with a military victory for Israel, it would ultimately constitute a diplomatic failure. Despite this, he strove, along with Eban and Shiloah, to keep the Presidents' Conference from publicly expressing criticism and to create a united front of American-Jewish support for Israel. This support was forthcoming throughout the period of

17. Telegram from Irving Miller and Philip Bernstein to Silver, October 29, 1956, AHSP I.

political struggle that followed the Suez Crisis and encompassed most of the American-Jewish organizations—both those that, like B'nai B'rith, the Central Conference of American Rabbis, and the American Jewish Congress, were members of the Presidents' Conference, and those that, like the American Jewish Committee, were not. The united American-Jewish front displayed support for Israel and opposed any threat of sanctions against it. Many of the Jewish organizations did express hope that the current situation would be utilized to advance an American peace initiative, but they refrained from any statement liable to be interpreted as criticism of Israel for its refusal to withdraw from the Sinai Peninsula or the Gaza Strip (Alteras 1993, 290–93; Eban 1977, 213; Goldmann 1969, 298–99).

Silver exhibited a similar approach but with one difference: in his case, the discrepancy between private criticism of Israel and resolute public support for its policies was particularly striking. While most of the American-Jewish organizations strove to avoid any conflict with the Eisenhower administration, Silver, in his very first public statement on the day following the start of the Sinai War, subjected the administration's conciliatory Middle East policy to a scathing attack. He denounced Eisenhower and Dulles personally; he blamed the president and the secretary of state for having issued warnings to Israel and denying it military guarantees and the opportunity to purchase arms for its own defense rather than condemning Nasser's seizure of the canal and his formation of a military pact against Israel. This personal attack was reminiscent, in its vehemence, of his denunciations of Roosevelt and Truman. It also positioned him unequivocally on the Israeli side, placing him in direct opposition to American policy (*The American Zionist* 1956).[18]

18. Statement of Dr. Abba Hillel Silver, Cleveland, Ohio, October 30, 1956, AHSP I; "Silver Assails Appeasement," October 30, 1956, AHSP V 929.

11

Unequivocal Support for Israel during the Suez Crisis

Silver's involvement in US-Israeli interactions during the Suez Crisis began the day after hostilities broke out, on October 30, 1956, and continued intermittently until Israel's withdrawal on March 7, 1957. Silver suddenly found himself in a position of senior mediator—the very position that he had so coveted since Israel's foundation. Yet now, when he could, presumably, have given expression to a separate Zionist agenda, he chose to speak in two voices, neither of which was his own—an admonitory "American voice" in his private talks with Ben-Gurion and Eban and an accusatory "Israeli voice" in his public statements and interactions with the Eisenhower administration.

Silver's sudden ascension to the status of senior "mediator" resulted from the collapse of direct talks between the administration and Israel's official echelon during the first two days of the war—a communication breakdown that reflected deep anger toward Israel on the part of the White House. When the first reports of Israel's Sinai incursion reached the president, he was in the middle of an election campaign trip to Florida. This was during the critical eight days prior to the elections, and Eisenhower, who was promising the American people "peace at any price," felt betrayed and deceived; he raged against what seemed to him an attempt by Israel to interfere in American politics during an election season. If this was indeed Israel's intention, it quickly proved to be a misguided one. The president cut his campaign trip short, called an emergency meeting that very evening, and announced that he would work to thwart the Israeli aggression even if it meant losing the election. He instructed Dulles to send a telegram to Ben-Gurion warning that the United States would take all measures, including sanctions, to end the Israeli operation. He even went so far as to quote the American-British-French Tripartite Declaration of May 1950, in which the United States pledged to take action against any side that tried by force to change the borders delineated by the Arab-Israeli armistice agreements. The Declaration's original intention had been to calm Israeli fears of a possible Arab attack; now the president was threatening to use it against Israel. Eisenhower's indignation increased the next day when Great Britain and France submitted their fictitious ultimatum to Egypt and Israel; it now became clear to the administration that it had been deceived not only by Israel, but also by its two closest international allies (Alteras 1993, 223–29).

During the two-day period of October 30–31, the administration expressed its anger by cutting off its direct channels of communication with Israel's official diplomatic cadre. At the same time, senior White House and State Department personnel conveyed harsh messages to Israel via a broad range of mediators drawn particularly from the American-Jewish leadership.[1] Of the various potential mediators, Silver was unquestionably the most vociferous in his public support of the Israeli position; paradoxically, it was this fact that prompted the administration to view him as the most suitable person to lay the situation before Ben-Gurion in all of its gravity. As Silver noted in his journal, he received a phone call from White House Chief of Staff Adams on the afternoon of October 30, after he himself had issued a public statement supporting Israel and criticizing American policy. Adams explained to Silver that the president was planning to deliver a special radio address the following evening. He asked Silver to telephone the Israeli prime minister and inform him that the president's speech would directly reflect Ben-Gurion's degree of willingness to pull Israeli forces back to the armistice lines.

In response, Silver sent Adams a draft of the radio speech that the president would, preferably, deliver in exchange for a commitment to

1. Apart from Silver, the administration conveyed harsh messages to Israel via Boustein, Proskauer, Elli Ginzberg, Phillip Ehrlich, and James Zellerbach.

withdrawal by Ben-Gurion. In this draft there was an implied demand to absolve Israel of any responsibility for the war and to cast off the "friendly neutrality" policy to which the United States had been adhering for nearly four years. Silver wanted Eisenhower to justify Israel's retaliatory actions and reprimand the Arab countries for having formed a military pact against Israel as well as for their economic embargo and blockage of Israeli shipping. Finally, Eisenhower was to demand that the Arab leaders enter into direct negotiations with Israel for a permanent peace treaty. What was particularly daring about Silver's draft was that it came as a response to Eisenhower's ultimatum. A few days later, on November 3, the former and present presidents of the American Jewish Committee sent a letter to Dulles with a similar tone; this letter, too, laid the blame on the Arab countries and demanded that the United States urge them to enter into negotiations for a permanent peace treaty with Israel (Alteras 1993, 292). However, unlike Silver, the AJC leaders did not aspire to put words in the president's mouth; they contented themselves with presenting their viewpoint regarding a desirable American foreign policy. Silver, by contrast, not only dared to formulate a presidential promise of policy change, but he did so in a way that constituted an ultimatum that the president would have to satisfy in return for the withdrawal commitment that Silver was to elicit from Ben-Gurion.

In fact, Silver did not stop there. He made a point of contacting presidential advisor Martin in order to confirm the president's approval of the proposed speech draft. According to Silver's journal report, Martin replied, in Adams's name, that the draft was, indeed, consistent with what the president was willing to say; it was solely on the basis of this promise that Silver went on to call Eban and Ben-Gurion. It should be noted, however, that the existing documentation in no way confirms the presidential commitment offered by Adams, nor is there any reason to think that Adams actually consulted with the president on this matter. Adams's answer was sufficiently general not to pin the president down in any concrete way; in any case, regardless of whether Adams consulted with Eisenhower, Silver's oppositional tone surely came as no surprise to him. Silver's overt disapproval was by now a given, and this was regarded in the current crisis as a means of ensuring that the ultimatum to Ben-Gurion would be taken as seriously as the president meant it to be.

Silver was no less blunt in his telephone conversations with Eban and, later, with Ben-Gurion, but this time his criticism was directed toward Israeli policy. As Eban noted in his memoirs, Silver—who, according to his own journal entries, had not spoken with Eisenhower—quoted the president as doubting the soundness of Ben-Gurion's judgment, even adding, supposedly in Eisenhower's name, that Israel needed to remember that its future and fate depended on the United States. Silver reiterated this position in a telephone conversation with Ben-Gurion at 8:30 a.m. the following morning. He reminded the Israeli prime minister that Israel was economically dependent not only on the United States, but also on American Jewry. Ben-Gurion, it should be noted, was not particularly impressed by this warning; he told Silver that he could not speak with him because the enemy might be listening in and demanded that he express his Zionist solidarity by immediately leaving for Israel. Eban, also concerned that Ben-Gurion acknowledge the gravity of the situation, verified Silver's message in a phone call of his own, and received the same "enemy eavesdropping" response. Many years later, he recounted with considerable humor that in another conversation later that day the enemy had apparently ceased to eavesdrop, and that Ben-Gurion spoke with him freely about the answer that should be conveyed via Silver to the White House (Eban 1977, 217–19; 1992, 268).

Silver's subsequent interactions with the White House and Israeli officials indicate that while he continued to exercise the utmost discretion in his criticism of Israel, his opposition to White House policy became increasingly public and harsh in its expression. Apparently, Silver realized that his first duty was not one of mediating between the two countries, but of defending Israel whether or not he agreed with its policy. This duty came to be acknowledged by a long list of American-Jewish figures over the course of the Sinai campaign. The greater the threat of an American ultimatum became, the more well-known American Jews—many of them unaffiliated—mobilized unequivocally on Israel's behalf. The reason for this mass mobilization appears to have been a strong sense within American Jewry that Israel's very survival depended on American economic and military support. For a generation still struggling with memories of Jewish collective powerlessness during the Holocaust, the American ultimatum seemed to challenge the very legitimacy of collective Jewish existence and, therefore, became a force for virtually unconditional support of Israel.

As events unfolded, Silver's commitment to serving the Israeli agenda became even clearer. After his telephone conversation with Ben-Gurion on the morning of October 31, Silver had to spend the rest of the day in great suspense, awaiting the Israeli prime minister's response. Over the course of this nerve-racking day, Silver's frustration was particularly acute. He knew that the answer that he would to be conveying to the White House would likely herald a turning point in US-Israeli relations; however, he possessed neither the authority nor the ability to affect the answer's content or tone. He now realized that despite his return to the nerve center of political activity, his real position was that of a soldier being deployed in Israel's defense rather than a member of the senior decision-making echelon. It was only at 4:30 p.m., just two and a half hours before the president's speech, that Eban telephoned Silver with the translated version of Ben-Gurion's evasive reply to Eisenhower, which Silver hastened to telegraph to the White House (Eban 1977, 217–19). Silver was worried about the response's likely reception by the White House, but just a few minutes before the president's speech, he managed to contact Adams by telephone and obtain from him a reassuring message that Eisenhower would refrain from harshly criticizing Israel.

Silver's fears were indeed well founded. Not only had Ben-Gurion withheld his answer until the last possible moment, but the answer itself was far from meeting the conditions that the president had set. Although Ben-Gurion emphasized the importance of friendly relations with the United States, even agreeing to "propose" to his government that the Israeli forces withdraw, this latter proposal would go into effect only if Nasser agreed to certain conditions that would have amounted to an Egyptian declaration of surrender.[2] At the end of the letter Ben-Gurion

2. Before an Israeli withdrawal went into effect Nasser would have to commit to refraining from any act of aggression against Israel, to cease the blockade on the Straits of Tiran and the Suez Canal, and to annul all anti-Israeli military pacts.

added that, before any decision to withdraw, Israel would have to consult with its allies, France and Great Britain. This was not in any way the kind of response that Eisenhower had demanded, and Silver could only hope to prevent an overly harsh American reaction. He was relieved to find that the president had not laid all of the blame on Israel and had mentioned Egypt's violations of UN resolutions. Eisenhower also referred to Israel as an ally and stressed his desire to put US-Israel relations back on track. At the same time, however, the president insisted on Israel's unconditional withdrawal. The president also stated his intention of turning the UN General Assembly—where Great Britain and France wielded no veto power—into an arena that would force Israel to withdraw. Under the circumstances, Silver's only solace was that the worst-case scenario—unequivocal condemnation accompanied by immediate sanctions—had not yet materialized.

At the same time, however, it was clear that the danger had not passed and that the immediate future held further pressures and threats to Israel. The pressure campaign had actually begun even before the president's radio address. A trip to Israel by an Import-Export Bank delegation was suspended, leaving a $75 million loan to Israel hanging in the balance. Also frozen were grant and food surplus agreements, as well as various economic aid programs. Thus, while the Israeli military campaign was meeting with success, the diplomatic campaign was proving to be a total failure. The Israelis had been wrong to assume that the British and French veto power in the Security Council would keep the United Nations from taking action. The United States was determined to bring the matter up before the General Assembly, where no country enjoyed veto power. In vain Eban attempted to persuade Dulles before the General Assembly convened on November 1 that the status quo ante ought not to be restored, and that the recent developments should, instead, be used to advance Western interests and regional peace. Dulles's position, which he reiterated in his speech before the United Nations, was that although Israel was justified in feeling itself to be an injured party, particularly in light of Egypt's disregard of a 1951 UN resolution on freedom of navigation in the Suez Canal, this was not enough to justify replacing UN mechanisms and attempting to resolve international conflicts by violent means. He argued that such retaliatory methods would necessarily mean undermining the United Nations as a decisive player in international relations and would plunge the international community into chaos and the danger of an all-out war.

Whether this argument reflected a consistent position on the part of Dulles and the State Department regarding the importance that the United States should attach to the United Nations and its mechanisms in the international sphere—a position that Silver consistently supported in all areas except those related to Israel—or whether it was a cynical use of the United Nations to advance US foreign policy goals, albeit at Israel's expense, Silver realized that he was merely a pawn wielding very little influence. All that he could do was observe, as an outsider, the actions of a complex international system for which the prevention of a third world war naturally took priority over the interests of the tiny State of Israel. Thus, the explicit Soviet threats to Israel's existence, at a time when Soviet forces were suppressing the Hungarian revolt, were perceived internationally not as a grossly unfair means of pressuring Israel, but as an indication of the urgent need to prevent a new world war from erupting and, thus, as yet another motive for immediate resolution of the crisis. Against this background, not even Eban's eloquent address before the General Assembly sufficed to prevent the passing, by an overwhelming majority (sixty-four to five), of a November 2 resolution calling for a cease-fire and the immediate withdrawal of all forces occupying Egyptian territory. Additionally, the American public's fear of an interbloc war made the struggle to turn public opinion against the Eisenhower administration hopeless. In fact, the danger of a world war improved Eisenhower's odds of winning the election; having been widely credited with extracting the United States from the Korean War, he was now deemed capable of sparing the country yet another conflict. Moreover, his status as the architect of the Allied victory in Europe placed him in a position that would elicit the trust of the American public in the event that current efforts failed and another war broke out.

In certain respects, the inability to conduct an effective public campaign on behalf of Jewish collective interests was reminiscent of the Holocaust era; this time, however, the endangered population was not

European Jewry, a powerless group lacking any form of political representation, but rather the sovereign State of Israel. Silver's task was not to give voice to a Jewish collective struggle, but rather to support a struggle being waged by highly skilled and officially recognized personnel. In this situation, Silver's close relationships with key Republican figures became yet another tool in the public and political struggle being conducted by Israel. Indeed, the journal entries that followed during this period confirm that Silver's main aspiration was to put his White House and State Department connections to use on Israel's behalf. In nearly all of these entries, Silver emphasized that his interactions with the administration were not taken on his own initiative, but were, rather, prompted by Israel. He thus noted with satisfaction that Eban invited him to Washington for a briefing on November 26.[3] In a later entry, on December 2, he included in full the memorandum that Eban had prepared for him, and which set forth in detail the points that Silver needed to stress in his talks with the administration. The following week, on December 10, Silver met in Washington with Adams, Martin, and Senator Clifford Case II of New Jersey. Silver also took part in a more formal meeting with Adams and Martin, at which he presented the main points of Eban's letter. In his journal, he took the trouble to emphasize that he had made sure to set forth the Israeli positions on the Sinai, the Gulf of Eilat, and the Gaza Strip, and that he had done so in near-total adherence to the section headings that Eban had provided in his December 2 memorandum.

The briefings that Silver received prior to his meetings with White House advisors were just one component of the new campaign that Israel launched during this period. This was against the background of Ben-Gurion's December 3 announcement that Israel intended to take the first step toward a withdrawal from the Suez, and that it would do so on a voluntary basis and without prior guarantees. From Israel's perspective, this measure was meant to ensure that subsequent withdrawals took

3. Even the fact that Eban was obliged to leave Washington at the last minute and was replaced by Shiloah did not detract from the importance that Silver attached to this briefing.

place only after suitable guarantees had been obtained. Indeed, on January 10, the day of Silver's White House meeting, Israel pulled back to the El Arish line, and three days later, on January 13, it executed an additional pullback. Now that this stage of the withdrawal had been reached, Israel's main effort was concentrated on obtaining guarantees prior to any further withdrawals. In fact, Foreign Minister Golda Meir and Ambassador Eban met on December 28 with Arthur Dean, Dulles's law practice partner and a friend of Israel, to discuss the guarantees that Israel wished to receive prior to full withdrawal. The next day, at a meeting with Dulles, Meir requested guarantees that the Straits of Tiran would be open to Israeli shipping, as well as an American commitment to preventing Egypt's return to Gaza. The Israeli officials quickly discovered that, apart from the Straits of Tiran issue, Dulles did not support the Israeli position; on the contrary, he harshly criticized it for its implicit nonreliance on the United Nations, opining that Israel's dependence on military action not only distanced it from peace, but actually constituted the gravest long-term threat to the country's survival (Alteras 1993, 254–55).

These latter statements by Dulles were indicative of the serious problems Israel was facing at the time. Over the following two months, Israel fought a losing battle to transform even a small portion of its military attainments into diplomatic assets. As time went by, the danger of UN sanctions, with American backing, was becoming ever more palpable. Paradoxically, this danger peaked just as Israel's standing in American public opinion was improving significantly. Once Israel began withdrawing its forces, a considerable number of voices—in both houses of Congress and on the editorial pages of the more prominent newspapers—called for Israeli demands to be met.[4] However, this public-relations success was

4. The public American threats of sanctions aroused strong opposition in Congress: Senate Minority Leader William Knowland, a Republican from California, spoke out against the "double standard" to which Israel was being held, at a time when the Soviet Union's actions in Hungary were going unprotested. Alexander Wiley, a Republican senator from Wisconsin and a member of the Senate Foreign Relations Committee, averred that it would be unfair to impose sanctions on Israel and that Israel was entitled to demand reasonable guarantees prior to withdrawal. Similar arguments were made by key Democratic

not translated into a revised White House position. On February 2, an American representative to the United Nations explicitly mentioned the possibility of imposing sanctions on Israel, while the next day Eisenhower sent a harshly worded letter to Ben-Gurion, affirming that Israeli obstinacy would result in UN sanctions and a major crisis in relations with the United States. During a February 5 press conference, Dulles reiterated that the United States would seriously consider supporting a UN resolution to impose sanctions on Israel. On February 11, Dulles called a meeting with Eban and Shiloah, and, subsequently, a memorandum was issued reiterating that the United States was prepared to guarantee unhindered Israeli shipping in the Straits, but also reaffirming Dulles's position on the Gaza Strip, namely, that Israel should settle for the stationing of an emergency UN force there. The memorandum did not satisfy Ben-Gurion; when Dulles received the Israeli premier's negative response, he decided, in consultation with the president, that the United States should make no further gestures toward Israel, and that no choice remained but to impose economic sanctions, both in the form a prohibition on UIA and Israel Bonds donations and in the form of American support for UN sanctions.

Silver was, by this time, entirely engrossed in the Israeli diplomatic effort. On February 18, he was summoned to a meeting with Eban in Washington, just prior to the latter's departure for Israel. At this point, Eban was well aware that the effort to obtain American guarantees prior to Israel's complete withdrawal had already exhausted itself and that his job was now to persuade Ben-Gurion to rely on the general assurances extended by Dulles and Eisenhower. Two days earlier, on February 16, Eban had been called to Dulles's apartment, where the latter explained to him just how critical the Israeli response was. Should Israel respond positively, the United States would be greatly in its debt; however, should Israel refuse to cooperate, it would suffer the consequences. Eban, whose own testimony indicates that he knew Dulles's memorandum to be the best offer Israel could hope to receive, "invented" an urgent summons

---

figures such as Eleanor Roosevelt, former President Truman, and Senate Majority Leader Lyndon Johnson.

to Jerusalem as a means of buying time, so that he could persuade Ben-Gurion to accept the American dictates. Dulles, for his part, agreed to add certain gestures, thereby providing Eban with additional ammunition for his persuasion campaign. These gestures were meant to express a degree of sympathy with Israel; at the same time, however, they conveyed that, with the White House having recognized the legitimacy of Israeli claims, it was now Israel's turn make concessions and announce the completion of its withdrawal.[5]

Silver was well aware that Eban had summoned him to Washington because he required a well-connected person of high stature to buy a little more time for Israel and thereby prevent a complete breakdown of US-Israeli relations during the critical days that Eban would be spending in Israel. This was a time in which the Eisenhower administration was bringing all possible pressure to bear on Congress and the American-Jewish leadership to ensure their support for its punitive approach to Israel (Alteras 1993, 265–69; Eban 1992, 279–81). Additionally, the General Assembly session was scheduled for February 21 to deliberate on the Arab draft resolution regarding disciplinary action against Israel. Silver's task was to help Shiloah and the embassy staff in their effort to forestall any announcements of condemnation or sanctions until after Eban's return. Indeed, Silver's aid was required almost immediately after Eban left for Israel. The very next morning, on February 20, Silver was notified that the president planned to deliver a televised address regarding the situation in the Middle East. Shiloah also informed him that the president had sent an admonitory letter to Ben-Gurion, in which he wrote that Israel would be ill advised to disobey the UN resolution. Shiloah also provided

5. Dulles agreed to affirm that, upon Israeli withdrawal, a UN force would be posted in Gaza (regarding what might follow, he agreed only to state verbally that in all likelihood Gaza would not be returned to Egyptian control). He also committed to a public statement by the United States regarding Israel's shipping rights in the Straits, and to sending American vessels to Israel via the Straits to ensure that these rights might be exercised. Dulles also obtained for his memorandum a personal endorsement by the president, who issued the next day from his vacation venue in Georgia a statement regarding American responsibility to ensure shipping rights and the justifiability of Israeli demands.

Silver with the response that was sent to Eisenhower in Ben-Gurion's name, via William Rountree, the assistant secretary of state for Near Eastern affairs. In this letter, Ben-Gurion asked the president for more time until Ben-Gurion could have the opportunity to hear Eban's update and deliberate on it with his cabinet. Shiloah, on his part, asked Silver for help on two fronts—keeping the president's speech free of the kind of harsh tone that had characterized his personal letter to Ben-Gurion, and doing whatever he could to secure an additional delay of the General Assembly deliberations.

Silver mobilized immediately for the task. He contacted Martin and asked to have a request conveyed to Eisenhower that the word "sanctions" not appear in his speech that evening; he also asked that the speech be formulated in such a way as to leave Israel enough time to come back with a positive response. Martin called Silver later, after he had spoken with Dulles and Adams, and promised him that the word "sanctions" would not appear and that the president's speech would be formulated in a way that left the doors open. After watching the presidential broadcast that night at 9 p.m., Silver issued a complex and crafty statement of his own (Silver 1957f). On the one hand, he attacked the speech with unprecedented bluntness, decrying its "deficiency of logic" and self-righteousness. In particular, he deplored the contrast between the hard line taken toward Israel and the more nuanced attitude toward the Arab countries, as well as the president's failure to acknowledge American responsibility for the crisis. On the other hand, Silver also called attention to what, for him, were the more pro-Israel portions of the speech. In particular, he noted the president's promise to ensure that the United States and the United Nations made every effort to address Israel's concerns over shipping in the Straits and the Suez, as well as the request for guarantees regarding possible Egyptian attacks from Gaza. Silver pointed out that the president had been unwilling to specify the measures that he would take to bring all these things about and that he was essentially asking Israel to rely on American goodwill. In his eyes, this appeal to Israeli trust placed a moral burden on the United States to ensure that Israel not suffer for its willingness to execute a full withdrawal. In other words, Silver was conveying two messages at once: he was letting the president know that, ultimately,

Israel would indeed have to accept his dictates and that sufficient time should therefore be allowed to enable the correct decision to emerge; he was also clarifying that this forthcoming Israeli acquiescence would place a weighty burden of responsibility on the United States, and on the president personally, to ensure that Israel receive the guarantees that it had not managed to obtain prior to the withdrawal.

The next afternoon, at 2:00 p.m., Silver spoke with Martin about the president's speech. He expressed dissatisfaction with the president's threat to support the Arab General Assembly draft resolution. He also pointed out that a friendlier tone toward Israel would make it easier for the Israeli government to make the desired decision. Silver's efforts were made in the face of the administration's growing impatience and its desire to force Israel into compliance with UN resolutions. That same day, on February 21, Dulles convened a group of Jewish leaders and businessmen, at least some of whom were uninvolved in Jewish or Zionist public activity, which he hoped meant that they would be more strongly inclined to side with the administration. However, despite the fact that the group was headed by a well-known Hollywood producer and close friend of the secretary of state, Dulles was surprised to find the group as vociferous in its condemnation of the president's speech as Silver had been. Even more surprising, the group members expressed their unwillingness to meet with the president for fear that they would be seen as supporting actions by the administration that they regarded as threatening to Israel's existence (Alteras 1993, 271–72). Later that same day, at 3:45 p.m., Shiloah telephoned again to notify Silver that Ben-Gurion's answer was negative but had left the door open; he also reported that Eban was already on his way back to the United States from Israel. The main task now was to prevent a crisis from erupting prior to Eban's arrival in Washington—not only to keep the White House from issuing a harshly worded statement, but also to delay, at all costs, a General Assembly meeting at which the administration could be expected to support the imposition of sanctions on Israel. Silver, accordingly, called the White House. After a few conversations with Martin, he was assured that, although it would be impossible to obtain an additional postponement of the General Assembly meeting, US Ambassador Lodge would refrain from speaking until two days later, thus giving Eban enough time to return to his post and try to resolve matters with Dulles.

This in fact concluded Silver's involvement in the Suez Crisis. It should be noted that Silver was never, even at the most critical moments of the crisis, more than an auxiliary to the main diplomatic effort being conducted by the Israeli government. Despite being updated in real time and receiving copies of confidential correspondence between Eisenhower and Ben-Gurion, Silver under no circumstances regained the status that he had enjoyed in 1947–1948 as a member of the decision-making elite, however narrowly or broadly defined. From this point of view, Eban's description of the events of this period in his autobiography is, in its paucity, a more faithful reflection of reality than Silver's journal. Eban devoted a mere half sentence to Silver's efforts, noting that Silver aided the Israeli campaign greatly during those critical days. What actually prevented a harsher White House response to Ben-Gurion's Knesset speech was not Silver's urgent telephone calls to the White House, but the fact that Ben-Gurion moderated the categorical message of his speech with a much more conciliatory telegram to Dulles, in which he requested that the UN vote be postponed so that Eban could have time to discuss a compromise with him. From this moment on, it was clear to the administration's senior echelon that the Israeli premier had capitulated; thus, from their perspective, the danger had passed, and Silver's involvement came to an end. Of course, various last-minute difficulties did arise. Eban and Golda Meir still strove to obtain terminology more favorable to Israel regarding the nonreturn of Egyptian forces to Gaza. Moreover, in the wake of Lodge's concluding speech before the General Assembly—which, from Israel's perspective, had deviated from the agreement between Eban and Dulles—Ben-Gurion called an emergency cabinet meeting and threatened to delay the withdrawal. By now, however, there was no turning back. Eisenhower sent Ben-Gurion a letter thanking him for his decision to withdraw and promising that the United States would work to ensure that Israel's hopes were fulfilled, while Ben-Gurion, in a speech on March 5, announced that Israel would comply with the UN resolution, despite concerns that an Egyptian civil or military government would return to Gaza.

Ultimately Ben-Gurion's fears were realized. Almost immediately after the Israeli withdrawal, on March 11, Nasser sent a civil governor to the Gaza Strip with an administrative staff, while the United States contented itself with expressing regret over the measure. Despite this, from an Israeli point of view, the diplomatic struggle had not ended in failure. Although Israel did not obtain the prior guarantees that it requested, in the long term, it gained assets of incomparably greater value. The agreement brought Israel a decade of a relatively quiet border and a period of stability and economic development. In addition, the agreement prompted a rapprochement between the United States and Israel, at a time when American relations with the Arab world, then enjoying ever-greater Soviet patronage, were cooling.

Paradoxically, the overall positive outcome for Israel underscores Silver's marginality in relation to the diplomatic effort—a marginality that also characterized the other American Jews who mobilized wholeheartedly for the diplomatic campaign of 1956–1957. In contrast to the Holocaust years when American Jewry struggled on behalf of a powerless population seeking to determine its own fate, the issue was now one of aiding a sovereign state with a voice of its own in the international arena. The rules of the game within this sphere were complicated, and it was difficult for anyone not belonging to the decision-making echelon to understand their implications in real time. This being the case, all Silver and his American-Jewish colleagues could do was to offer Israel their support and to hope that the Jewish state was acting wisely. In this respect, Silver had no choice but to reconcile himself to a secondary status; had yet another crisis erupted in US-Israeli relations, he would once again have mobilized unequivocally on Israel's behalf, whatever his personal opinion of Israeli policy might be.

Paradoxically, it was Silver's short "return" to the center of the diplomatic campaign on behalf of Israel that underscored the marginality of his Diaspora-Zionist leadership. Indeed, it seems that Silver himself gradually understood this, and it is safe to say that the Suez Crisis forced him to seek alternate means for expressing his separate Diaspora approach to Zionism. He had to find new means that would act as a counterbalance to the survivalist mode that became such a dominant characteristic of his own Diaspora identification with Israel. If not counterbalanced, this survivalist mode could compel Silver to mobilize solely for a renewed struggle over national Jewish existence instead of seeing the State of Israel as a scaffold for the implementation of a universalistic Jewish vision.

In this context, it is worth noting the interpretive modes that Silver used during this period, attempting to see Israel's existential struggles in a Diaspora-Zionist perspective. A notable example of this interpretive mode may be found in an April 11, 1957 speech inaugurating a joint fundraising drive by the Jewish Welfare Fund of Cleveland (Silver 1957b). The speech was delivered just a month after diplomatic efforts by Israel and its supporters had failed to counteract pressure on Israel to complete its withdrawal from the Sinai Peninsula without prior guarantees. Silver's speech featured a bitter reaction to what he regarded as unfair US pressure on Israel. In Silver's view, Israel had waged a preemptive war against the Egyptian forces that were preparing to destroy it, before the United States and the United Nations had succeeded in coercing a withdrawal and neutralizing its victory. He depicted the American intervention as an outburst of self-righteousness that played into Soviet hands just when the Soviet Union was invading and destroying Hungary. He was especially outraged by the administration's inaction regarding the problem of the Egyptian-Jewish refugees. He deplored the fact that, in contrast to its policy toward the Hungarian refugees, the United States had neither eased its immigration restrictions in favor of the Egyptian Jews, nor did it call for a UN investigation of Egypt's human rights violations regarding its Jewish residents.[6]

This speech thus expressed Silver's grave disappointment with the Eisenhower administration in a manner reminiscent of his harsh denunciations of the Roosevelt and Truman administrations during the 1940s.

6. On November 1, 1956, Nasser authorized the expropriation of British and French property, and two days later he expanded the order to include the property of Egyptian Jews. Many leaders of the Jewish community were arrested, and anti-Jewish riots took place in several locations. About two thirds of Egypt's forty thousand Jews emigrated.

However, a more careful reading of the speech reveals that its main purpose was to refute any pessimistic conclusions that might be drawn regarding what seemed to be a recurrent Jewish impotence in the face of the American government's willingness to sacrifice yet again—as it did during World War II—Israel and Jewish refugees. For this purpose, Silver was careful to convey Jewish self-confidence. His main effort at communicating optimism went into the speech's opening and closing sections, where he presented Jewish continuity as a religious imperative entailed by solidarity with the State of Israel's ongoing struggle for survival.

In the introductory portion of the speech, Silver welcomed Robert Briscoe, the Orthodox Jewish mayor of Dublin,[7] who was the event's guest of honor. Silver drew a comparison between the longtime Irish struggle for sovereignty and the Zionist struggle for a Jewish state, and called attention to the optimism and dedication that had characterized both endeavors: the Irish had had to endure centuries of repression and persecution in which many had died, been imprisoned, or exiled. And yet, he noted approvingly, they had never despaired, and, against all odds, had held steadfast to their belief in ultimate victory. The determination and confidence that Silver found so admirable in the Irish became a quasi-religious obligation where the Jewish people were concerned. Silver quoted a midrash in which Moses was taken to task for fearing that the Israelites would doubt that God had sent him to take them out of Egypt. According to the midrash, Moses's fear was misplaced in that it reflected a lack of confidence in the Jewish people. Silver intended this to be an analogy to the American-Jewish community, which, he felt, was duty bound to express confidence in the State of Israel at all costs—even when current conditions made this confidence appear unjustified.

In the concluding section of the speech, Silver appeared personally to have fulfilled this latter commandment. He recalled a visit that he had made many years earlier, in August 1935, to the Winter Palace in Leningrad—the former residence of the Russian tsars that had been turned

7. Robert Briscoe served as Lord Mayor of Dublin from 1956 to 1961. His son, Ben Briscoe, held the same office in 1988.

into a museum, preserving all of the imperial family's effects just as they had left them prior to their execution. In the library adjacent to the tsar's bedchamber, he was amazed to find a copy of Israel Zangwill's *Children of the Ghetto* (1892). The plot of Zangwill's novel, which at the turn of the twentieth century had enjoyed enormous popularity among the British- and American-Jewish immigrant communities, was still familiar even half a century later to most of Silver's audience. Contrary to what its title might indicate for today's readers, the book was not about Russian Jewry's generations-long dream of escaping the shtetl and immigrating to Palestine; rather, it dealt with the dream of the immigrant Jews in their western European and American ghettos to become fully integrated in their new, modern environment while still maintaining their Jewish identity.[8] Using Zangwill's book, the Diaspora's unequivocal support for the State of Israel had become a vision that celebrated the possibility of a free Jewish existence inextricably embedded within the non-Jewish democratic environment. Silver described the feeling of exaltation elicited by discovering this book, which symbolized for him the invincible nature of the Jewish vision. Choosing to conclude his 1957 speech with this moment of rapture from 1935, he pointed out that, long after the Jew-oppressing Romanov dynasty had been killed off, this little book of Zangwill's could still be found in the imperial palace, testifying to the fact that the Jews had at last escaped their dark ghettos and, by dint of faith and courage, realized their dream of finding a free home for themselves: "The Tsars are dead but the dreamers of the Ghetto . . . live gloriously and creatively." Silver concluded by turning to his audience of American Jews and, in the first-person plural, proclaiming "our determination" to share in the dreamers' hope "and in their sacrifice, even as we share in their pride" (Silver 1957b).

This Diaspora-Zionist interpretive stance replaced Silver's earlier approach of overtly criticizing Israel-centric Zionism, with its pessimistic

8. The novel describes Jewish life in the London immigrant ghetto. It was translated into a number of languages and was the basis for various dramatic productions and films. For an analysis of how Zangwill depicts the Jews' effort to straddle tradition and modernity, see Udelson (1990).

prognostications for Diaspora life. It should be noted, however, that an element of criticism still remained, covert though it had become. This may be seen in the humorous tone taken by Silver in his welcoming remarks to the visiting Jewish mayor of Dublin, as he described the sort of "miracle" of an Orthodox Jew being chosen to lead the capital city of an overwhelmingly Catholic country. He went on to talk about the Jewish tradition of a messiah descended from Joseph who is expected to precede the Davidic messiah, concluding playfully that the miracle of a Jewish mayor of Dublin proved that *Mashiach ben Yosef* had already arrived, and that when the counterpart miracle—the election of a Catholic mayor in Jerusalem—finally occurred, it would be a sign that *Mashiach ben David* had appeared as well. Silver's comments were, of course, meant to be taken in a jovial light, and one can almost hear the bursts of laughter with which Lord Mayor Briscoe and his fellow attendees must have greeted Silver's remarks. It should, however, be acknowledged that these remarks were based on certain very serious assumptions regarding the differences in mentality between the American "new world" and the "old world" of Europe and Israel. In the eyes of Silver and his audience, the idea of an Orthodox Jew being elected mayor of a Catholic city in Europe, or of a Catholic being elected mayor of Jerusalem, was almost inconceivable. This was despite the fact that similar situations were by no means inconceivable in the United States—it would hardly have occurred to Silver to joke about the election of a Jewish mayor of Boston or a Catholic mayor of one of New York City's predominantly Jewish boroughs. Silver's jocularity thus presupposed very different expectations regarding social reality in Europe and Israel compared with the United States. Together with the "children of the ghetto" vision with which he concluded his speech, Silver's humorous remarks underscored his view that Jewish aspirations to integrate within the non-Jewish world were still nearly inconceivable in the "old world."

It is important to take notice of Silver's embracing tone toward Israel. Rather than falling into the trap of head-on confrontation with the Israeli symbols around which Jews the world over rallied in solidarity, efforts were now invested in changing the way in which these symbols were interpreted. Another instance in which this inclusive tactic was employed was Silver's address, five months later, at the inaugural event of the ZOA convention held in New York on September 14, 1957 and dedicated to the sixtieth anniversary of the first Zionist Congress in Basel (Silver 1957h; see also *The American Zionist* 1957; *HaBoker* 1957). The Israeli oppositional newspaper, *HaBoker*, characterized the speech as polemical in nature and reminiscent of the intra-Zionist debates of the early 1950s. However, a comparison between the original speech and the text in *HaBoker* indicates that the Israeli newspaper quoted the speech only in part and misinterpreted its meaning. Although Silver did indeed say that the attempt to turn Zionism into a synonym for personal commitment to *aliyah* represented a narrow interpretation of Zionist ideology, this remark was by no means the crux of his speech. Upon closer inspection, it becomes clear that Silver insisted that this internal Zionist debate would have no effect on the unconditional American-Jewish support for Israel's well being. Rather than intensifying the ideological dispute, the speech sought to express the kind of optimistic and faith-oriented attitude that, in Silver's view, should be unifying American Jewry around the Zionist ideal. He declared that the duty of American Zionists was twofold: on the one hand, unconditional support for Israel—seeing it as the main focus of American-Jewish identification; on the other hand, teaching the "true" religious and social universalistic interpretation of Israel's existence.

Silver devoted the major part of his speech to the second of these goals, and already in the opening paragraphs focused on the universalistic context of Israel's founding.[9] He began with an attempt to provide a broad context for the sixty years that had passed since the first Zionist Congress, describing it as a period that witnessed the exciting modern revolutions of nationalism and enlightenment, but also the agonizing catastrophic crises of human suffering that came in their footsteps. On the face of it, these crises ought to have generated disappointment in enlightened values and pessimism regarding their ultimate triumph. In Silver's view, however, the past sixty years of Jewish history actually contradicted these dismal conclusions. The Jewish people had paid a higher price than

9. The *HaBoker* translation omitted most of the opening paragraph and failed to note that former US President Harry Truman was present at the gathering.

any other ethnic group for the social and political upheavals of modernity; nevertheless, it had survived to undertake a cultural and religious renaissance. That fact ought to counterbalance any feelings of pessimism; indeed, it ought to inspire renewed faith that progress would ultimately prevail. Israel's rebirth thus served as a living example of the human ability to overcome the most formidable hardships and failures in a way that leads to the ultimate victory of the universalistic values of enlightenment and democracy.

This transformation of Israel into a quasi-utopian ideal heralding progress and enlightenment for all mankind featured even more prominently in two speeches by Silver marking the tenth anniversary of Israeli statehood. The first of these was delivered at Silver's "home" synagogue upon his return from yet another visit to Israel (Silver 1958c). Interestingly, Silver chose to call his trip a "pilgrimage," thereby underscoring the State of Israel's sanctity and its status as a focal point for solidarity and faith. It should be noted, however, that this exaltation of the Jewish state also contained an element of distancing from the political Israel and could perhaps be seen as harking back to the pre-Zionist era, when a sacred and spiritualized Palestinian-Jewish community stood in stark contrast to the material world in which everyday life took place. From Silver's point of view, this was a major turning point in relation to Diaspora Zionism's earlier demand to be critically involved in the Israeli political arena. Differently from his early post-1948 criticism of Israeli politics, he now limited himself to an admiring description of Israel's spiritual role. This was most evident in his description of the spiritual atmosphere that he found at the dedication ceremony of the new Hebrew University campus at Givat Ram, Jerusalem. As the sun set, the attendees lit thousands of candles that studded the surrounding hills with light, symbolizing, in Silver's eyes, the triumph of reason and enlightenment. He used Ben-Gurion's address at the ceremony as a source for reflection on the State of Israel's overall spiritual-utopian character. Ben-Gurion had quoted Zechariah 4:6, "Not by might, nor by power, but by my spirit, says the Lord," and Silver explained his interpretation that despite Israel's need to rely on its military strength in its fight for survival, the real power and destiny of the Jewish people lay in the country's spiritual aspirations.

Silver made similar points in another talk two months later (Silver 1958b). This speech, delivered at a gala event marking Israel's first decade of statehood, aptly demonstrated how exaltation of Israel—rather than polemics—could enlarge key Zionist concepts and make them compatible with a Diaspora-Zionist orientation. Silver began his speech by celebrating Israel's establishment and attaching a larger meaning to it, calling it not merely a local event of limited importance, but rather an ongoing process with far-reaching consequences for world Jewry and humanity. Zionism, in Silver's view, was a revolution of similar magnitude to such scientific advances as the breaking of the sound barrier and the achievement of space travel; in the cultural-political realm he compared it to the Renaissance and the American and French revolutions, while on the Jewish-historical plane he likened it to the Exodus from Egypt, the giving of the Torah, and the advent of prophecy. These comparisons, while underscoring the importance of the Zionist redemption, also removed it from any Israel-centric context. The very fact that Silver classed Israel's establishment with other revolutions that had broadened humanity's horizons meant that the Zionist redemption could be conceived as part of an ongoing process whose main importance was not limited to one specific location or to one concrete people. Silver noted that the broad revolutionary character of Zionist redemption became all the more striking against the background of the Holocaust. In his view, the founding of Israel saved the Jewish people from the disbelief in humanity brought on by the Holocaust. It boosted a sense of national pride, which was not focused on Israel's physical might but on its universalistic heritage and mission.

Silver chose to conclude his sermon with a quote from a speech that he had given twenty years earlier, in 1937, before the Central Conference of American Rabbis in Columbus, Ohio. This was the conference at which Reform Jewry famously adopted an alternative platform to the anti-Zionist Pittsburgh Platform of 1885. Silver quoted the part of his speech presenting the Jewish national commitment as only one aspect of the core Jewish religious commitment to the principles of enlightenment and progress. In 1937, he directed this universalistic emphasis against his anti-Zionist Reform colleagues, who saw an unbridgeable gap between the universalistic message of the Jewish religion and Jewish nationalism. Now, in 1958, he used this same message in order to present an alternative brand of Diaspora religious-national solidarity—one that saw Israel's founding as an intrinsic part of Judaism's universalistic religious commitment:

> It is the total program of Jewish life and destiny, its vast inclusiveness and completeness that religious leaders of our people should dwell on today—the religious and moral values, the universal concepts, the mandate of mission, as well as the Jewish people itself. (Silver 1937)

This approach found notable expression half a year later, during a domestic Israeli political crisis over the question of "who is a Jew." The crisis broke out between the Israeli ruling party and its religious Orthodox coalition partners in June 1958, after the Israeli government approved a previous ordinance of the interior minister, allowing every citizen to register as a Jew based on a personal declaration, even in cases contradicting Halachic Jewish law. On July 20, the Israeli government decided to approve the instructions, thereby sparking a coalition crisis with the religious parties who perceived the ordinance as liable to create a rift within the Jewish people. In an attempt to resolve this crisis, Ben-Gurion appealed to fifty Jewish leaders from Israel and the Diaspora, including Silver, for their opinions on how to handle the registration of children whose Jewish father and non-Jewish mother wished to register them as Jews.[10] Silver chose to answer Ben-Gurion via a sermon to his own community, taking the opportunity to set forth his own American religious perspective on Jewish identity (Silver 1958d).[11] In the opening portion of the sermon, he distinguished between the political crisis in which Israel was then mired and the religious-philosophical question of "who is a Jew." In his view, the State of Israel had no authority to rule on this religious issue, just as the US government was authorized only to define who was an American—not who was a Christian or a Jew, or any other religious affiliation. Although

10. On Ben-Gurion's appeal regarding the "who is a Jew" question, see AHSP I.

11. Silver never responded directly to Ben-Gurion, and this sermon was his sole statement on the issue. On the various responses received by Ben-Gurion, see Ben-Rafael (2001). Ben-Rafael covers forty-seven respondents, among whom Silver does not appear. For an overview of the topic, see Don-Yehiya (2002).

Silver addressed the Israeli political crisis in his speech,[12] this amounted merely to defining it as a domestic Israeli affair, distinct from any religious-philosophical agenda of interest to world Jewry. Thus, in contrast to his approach during the early years of the state, Silver now decided not to interfere with Israel's internal politics. He preferred to elucidate a religious-philosophical agenda of relevance to the entire Jewish people.

Silver chose to do this by means of an implied challenge of the accepted Israeli-Zionist religious-historiographical interpretation of the Maccabean struggle—one that saw the Hasmonean revolt as a model struggle for national independence. By contrast, Silver saw the Hasmonean struggle primarily as a religious-moral challenge. The Maccabees were faced with a phenomenon of Hellenizers who, though formally Jewish through Halachic law, behaved, for all intents and purposes, like pagans, turning their backs on the Jewish code of moral conduct and commitment to social justice. By their immoral behavior, the Hellenizers had destroyed Judaism from within; therefore, the Maccabees saw no alternative but to fight them. In other words, the Maccabees had fought on behalf of the universalistic Jewish religious-moral code, and their criteria for defining "who is a Jew" were based not on formal Halachic categories, but on the individual's willingness to remain loyal to Jewish values. This moralistic Jewish approach attached prime importance to a pan-Jewish agenda, one that was far more comprehensive than the political-legalist controversy within Israeli society:

> That's the problem which the Jewish people in the entire world—inside of Israel and outside of Israel—face today, not a legal problem. Not to define a Jew in relation to a "Law of Return" . . . but how to be a Jew in relation to their great historic destiny. And the Maccabees have told us how to be such loyal Jews. . . . Not to be afraid because we are few in numbers . . . to preserve the integrity of our spiritual heritage and to transmit it to the world. (Silver 1958d)

12. Silver identified the roots of the crisis in Israel's failure to uphold a separation between religion and state. This situation, in Silver's view, could be solved only by instituting civil courts to deal with marriage issues.

In effect, Silver used his alternative interpretation of the Hasmonean revolt to enhance the universalistic meaning of the Jewish existence as a minority in the Diaspora. The last Hanukkah sermon that he delivered before his passing strikingly exemplified this approach (Silver 1972f). As in many of his Hanukkah sermons, here as well, Silver drew parallels between the Zionist ethos and the idea of "the few against the many." However, in his 1962 sermon he used this ethos as the basis for an alternative Zionist historiography that elevated the status of the minority people in exile, presenting it as an ideal situation that could serve as a model for Jews and non-Jews alike. He opened his sermon by reflecting on the importance of the minority group as the standard-bearer of social progress. He quoted the historian and philosopher Will Durant (from his monumental work on the Renaissance) to the effect that cultural progress is always the product of the select few. Silver took this notion even further, contending that the Jewish people's lofty mission was inextricably connected with its minority status, and that the creation of the State of Israel had given the Jews both an opportunity and an obligation to realize this mission.

> For it is true that the precarious position of a minority, and the many disadvantages which its status imposes upon it, forces its members . . . to rely upon their single intellectual and spiritual energies and inventiveness. Members of a minority group are prone to develop independence of judgment and a valuable patience and persistence. . . . [T]hey are likely to entertain a greater passion for social righteousness, for brotherhood, for humanity, for peace. (Silver 1972f)

Silver turned the minority experience into a key concept for understanding Jewish history. He averred that the Jews had never been disheartened by their inferior political status as a minority; to the contrary, they had transformed this situation into a moral-spiritual mission. The Jew should view Israel's foundation as an opportunity to turn his minority status into a social-religious commitment. He must look back to his past history with pride, understanding it as a heroic story of a people who were always faced by unfavorable odds, but were never fazed by it. He must understand that the minority status is in fact a universal reality, for almost every person may feel disadvantaged by adverse circumstances, and when the odds are against him, he must take heart from the life experience of the Jewish people:

> Bravery in wartime is commonplace. . . . But courage in the face of day-long, year-long and life-long frustrations, injustices and discrimination is of an even higher order. To be fenced in on all sides by untoward circumstances, whether social, economic, racial or otherwise, and yet to remain unconfined and unimpaired in mind and spirit . . . that is to display manhood at it noblest. (Silver 1972f)

To conclude, one may say that Silver sought to give new meaning to Zionism and to the heroic imagery associated with it, making it the focal point for a universalistic Jewish identity. Silver hoped to advance a Diaspora-Zionist ideology that identified with the State of Israel but maintained its own distinct Jewish agenda. The extent to which he succeeded in this endeavor is a question that is not easy to answer. In the concluding chapters I hope to set forth a few parameters that may facilitate some possible answers.

EPILOGUE

Reform Jewish Prophet or Zionist Leader?

12

Silver as a Progressive Visionary

It should be recalled that when Silver strove to demonstrate the importance of Israel's establishment, he depicted it as an act aimed at ensuring an adequate air supply. Israel was now supposed to become transparent, like air; essential though it was to Jewish survival, it could by no means be regarded as the ultimate purpose of Jewish existence. In reality, however, Israel's survival became neither transparent nor self-evident. The ongoing threats to its existence could be compared to the malfunctions that might afflict an oxygen tank. It is against this background that one should understand Silver's attempts to delineate a stance that, while assigning a central role to the struggle for Israel's survival, nevertheless interpreted it as the means by which to mobilize American Jews for a more encompassing struggle on behalf of Judaism's prophetic-universalistic vision. For Silver, pledging unconditional loyalty to the Jewish state as the basis for a commitment to this universalistic mission was the most suitable means by which American Jewry could contend with the post-statehood reality.

This approach is clearly seen when we compare a Hanukkah sermon that Silver delivered at the beginning of the Holocaust era, in December 1939, with his last Hanukkah sermon of December 1962 (Silver 1972e, 1972f).[1] As in its 1962 counterpart, the 1939 sermon presents a religious-moral, rather than national, interpretation of the Hasmonean rebellion. In answer to the question "Why did the Maccabees fight the Greeks?" he notes that the Jews had lived in a state of political subjugation for

1. The main features of this speech were discussed at the end of the previous chapter.

over two centuries without mounting a revolt, and that it was therefore implausible that the Maccabees suddenly rebelled for the sake of political independence. He claimed that the Maccabees saw it as their task to place the concept of social solidarity within a binding religious context; they rebelled because they could not reconcile themselves to the social corruption that they associated with Greek culture. On the face of it, this religious-social interpretation of the Hasmonean revolt bore similarities to Silver's last Hanukkah sermon of 1962. Nevertheless, a closer reading reveals an important difference: in 1939, Silver sought to plant the seeds of hope into an apparently desperate situation, pointing out similarities between the Maccabees' victorious few-against-many campaign and the current Jew-versus-Nazi situation. He argued that Antiochus, like dictators in every generation, including Hitler, had sought to crush the Jewish spirit because of his fear of the moral challenge that Judaism embodied. He stressed that although "the lot of the weak seems to be as tragic today as it ever was,"

> we Jews ought to ask ourselves even as Judah and his followers asked themselves: "just how weak are we?" . . . The Jewish people is being liquidated with fire and sword. Yet, by all records of history, we are not weak at all but strong, so strong to frighten the Antiochus' of our day. . . . They are afraid of our classic and still vigorous ideas of freedom, the rights of man, human brotherhood, peace. (Silver 1939)

Unlike the 1939 sermon, Silver's 1962 Hanukkah address did not strive to alleviate fears regarding Jewish survival, but rather to transform them. Silver used the image of the few against the many, not to inspire courage in the face of potential physical annihilation, but rather to persuade his fellow Jews that it was within their power to rise above the survivalist concerns and to mobilize for Judaism's prophetic mission. Silver's goal was to exhort his listeners to devote themselves to the struggle for universalistic values of freedom and social justice, and to do this even if it conflicted with the prevailing social norms of the majority society. In Silver's view, this was the essence of the prophetic ethos, and he saw it as his duty to personally fulfill it. Although he had previously understood the prophetic ethos as Judaism's core feature, this original appreciation intensified dramatically after the establishment of the State of Israel. In Silver's view, the founding of the state ought to have triggered a fundamental change in the character of Zionist leadership. The role of the Zionist leader in the post-statehood period was to educate his people about Zionism's revolutionary character by serving as a prophet of universal social progressivism striving to eradicate injustice, oppression, and war.[2]

Silver's last book, which appeared in 1961 and dealt with the originality of Moses's prophetic message, testified to this preoccupation with the religious-social role played by the prophets (Silver 1961b, 1961d, 1961h, 1967c). According to Silver, the innovation of Moses's prophetic activity lay not in the invention of a moral code, but rather in that code's transformation into religious obligation. The prophets who came afterward conferred on Israel an additional function of serving as a light unto the Gentiles. According to this interpretation, the prophet was a religious and a social leader who meant to awaken the nations of the world for a struggle against social injustice, to quench the fires of hatred and war, and to advance the goal of a community of nations bound by a universal ethical-social constitution.[3] Silver strove to exemplify this pursuit of Judaism's religious-prophetic mission in his own conduct. He proclaimed that the prophetic ethos obligated its adherents to challenge all dictators and repressive regimes, and that the future of the world depended on the willingness of political activists to adopt the prophets' code of conduct and to fearlessly combat immoral social practices:

> And if ever our world, which is still so steeped in barbarism, in hate and exploitation . . . is to be saved from the abyss, it will only be by men and women who remain faithful to the teachings of these prophets . . . who raise their voices fearlessly against those . . . who cry in the faces of the poor, who shed innocent blood. (Silver 1961h, 14)

2. On Silver's identification with the role of the prophet, see Schindler (1997, 7–8).

3. Silver explained that, unlike the obligation to protect the poor and the stranger, the concept of universal peace among the nations could have sprung up only after the Jewish people had lived for generations as a nation among the other nations of the world, and not during Moses's generation, which had yet to undergo that formative national experience.

Silver's self-appointed role as prophet to the Gentiles was evident in his sermons against the South African apartheid regime. In a January 1961 address on the originality of the Hebrew prophets, he discussed his recent visit to South Africa, cautioning that, should a cadre of prophetically inspired citizens fail to emerge and challenge the Afrikaner authorities, a bloody revolution of apocalyptic proportions would likely take place. In an earlier Passover sermon from April 1960 (Silver 1960a), he compared the repressive South African regime to those of Nazi Germany and ancient Egypt. He drew an analogy between the Pharaoh's decree ordering the murder of Jewish male infants, the Nazi practice of putting Jewish children to death in gas chambers (here he inserted chilling quotes from Rudolph Hess's recently published journal), and the Afrikaner policy of banishing blacks not needed for labor to specially designated "homelands" and keeping those needed for labor in conditions of social isolation. He particularly denounced the transit pass required of black workers, which he likened to the yellow star mandated for Jews by the Nazis.

Silver's comparison culminated in a discussion of Moses's ancient battle cry, "Let my people go." According to Silver, this slogan had denoted the first social revolution in history; even three thousand years later, it remained relevant and inspiring. He identified its strong echo in Alan Paton's *Cry the Beloved Country*; the South African author had recently published an article calling for black suffrage, a dismantling of the homelands system, and the abandonment of apartheid. Silver added that, should South Africa fail to produce a prophet capable of swaying the repressive minority, a violent rebellion by the black majority would inevitably ensue. Although he generally deplored violence, in his view any future revolt against the apartheid regime would have to be seen as analogous to Moses's smiting of the Egyptian slave master—a situation in which injustice could no longer be met with silence. In his stirring conclusion, Silver called for the emergence of South African leaders comparable to Moses and Abraham Lincoln—leaders capable of guiding both the black majority and the white minority toward freedom and coexistence.

Silver's identification with the prophetic message intensified in the context of the Cold War. In this case the issues at hand concerned not faraway South Africa, but Silver's immediate American environment.

Silver's opposition to the Cold War was not new; however, his position strengthened during the early 1960s—a time of widespread fear among the American populace that tensions in Cuba and Berlin might lead to a nonconventional world war. His tone of reproof is exemplified in a sermon from November 1961, in which he discussed the Berlin Wall that had been constructed four months previously and the danger of war that it represented (Silver 1961a). Silver minced no words in denouncing those engaged in erecting walls of fear, calling it an act of heresy. His condemnation extended not merely to nondemocratic regimes whose walls of hostility were being built in the name of race, religion, and class, but also to those building walls in the name of humanism and democracy. Both, in his view, were sowing the seeds of fear and hatred, and reaping conflict and prejudice. Both sought to portray themselves as constructing fortresses of freedom and justice, whereas in reality, the only reason for the erection of walls between nations was mutual hatred and fear. He concluded by noting that fear and hatred could not be a basis for the "good society" that Soviet communism and American democracy, each in its own way, aspired to build.

In the second part of the speech, Silver focused on what he called warmongering propaganda, which portrayed the Berlin Wall as a danger to the free world. Silver rejected this premise, averring that not only was the wall not a threat to the West, but that it actually underscored the weakness of the Communist regime. Had that regime been truly confident in its ability to threaten the West, it would not have built a wall around itself. The tens of thousands of Germans who had fled to the West prior to the wall's construction were proof of the Communist regime's inability to survive with open borders. Silver reserved special vitriol for the pictures of German women weeping on the wall's western side that had been published in the American press. He saw these pictures as propaganda aimed at inciting the West to war, and asked whether those same women had cried by the barbed wire fences that had encircled the Nazi concentration camps.

> I haven't any tears to shed over these Berliners. . . . They are not starving, nor dying, nor doomed, nor facing gas chambers. . . . I would not wish to see the world destroyed by atomic fire in order to give these

> West Berliners . . . a re-united Germany. . . . Let these past masters in the demonic art of building walls around other men now learn the difficult art of removing them from around themselves. (Silver 1961a)

Clearly, Silver incorporated his ingrained anti-German perspective into his jeremiads against any society that based its ideology on fear and warmongering.[4] In the same spirit he deplored the hysterical fear that had gripped the American populace and drove them to build underground bomb shelters. He noted how a proud and lofty American civilization had been "driven underground by fears which have resulted from the evil work of our own hand," and pointed out that, should nuclear war indeed break out, no shelter would be able to prevent the total destruction in store for American society. Thus, anyone truly interested in preventing such destruction would be better off working to counter the demonization and fear of the other side. "Let it never be said that the fault is theirs and not ours," he declared. "Let us not add the sin of self-righteousness . . . to the desperate crisis . . . for which we are all responsible" (Silver 1961a). Silver concluded by exhorting the American public not to place its trust in the false security of bomb shelters, but rather to pressure the leaders of the two great powers to sign a nuclear disarmament treaty. He blasted the United States and Britain for voting against a UN resolution prohibiting the use of nuclear weapons. Neither did he spare the Soviet Union, which, though it voted for the resolution, had compromised the value of its vote by conducting nuclear tests several months earlier. He rejected the claim made by each side that its nuclear weapons were intended merely to defend the world from its rival; peace, he insisted, would come not through a nuclear arms race, or the false security of underground bunkers, but rather through abandonment of aggression and hatred in favor of mutual tolerance.

4. A month later, in response to the Eichmann verdict, Silver again observed the necessity of punishing Germany. Referring to the Nuremburg trials as a legitimizing precedent, he opposed any attempt to commute the death sentence, even if it placed Israel in a positive light (Silver 1961i).

Silver directed his strongest words of censure toward American foreign policy, as exemplified by a speech that he delivered in advance of the Eisenhower-Khrushchev summit scheduled for mid-May 1960 in Paris (Silver 1960d). This summit, which had been planned when the two leaders met in the United States in 1959, raised hopes for a defusing of Cold War tensions. However, two weeks before the summit, on May 1, an American U-2 spy plane had been shot down over Soviet territory; when the United States refused to apologize for the incident, Khrushchev decided to abandon the summit. Though he directed considerable criticism toward Khrushchev, whom he accused of exploiting the situation, he reserved his harshest condemnation for Secretary of State Christian Herter for declaring the surveillance flights in question to be defensive operations, which the United States was morally entitled to mount. Silver denounced this statement, asking how the United States would react if the Soviet Union were to make similar claims prior to a summit intended to defuse tensions. He added that, even if it were true that Khrushchev was looking for a way out of the summit, the United States ought not to have provided him with a convenient excuse. Moreover, the United States was to blame, not because of a mere error of judgment, but rather because the religious-moral compass that should have been guiding American policy had been discarded. American policy at its best ought not to be based on selfish, power-seeking interests, but on a deep commitment to advancing social justice and democratic values throughout the world.

> Where have we failed the free world, in spite of our Marshal plan . . . in spite of our sincere desire to be helpful and to advance the cause of peace and freedom in the world. Why . . . have we made so few friends. . . . Have we perhaps lost the larger mission of our national destiny. . . . We ought to recapture the vision which was ours, which made America the glorious hope of mankind. (Silver 1960d)

Silver did not withhold his criticism of the Soviet Union; he accused the Soviet leaders of betraying communism's basic ideological commitment to building a "good society." A few months later, he even went so far as to call on the Soviet people to oust Khrushchev (Silver 1960e). In this instance, Silver's remarks were occasioned by the famous shoe-banging incident during the fifteenth session of the UN General Assembly. Silver accused Khrushchev of having planned this spectacle in advance in order to show his disdain for the UN's parliamentary processes. The incident, as he saw it, exemplified a well-known Communist tactic of disrupting, from within, the parliamentary procedures of democratic organizations. Such a tactic was, in Silver's opinion, an intolerable effort to subvert the sole mechanism capable of fostering international dialogue, and an indication that the Soviet leader had no interest in coexistence. The Cold War, Silver felt, would be resolved only when the populaces of both sides demanded foreign policy based on the ethical principles of their respective national ideologies. In this context, he quoted President Lincoln's answer to the question of whether God was on his side of the Civil War. To this the president answered that his concern was not whether God was on his side, but "whether we are on God's side, on the side of humanity, on the side of progress . . . and that we are prepared to seize every opportunity to bring these moral sound objectives to pass" (Silver 1960e).

Silver used similar religious-moral criteria to assess John F. Kennedy and Richard Nixon as US presidential candidates. In a sermon delivered a week before the November 1960 elections (Silver 1960b), he accused both candidates of competing in their displays of abhorrence of communism while all but neglecting to discuss disarmament or ways of enabling the United States and the Soviet Union to coexist peacefully. The American president who embodied Silver's leadership ideal was Abraham Lincoln; he described this ideal at length in a particularly compelling sermon a month after Kennedy took office (Silver 1961c). Silver noted that, although Lincoln opposed slavery's extension into new American territories, he originally had no intention of abolishing it in the states where it already existed. Lincoln's greatness lay not in his determination to eradicate slavery at all costs, but in his readiness for compromise, even if it meant that slavery would continue to exist in the southern states. This willingness to compromise, even at the price of an undemocratic South, set an example for the current American president as he contended with the communism–capitalism conflict. Silver explained that even those who viewed communism as the embodiment of evil had to acknowledge the degree to which the system had become entrenched in substantial portions of the world, and that it could not be eradicated by force without devastation on both sides. He noted that although the United States had survived the Civil War, it was doubtful whether either America or the Soviet Union would survive a war between the two nuclear powers. The measure of the new president's greatness would be his ability to teach America to coexist with the Communist regime.

Silver believed that a willingness to coexist was the truest reflection of a religiously inspired commitment to humanist and democratic values. This belief was itself based on the premise that peace would necessarily generate social change on both sides—change that would bring the Communist societies closer to democracy while strengthening humanist tendencies in the capitalist West. In this context, Silver wanted the competition between the two blocs to undergo a fundamental change; by calling on the two political systems to compete with each other not for power, but for the sake of demonstrating greater tolerance and social justice, Silver recalled the "bridges and walls" religious vision. These exhortations countered the "practical" considerations of realpolitik with a deep faith in the power of universal values of freedom and social justice to carry the day once they become central to public discourse.

Silver wanted to demonstrate this latter approach by emphasizing the social-moral achievements of each bloc in its own terms. One example of this was the way in which he reported on his visit to the Soviet Union in July 1961 (*Cleveland Plain Dealer* 1961; Silver 1961e, 1961f). He returned from this trip at the height of the crisis sparked by the construction of the Berlin Wall. Aware of the situation's sensitivity, he chose to present the Soviet Union as posing a "positive" social-moral challenge to the United States rather than a threat. He noted that, in contrast to the humiliations that nonwhite visitors had to endure in all-too-many American hotels and restaurants, he encountered no discrimination while traveling in the Soviet Union. He went on to extol the way in which women were involved in nearly all existing occupations, including the hard physical labor of construction and road paving. He also credited the Communist government with stamping out illiteracy, a social ill that had afflicted 70 percent of the populace under tsarist rule. Although he described universities full of students, he expressed disapproval of the Soviet bias toward the sciences over the humanities and the lack of full intellectual freedom. He concluded by declaring the Soviet Union to have made remarkable progress since his earlier visits in 1926, when the country was still recovering from its civil war, and 1935, just prior to Stalin's show trials and purges. After his three-week stay, he declared that, although he had seen many things of which the Soviets could hardly be proud, nevertheless, if one arrived there with an open, unprejudiced mind, one could learn much from the exciting new world that they had built—a world that could open new horizons for all humankind.

Silver was not indifferent to the fact that the Soviet Union was a dictatorship; however, he found it important to note that, despite its government's propaganda, the Russian populace was not anti-American. On the contrary, most Russians, he assured, harbored "a secret admiration for the great achievements of our country. . . . They want to live in peace and friendship with us" (Silver 1961f). Silver believed that friendship and a desire for peace also existed within the American public, and that the current atmosphere of mutual suspicion had been generated by the two governments. During his visit, he told the Soviets that Americans found it hard to reconcile Russian desires for coexistence with the Soviet Union's invasion of Hungary, its refusal to subject itself to nuclear inspection, and its efforts at disrupting UN activity. At the same time, he reported to the American public that the Russians could not understand why the United States insisted on arming Germany, sent its U-2 spy plane just before the Paris summit, funded and equipped the Bay of Pigs invasion force, and opposed Communist China's entry into the United Nations. Silver concluded his speech by calling for an end to the mutual suspicion, noting that it was better to learn from one's enemy than to try to humiliate him.

> We must learn to live on the same globe with the Soviet people, and they with us. . . . Let us not be afraid to trade with each other in goods or in ideas. Let us compete in only one way—which system can do more for its people. The problem before the world is not which system is the better, but how the two can keep from destroying each other—and mankind. (Silver 1961f)

These remarks indicate that Silver saw himself not merely as a prophet of doom, cautioning against war and the destruction that it would bring in its wake, but also as a prophet of hope, working to strengthen his constituency's faith in progress and democracy. This approach was reflected in Silver's "Taking Stock" speech of 1961 (Silver 1961i). At the beginning of the sermon he expressed bitter disappointment in the rising tension between East and West, and warned that a descent into apocalyptic conflict must be avoided. He was particularly concerned by recent signs of the United Nations' deteriorating status,[5] recalling that World War II broke out a short time after the collapse of the League of Nations. These concerns notwithstanding, Silver also made sure to include portions of his original 1950 "hope speech" in his sermon—those affirming his faith that current social trends were positive on the whole and destined to make the world a better place. He even updated the original version of the speech by adding a number of events that, in his opinion, pointed to the generally progressive tendency of world affairs. These events included the establishment of the European Economic Community in 1957, the United States' billion dollar, ten-year aid commitment to Latin America, and the Kennedy administration's endeavors on behalf of civil rights for African Americans. Above all, he was thrilled by Kennedy's Peace Corps initiative, which he likened to the gathering of a cloud that heralds the end of a drought. He saw the Peace Corps as an expression of America's exalted sense of mission—one concerned not with eradicating communism or with rescuing democracy via military pacts, but rather with helping victims of war, poverty, and natural disasters to help themselves.

Silver took a similar tone in his last speech—a eulogy for President Kennedy that he composed a week after the assassination, but which Silver did not live to deliver. It was ultimately included in the memorial service held for Silver, and may thus be seen as a kind of spiritual last will

5. Silver denounced India's invasion of the Portuguese colony of Goa. In contrast to his support five years earlier for a similar action by Israel in the Suez conflict, in this instance he declared that, however strong India's territorial claim to Goa was, the United Nations could not condone an act of aggression, even for justifiable reasons.

and testament. It conveyed Silver's frequently iterated belief that the public agenda should be dictated not by a sense of crisis or fear, but by a sense of commitment to progress (Silver 1972c). Accordingly, Silver described Kennedy as one whose message of hope had derived from the "unbroken chain of fervent human aspirations . . . the unremitting struggles of men for larger freedom, for their basic human rights, for the dignity of man." In his eyes, and doubtless in the eyes of those who participated in the memorial service, it was the last portion of the address that communicated the vision that Silver himself had spent most of his life striving to advance:

> Here is high sorrow for all of us—but also high hope, hope that his life will inspire other lives—that our people will look to his example, his message and his mission and, in a chastened spirit, will forego the hate which turns brother against brother, and people against people; hope that they will resolutely preserve in the ways of progress and peace. (Silver 1972c)

13

Nonetheless, a Zionist Leader

An additional, quite surprising, dimension of Silver's self-assigned prophetic role could be seen in the special relationship he developed with the North American financier Cyrus Eaton—a 1960 Lenin Peace Prize recipient known in the height of the Cold War as "the Kremlin's favorite capitalist." During the 1950s, Eaton had become an ardent critic of US foreign policy, particularly as it related to the Soviet Union. His best-known effort in this area was the funding of the Pugwash Conference on Science and World Affairs, an endeavor composed of scientists from the two blocs. The endeavor was initiated in July 1955 by a joint announcement of Albert Einstein and Bertrand Russell and, starting in 1957, convened annually to discuss ways of addressing the nuclear arms race. The organizers, Eaton among them, were accused during the Cold War era of serving as a Soviet propaganda tool, and only years later, after the 1995 Nobel Peace Prize was awarded to their endeavor, was their reputation fully rehabilitated.

Silver had openly aligned himself with Eaton as early as the late 1950s, at a time when the latter's efforts at personal diplomacy and rapprochement between the two blocs had still aroused harsh public condemnation.[1] The two began to correspond after a sermon delivered by Silver on the Cold War appeared in the *Plain Dealer*, Cleveland's daily newspaper. Eaton sent Silver a letter of support immediately upon the sermon's

1. It should be noted that Eaton's progressive views had been shaped by the Protestant Christian Social Gospel movement, which, during the early twentieth century, had influenced Reform Judaism and, by extension, Silver.

publication on December 9, 1957; from that time until Silver's death the two met and wrote each other frequently. Eaton sent Silver numerous letters of appreciation for his sermons on the Cold War. Silver, for his part, frequently lauded Eaton's initiatives and stood by him at times of public condemnation.[2]

In December 1960, the Israeli consul in Chicago asked Silver to use his friendship with Eaton on behalf of Jews wishing to immigrate to Israel for "family reunification" purposes.[3] Although Silver devoted significant attention to the affair, his role in it was actually quite marginal. Most of his efforts focused on an ill-fated initiative to have a delegation of American-Jewish businessmen meet with Soviet officials. In his private journal he reported on his efforts, together with the Israeli consuls in Chicago and New York, to draw up a list of fifteen leading Jewish figures in the financial sector[4] and on his cooperation with Eaton to compose a personal appeal to Khrushchev. Ultimately, after preliminary discussions with the Soviet ambassador in June 1962, Eaton decided not to send the letter and to abandon the initiative altogether, owing to the Soviet precondition that the American-Jewish delegation place pressure on President Kennedy regarding Berlin prior to their meeting with Khrushchev.[5]

2. Letters between Silver and Cyrus Eaton, December 9, 1957–March 21, 1962, AHSP I; Silver's Diary, 1949–1963, January 6, 1961–March 1, 1963.

3. The "family reunification" endeavor concerned families divided by the Holocaust. Starting in the mid-1950s, Israeli members of such families would send notarized documents (nine thousand by the early 1960s) to their relatives in the Soviet Union, as the basis for visa requests by the latter. Most of the requests were denied.

4. The list included the banker Edward Warburg; Fred Lazarus, owner of Federated Department Stores (subsuming, among others, Bloomingdale's and Filene's of Boston); Henry ("Colonel") Crown, owner of General Dynamics and the Hilton Hotel chain; and the Detroit industrialist Max Zivion.

5. After the failure of the businessmen's delegation initiative, Silver continued to document his involvement in related areas. On March 1, 1963, at the behest of the Israeli ambassador to the United States, Avraham Harman, and with Eaton's aid, he met with the Soviet ambassador, requesting that the latter intervene to accelerate the provision of exit visas for Romanian Jews.

Eaton also used his connections with the Soviet elite to help Silver plan his July 1961 visit to the Soviet Union. During his trip Silver raised the subject of Soviet Jewry in his conversations with Soviet functionaries, but instead of continuing his efforts on behalf of Jews wishing to immigrate to Israel, he focused on the cultural and religious rights of the Jewish minority, comparing them with those of other Soviet national minorities.[6] In December 1961, a few months after his return to the United States, Silver reported in his journal on two members of the Soviet delegation to the United Nations who had visited him at his home; on this occasion as well, Silver did not discuss the right of immigration for Soviet Jews, but rather their cultural rights as one of the Soviet minority groups. Finally, during the last days of Silver's life, a delegation of Soviet writers and journalists visited Cleveland; on November 25, Silver participated in a reception that Eaton had organized for them. Three days later Silver died, leaving the event unrecorded in his journal.

The fact that Silver chose to document, via a journal devoted to his pro-Israel activity, various endeavors on behalf of Soviet Jewry, and to do so in great detail, indicates that he regarded these endeavors as an important channel for American-Zionist solidarity. Although the battle for Soviet Jewry was not yet the galvanizing issue for American Jewry that it would become a decade later (Feingold 2007), Silver already appears to have understood the issue's potential. He was particularly aware that activity on behalf of Soviet Jewry was a major way of expressing solidarity with Israel, and of doing so in Diaspora-Zionist terms. One example of this is the manner in which Silver described his impressions of Soviet Jewry to his Cleveland congregants after returning from his July 1961 trip. He noted in great detail Soviet Jews' thirst for any information about Israel. He described the way in which worshippers at the main synagogue in Moscow congratulated one another on hearing that Israel had launched

6. In his reports on the trip, Silver related that he had met with the heads of the Soviet State Committee for Cultural Relations with Foreign Countries, and had pointed to the prohibition on the study of Yiddish and Hebrew as evidence of discrimination against Jews comparable to other national groups within the Soviet Union.

its first rocket—the Shavit 2—into space, and how thousands of Jews had stood in line for the chance to view a documentary film about Israel. In Silver's hands, Israel became a symbol of international Jewish solidarity, one that connected his congregation in Cleveland with the worshippers of Moscow's main synagogue. Significantly, no preoccupation with the idea of aliyah featured in that solidarity. The focus was, rather, on the right of the Soviet Jewish minority to develop its cultural life in the Soviet Union. Thus, in the context of activity to ease the plight of Soviet Jews, identifying with Israel became a means of expressing pan-Jewish solidarity in the spirit of Diaspora Zionism.

Moreover, Silver's endeavors on behalf of Soviet Jewry afforded him the opportunity to cast this Diaspora-Zionist solidarity in the light of a universalistic "prophetic" struggle to establish a "good society." During the period in question, this struggle's most active front was that of the Cold War; Silver's own contribution being his efforts along with Eaton's to prevent US-Soviet tensions from spiraling into a third world war. Indeed, linking the Zionist struggle with the universal religious-social endeavor was hugely important to Silver throughout his career. He had emphasized this connection as early as the 1920s and 1930s, while challenging the anti-Zionist stance of his Reform colleagues who regarded a progressive social vision as incompatible with Zionism's nationalist ethos. He had taken the idea even farther during the Holocaust years, when he used the Zionist endeavor to underscore the indispensable link between a lasting solution for the Jewish problem and the vision of building the "good society" in the aftermath of the war. Ultimately, this connection became a cornerstone of Silver's view of the creation of the State of Israel as a necessary precondition without which the Jewish collective could never hope to transcend its preoccupation with self-defense and to embrace its universalistic mission.

The supreme importance that Silver placed on connecting Zionist solidarity with a broader sense of a religious-social mission may be seen in a Purim sermon that he delivered in 1955. In this sermon, Silver denounced the anti-Zionism of the celebrated historian Arnold Toynbee (Silver 1972a), focusing particularly on Toynbee's criticism of the Jews in his *Study of History*. At first glance, the vehemence of Silver's denunciation seems excessive. Silver might, after all, have agreed with Toynbee's belief in the ultimate intermingling of cultures in a new, universal religion based on the ethical code of the prophets.[7] However, in this case, it seems to have been the very similarity between the two approaches that disturbed Silver. Silver was unwilling to accept that the kind of universalistic vision that he shared with Toynbee entailed negating Zionism or viewing the Jews in Israel as victims-turned-terrorists who treated Arabs the way the Nazis had treated the Jews. Focusing on Toynbee's conception of Judaism as a fossil that ought to have disappeared long ago, Silver stressed that Judaism's gift of monotheism to world civilization was, rather, an ongoing process; the Jewish contribution to world civilization, he explained, did not consist merely in a one-time bequeathal of various religious and ethical concepts, but rather in the fact that the Jews had preserved these ideals in the face of repeated persecutions, as exemplified in the story of Purim. Had they not done so, those ideals would have been mere flashes in the historical pan. Thus, Silver chose to respond to Toynbee and to affirm the legitimacy of Zionism and the State of Israel by focusing on the Jewish will to survive in exile, seeing it as a model of Jewish heroism—one to be emulated in the struggle to realize the universalistic Jewish mission.

The foregoing points to a change in direction for Silver: without abandoning his Diaspora-Zionist approach, he nevertheless ceased to call for an equal dialogue between it and the Israel-centric version, as he had done during the early years of the state. Rather, he began to employ Diaspora Zionism as a means of reinterpreting Israel's centrality—of giving it its proper place within the universalistic vision. The use of Purim in this context was not coincidental. The story of exilic heroism gave Silver a framework for elucidating Israel's significance while focusing the spotlight on Diaspora Jewry and its relations with the surrounding Gentile environment. This is further illustrated in yet another speech—one featuring both Purim and the State of Israel—which Silver delivered at The Temple in Cleveland five years later, in March 1960, upon his return

7. Silver could also agree with Toynbee's view of Diaspora Jewry as an exemplary community on which an ideal global state—one that offered a degree of autonomy to its component units—might model itself.

from another visit to Israel (Silver 1960c). He explained that, upon arriving in Israel from Rome, he had primarily been interested in seeing how a young nation, composed of myriad immigrant groups traumatized by recent events in their countries of origin, would react to Nasser's repeated threats of war.[8] The question that he had asked himself during his flight from Rome was whether Israel would display a new pattern of response—one not emanating from the bunker of existential anxiety. As an answer to this question, Silver proudly reported that he had found Israelis to be concerned but calm. He was particularly impressed by the widespread Israeli hope for peace and the absence of hatred for those who threatened the country's survival. He was pleased that the Purim parades had not degenerated into mass rallies against Jew-haters of the past and present. On the contrary, the theme of the main parade in Tel Aviv had been one of friendship and international cooperation, with floats featuring the United Nations, African countries, and even Great Britain—only recently the Jewish Yishuv's bitter enemy. The sole display that advanced an agenda of hatred or revenge was the one depicting the Purim story itself. Haman's hanging head had seemed to him to resemble that of Hitler, while one of the ten sons of Haman had borne a resemblance to Nasser.

It was clear that Silver intended no criticism by this latter remark. On the contrary, the Purim float had struck him as evidence of a welcome normality—a sovereign people expressing anger against its enemies in a proportionate way and evincing no undue preoccupation with hatred or revenge. In the same vein, Silver related with unconcealed delight the story of a soccer match in which Israel had defeated Greece, noting that, from the reaction of the Israeli radio, one might have thought that the Maccabees had once again triumphed over the Seleucids. The general rejoicing had denoted, in Silver's eyes, a welcome channeling of Jewish existential anxiety toward the relatively marginal spheres of Purim festivity and athletics. Now that a Jewish sovereign state had been established, the issues

8. In his discussion of threats to Israel's existence, Silver noted in particular Nasser's stationing of four divisions on the Gaza border and the rumors then circulating of impending war in the Middle East.

currently occupying a central place on the Israeli public agenda were not those of taking revenge for past persecution, or territorial expansion at the expense of current foes, but rather those of developing the country's economic, cultural, and educational systems. Among the topics of consuming interest to the Israeli public, Silver noted, were a large textile factory that had been built in the southern town of Kiryat Gat, a chemical plant envisioned for the southern Be'er-Sheva area, and a planned deep-water port at the city of Ashdod. He was particularly impressed by Alexander Zarchin's water desalination facilities, and predicted that they would bring about an economic revolution for Israel and the entire world.[9]

This use of the Purim story recurred in a 1961 sermon in honor of the holiday (Silver 1961g). Silver stressed that the basic situation known to Judaism—that of an *Amalek* (the Jews' eternal enemy) appearing in every generation—had not changed with the founding of the State of Israel; indeed, an Amalek might well return to endanger the Jews, their state, and perhaps the entire world. This being the case, the new message that Silver sought to convey was that although the age of war and conflict had not ended, a new means had emerged of coping with threats to the Jewish people and their universal mission. Silver gave expression to the anticipated new coping method by contrasting it to André Schwarz-Bart's recently published novel, *The Last of the Just*. The book told the story of a Jewish family that, from the Crusader period on, had produced a martyr in every generation; the last of these martyrs, whose turn came during the Holocaust, redeemed the entire world. Silver opposed this model, maintaining that the idea of "the last of the just" was unknown to Judaism, since the struggle against evil and war was an eternal one from which we are forbidden to desist. As Silver saw it, the answer posed by the State of Israel to the Holocaust and generations-long persecution was not a messianic one, heralding the end of war and the disappearance of existential

9. Most of the endeavors that Silver noted here in evidence of Israeli society's pioneering and technically advanced nature ultimately came to symbolize the opposite—failed initiative and wrongheaded policy. The textile factory closed, the chemical plants became major polluters, and the desalination plants came to be viewed by many as emblematic of Israeli policymakers' neglect of its increasingly problematic water shortage.

threats. On the contrary, even during the era of Israeli statehood, the Jewish people—and, indeed, humanity as a whole—would be called on in every generation to fight a new Amalek. The State of Israel's role was not to end the struggle, but rather to infuse it with a new spirit. Rather than fighting their ongoing battle as victims and out of a sense of existential anxiety, the Jews would now see it as part of their unceasing commitment to the establishment of a universal, good, and just society.

This idea resurfaced in the last Purim sermon that Silver delivered before his passing—a sermon that, once again, focused on the best way to respond to the Jew-hating Haman of every generation (Silver 1972g). In Silver's view, this hatred stemmed from a false sense of supremacy, gained by humiliating and persecuting those on the margins of society. He took as an example the recent demonstrations in Oxford, Mississippi, against the enrollment of an African American student, James Meredith, at the University of Mississippi. According to Silver, the white rioters had seen in Meredith a threat to their supremacy, which itself was based entirely on the humiliation and disenfranchisement of nonwhites. Mordechai and Esther's heroism represented, in Silver's quite creative interpretation, a model of proper Jewish response to hatred of this kind. They were the quintessential leaders who cared not only for themselves, but also for the rights of those belonging to oppressed minority groups. Rather than attempting to cure hatred, their message was that when people stop thinking only of themselves and start thinking about others and what can be done for them, then they cease to hate.

This use of the Purim story to reinterpret the existential Jewish struggle also sheds light on why Silver abandoned his demand of the early 1950s for American-Zionist participation in domestic Israeli political discourse. Silver was now placing Israel on a pedestal, highlighting only the admirable nature of its struggle—that which offered inspiration to the Diaspora-Jewish agenda. One vivid example of the latter approach may be found in the conclusion to the sermon in which Silver described his 1960 Purim visit to Israel (Silver 1960c). In contrast to many of his previous visits, this time Silver was able to report on his friendly interaction with Ben-Gurion, who had ceased to shun him after realizing that Silver no longer harbored any pretensions to involvement in Israeli politics. The topic of their discussion had been Ben-Gurion's planned trip to the United States and his scheduled talks with the president. Silver refrained from making any comments regarding Israeli policy; rather, he related with gratification how his private meeting with Ben-Gurion had resulted in an invitation to a discussion group on the Bible, which the prime minister held regularly in his home. Silver had found it particularly moving that, in the midst of preparations for an important trip to Washington, Israel's prime minister found time—four hours in whole—to summon a group of the elite Israeli leadership, including President Yitzhak Ben-Zvi, the prime minister, the IDF chief of staff, and various professors, to discuss the Bible. In effect, he presented Ben-Gurion as a legendary king-philosopher—an ideal leader of a utopian country, who combined in his conduct the heroism of King David with the wisdom of King Solomon. He concluded his sermon by recounting a conversation with a customs official immediately upon his return to the United States—an American Jew who had expressed his admiration for Israel and veneration of its mythical leader, Ben-Gurion. It seems that Silver purposely chose this ending in order to cause his listeners to identify with the view of Ben-Gurion and Israel as objects of exaltation belonging to a different plane from that of the everyday political reality.

This extraordinary change of heart, however, had not constituted an admission of failure on Silver's part in formulating a viable Diaspora-Zionist approach, distinct and independent from that of Israel. One may say that Silver decided, in effect, to challenge the Israel-centric approach precisely by turning it into an elevated sacred focus of pan-Jewish identification. One outstanding feature of this tactic is clearly seen in Silver's May 1963 acceptance speech for the Brandeis Award (Silver 1963b; see also Silver 1962, 1963c). The event, marking fifteen years of Israeli independence, was held by the American Zionist Council, which by that time had clearly become an operating arm of the State of Israel; the decision to give Silver the award may thus be seen as an indication of Israel's readiness to grant recognition to a leader who finally accepted its authority. Silver, for his part, had adopted a stance that underscored Israel's centrality for the Jewish people; this stance, however, gave him the legitimacy to denounce the anti-Diaspora trends, then current in Israeli society, for belittling the pan-Jewish significance implied by Israel's central and leading role. He predicted that as Israeli society overcame its immediate existential challenges, it would come to realize the inadequacy of Israel-centric nationalism and would be inspired to fulfill its universalistic spiritual mission. Thus, Silver posed an agenda no less polemical than that of his approach of a decade earlier; however, his current agenda was not one of opposing Israel-centrism, but rather of glorifying Israel's pan-Jewish, universal role.

This latter stance was succinctly expressed in the section headings of a programmatic speech entitled "Zionism" that Silver composed just prior to his passing (Silver n.d. [1963]).[10] Silver began by defining Zionism as a "two-way bridge" between Israel and the Diaspora,[11] "open at all time for spiritual and cultural traffic." He explained this new definition by dividing modern Jewish history into two eras: the "Age of Drift," followed by the "Age of Decision." This division alluded to a popular Zionist historiographical approach that saw Zionism as the answer to failed Jewish attempts at integration within non-Jewish society. While ostensibly adopting this approach, Silver used it in a different, subversive way. He depicted Zionism as a response not to failed integration but rather to a desperate intermediate state in which Jews were forced to choose between an isolated ghetto existence and assimilation within non-Jewish society. Hence the State of Israel's importance: it addressed the particularistic-universalistic tension inherent to Judaism, thus offering the Jews a new means of "integration without assimilation." Putting this capability into practice entailed a redefinition of Israel's centrality—one that would underscore the importance of Jewish life in the Diaspora and give inspiration to Diaspora Jewry in fulfilling the universalistic prophetic vision.

10. Based on the file's archive number, it appears to have been the first draft of a speech that Silver had worked on shortly before his death and had not managed to send to his secretary for retyping. Notations at the top of the first page indicate that the speech was to have been delivered at an event in the presence of Israeli Ambassador Avraham Harman.

11. Silver used the image of a two-way bridge in several of his speeches during this period; it may be conjectured that his sudden passing prevented him from developing a "two-way bridge" speech template that would have replaced his "two centers" and "hope speech" templates.

> The state of Israel is a great and glorious fact in Jewish life . . . but greater than the state of Israel is the people of Israel, and greater than the people of Israel is the immortal vision and hope which sustained our people through the long centuries, which made of it a covenanted people, pledged to the ideal . . . of the establishment of the Kingdom of God on earth.

This reinterpretation of Israel-centric Zionism has found a new and perhaps cruder echo in Jewish public life today. As in the early years of Israeli statehood, those who support a similar approach to Silver's now find themselves on the defensive, fighting a rearguard battle on multiple fronts—not only against Jewish national and religious extremists urging the exclusionist nature of the "walls" that separate Jews from their non-Jewish surroundings, but also against those who utterly reject the legitimacy of those walls. What makes these two fronts so very challenging is the question that they implicitly pose: Can Silver's "bridges and walls" vision be transformed into a goal capable of dictating a practical political-social agenda? Can a vision of an incessant journey toward a postnationalist utopia be expected to shape the agenda of a national state, particularly when the latter is still in the midst of a struggle for its very survival?

Against this background, the relevance of Silver's approach lies in his dual attitude toward the concept of "national walls" that separate Jews from other nationalities. This dual approach needs to be understood not as ambivalence regarding the necessity of national boundaries, but rather in terms of dual decisiveness: Silver exalted the need for national walls with the same conviction that characterized his desire to tear them down. It is this dual passion that explains Silver's complex relations with Israel and makes it difficult for contemporary Jewish observers to truly understand Silver's modes of thought. While one would normally expect to find an unbridgeable gulf between those favoring self-segregation—the erection of walls between faiths, cultures, and nationalities—and those favoring the destruction of such walls, this dichotomy does not apply to Silver. What is unique about Silver is that he fostered a Jewish-Zionist tradition predicated on an intermingling of these two choices. Silver regarded this complex ideology as a fitting answer to the tangle of contradictory existential fears: on the one hand, a fear that an excessive emphasis on "walls" may have a suffocating effect on personal or group creativity; on the other hand, when "walls" are absent or have been demolished, the sense of security and belonging they provide is lost and chaos ensues. Indeed, the call to simultaneously embrace and defy the "wall concept" is what characterized Silver's activity throughout his career as a Reform rabbi and Zionist leader. The call became increasingly urgent during the first decade of Israeli statehood because of Silver's prevailing perceptions of the state's founding as a turning point—one destined to profoundly alter the character of modern Jewish life. Israel's establishment was expected to engender the "new Jew" capable of encompassing the conflicting loyalties entailed by the "bridges and walls" ideal. As Silver saw it, an inability to cope with these internal contradictions was inherent to the exilic, pre-state period; it reflected the exilic mentality that Zionism sought to overcome.

Silver was well aware that during the pre-state period there was no choice for the Jewish people but to devote the major portion of their resources to the construction and reinforcement of Jewish national walls. However, even at the height of the Holocaust and in the midst of the fight for Israeli statehood, he repeatedly proclaimed that an attitude of sanctification regarding Jewish national walls lay at the heart of the negative, self-segregating Jewish mentality that the Zionist ideology proposed to counter, and that a sovereign Jewish state was desirable precisely in order to overcome this mentality. Silver repeatedly affirmed his hope that preoccupation with the existential struggle for statehood would prove to be merely a temporary stage, whose completion would usher in a new era of spiritual Zionist activism. He hoped that after centuries of struggling to fortify the walls of Jewish existence, the Jewish collective would now be able to turn to its spiritual and ethical mission. In its contemporary form, this hope placed three basic issues in opposition to one another. First, can we do without rebuilding and maintaining strong and protective walls? Can we ignore the possibility that even the tiniest crack in the wall will endanger our survival? Second, conversely, can we indeed continue to exist within walls, or are we building, with our own hands, a new ghetto that tolerates not the smallest manifestation of difference or otherness, whether within or without? And, finally, transcending these two conflicting views, can we—as certain modern Jewish leaders, including Silver, have averred—take a third path, one that advocates preserving the walls but in the form of *good walls*—walls that do not merely keep out but also let in? In relation to this latter possibility, yet another question arises—one that has hovered in the background throughout the present work: is such a concept as good walls even possible? Do all attempts to produce a desirable form of walls serve only to justify the existence and repressive objectives of various ideologies?

In contrast to the skeptical tone of the foregoing questions, Silver was an ardent believer in the possibility of good walls; he devoted his entire rabbinical and Zionist careers to promoting their construction and maintenance. This latter approach of Silver reflected the great importance attached by modern Jews, especially Diaspora Jews, to the "ruins" of the ghetto walls, that is, to those sections of the wall that, while still standing, no longer constitute a clear boundary between Judaism and its surrounding environments. It was precisely at those points when the stability of the Jewish religious-cultural walls were most threatened that Silver had to redefine those walls. The ability to simultaneously emphasize and blur the boundaries between Jews and their non-Jewish surroundings became, for Silver, the sole means of commitment to the social-moral Jewish endeavor. As Silver understood it, only by combining a commitment to walls with an ongoing questioning of their definiteness might the individual acquire the ability to have an impact on his surroundings, and thus the moral responsibility to do so.

This was the devoted yet skeptical philosophy that Silver cultivated over the course of his life, and it explains the many contradictions that characterized his Zionist and religious-social activities. He was both a believing Jew and a devout rationalist, and a Jew whose Orthodox religious-ethnic childhood had a decisive impact on his way of life. Yet, at the same time, he was a Reform rabbi whose faith and activity were strongly inspired by the spirit of nineteenth-century enlightenment and mission-oriented classical reform. A holder of progressive views in the social and economic sphere, he nevertheless openly aligned himself with the Republican Party and with a certain portion of its conservative ideology. Finally, Silver was both a passionate believer in full Jewish cultural and social integration into American-democratic society and a determined advocate for a separate and distinct Diaspora-Jewish existence. A common thread weaves through all of these contradictory elements: Silver acted out of a sense that there was no choice but to continuously reinvent *good walls*, even in the face of external and internal threats posed by exclusionary ideologies as well as by countless secularist, relativist, existentialist, and materialist ideologies, which he viewed as encouraging the wholesale destruction of all forms of walls. In retrospect, Silver's "bridges and walls" ideology poses to contemporary society a most important question: Can the polarization between the wall-sanctifying and wall-demolishing approaches be resolved only through an unambiguous victory for one side or the other? Or should the tension between the two be seen as the desired basis of a continuous, tireless struggle for a new social and political order?

References

Index

References

Ahad Ha'am. [1909] 1950. "Negating the Exile." In *Kol Kitve Aḥad Ha'am*, 399–403. Jerusalem: Dvir.

Al-Hamishmar. 1951a. "A Pompous Demonstration." April 26.

———. 1951b. "Silver's Self-Defense against Slanderous Propaganda." April 29.

Alteras, Isaac. 1993. *Eisenhower and Israel: U.S.-Israeli Relations, 1953–1960*. Gainesville: University Press of Florida.

American Public Welfare Association. 1956. April 15–18. AHSP V 938.

The American Zionist. 1951. "Identification—Issue or Smokescreen? An Analysis of the Record, The National Committee for Zionist Action within the ZOA, New York, 1952." July 1–3.

———. 1956. "Silver Assails Appeasement." 47, no. 2: 1–3.

———. 1957. "What We Must Always Remember—World Jewry—First Line of Israel's Defense." October, 4–5.

American Zionist Council. 1950. "Zionists View Big Three Statement on Middle East as First Breach in Wall—Assert Concern over Implementation of Announced Policy." Press Release, May 26.

American Zionist Emergency Council. 1944. March 21. AHSP V 645.

———. 1946. Minutes of AZEC Plenary Meeting No. 44, Washington, July 1–3.

Arad, Gulie Ne'eman. 2000. *America, Its Jews, and the Rise of Nazism*. Bloomington: Indiana University Press.

Arnold, Mathew. 1883. *Culture and Anarchy and Friendship's Garland*. New York.

Ben-Gurion, David. 1938. Speech, December 7. File 38/23, Labor Party Archive.

———. 1950. Speech at Meeting of the World Labor Zionist Movement, January 27. Speeches, Ben-Gurion Archives.

———. 1956. "Answer to Bevin at the Elected Assembly, 28 November 1945." In *Ba-Ma'arakha*, vol. 5, 9–32. Tel Aviv: Am Oved.

Ben-Rafael, Eliezer. 2001. *Jewish Identities: The Answers of the Sages of Israel to Ben-Gurion*. Sde Boqer: Ben-Gurion Institute.

Berlin, Isaiah. [1954] 1969. "Historical Inevitability." *In Four Essays on Liberty*, 49–82. London: Oxford University Press.

Berman, Aaron. 1990. *Nazism, the Jews, and American Zionism, 1933–1948*. Detroit: Wayne State University Press.

Bernstein, Barton J. 1971. "Election of 1952." In *History of American Presidential Elections, 1789–1968*, edited by Arthur M. Schlesinger, vol. 4. New York: Chelsea House.

Bialer, Uri. 1990. *Between East and West: Israel's Foreign Policy Orientation, 1948–1956*. Cambridge: Cambridge University Press.

———. 2002. "Top Hat, Tuxedo, and Cannons: Israeli Foreign Policy from 1948 to 1956 as a Field of Study." *Israel Studies* 7, no. 1: 22–33.

Brunner, Emil. 1954. *Our Faith*. Translated by John W. Rilling. New York: Scribner.

Caplan, Neil. 1997. *Futile Diplomacy*, vol. 4, *Operation Alpha and the Failure of Anglo-American Coercive Diplomacy in the Arab-Israeli Conflict, 1954–1956*. London: Frank Cass.

Chicago Jewish Chronicle. 1936. "Sinai Temple to Hold Its 75th Anniversary." October 16.

Cleveland Plain Dealer. 1961. "Rabbi Silver Reports on Russian Advances." August 10. AHSP V 1023.

Cohen, Naomi W. 1972. *Not Free to Desist: The American Jewish Committee, 1906–1966*. Philadelphia: Jewish Publication Society of America.

Davar. 1951a. "Abba Hillel Silver Comes to Israel." April 26.

———. 1951b. "Silver's Zionist Views and His Attitude towards American Policy." April 29.

Diner, Hasia R. 1997. "Zion and America: The Formative Visions of Abba Hillel Silver." In Raider, Sarna, and Zweig, *Abba Hillel Silver and American Zionism*, 45–69.

Dinur, Ben-Zion. 1978. "Galuyot ve-Hurbanan." In *Dorot ve-Rashumot: Mehkarim ve-Iyunim baeHistoriografiya Yisraelit*. Jerusalem: Bialik Institute.

Don-Yehiya, Eliezer. 2002. "Religion, National Identity, and Politics: The 'Who Is a Jew' Crisis, 1958." In *On Both Sides of the Bridge: Religion and State in Israel's Early Years*, edited by Mordechai Bar-On and Tsevi Tsameret, 88–143. Jerusalem: Ben-Zvi Institute.

Drory, Ze'ev. 2005. *Israel's Reprisal Policy, 1953–1956: The Dynamics of Military Retaliation*. New York: Routledge.

Eban, Abba. 1977. *An Autobiography*. New York: Random House.

———. 1992. *Personal Witness: Israel through My Eyes*. New York: Jonathan Cape.

Efrat, David. 1951. "A Greeting to Rabbi Silver." *Ma'ariv*, April 26.

Eisenstadt, S. N., and Moshe Lissak, eds. 1999. *Zionism and the Return to History: A Reassessment*. Jerusalem: Ben-Zvi Institute.

Eytan, Walter. 1958. *The First Ten Years: A Diplomatic History of Israel*. New York: Simon and Schuster.

Feingold, Henry L. 1995. *Bearing Witness: How America and Its Jews Responded to the Holocaust*. Syracuse: Syracuse University Press.

———. 2007. *"Silent No More": Saving the Jews of Russia, the American Jewish Effort, 1967–1989*. Syracuse: Syracuse University Press.

Feldstein, Ariel L. 2003. *Gordian Knot: David Ben-Gurion, the Zionist Organization and American Jewry, 1948–1963*. Sde Boqer: Ben-Gurion Institute.

Feuer, Lewis S. 1987. "Horace M. Kallen on War and Peace." In *The Legacy of Horace M. Kallen*, edited by Milton R. Konvitz, 39–40. Cranbury, NJ: Associated University Presses.

Fineberg, Solomon Andhil. 1943. *Overcoming Anti-Semitism*. New York: Harper.

Frank, M. Z. 1966. "The Silver–Ben-Gurion Affair." *HaDo'ar* 46/b, November 11, 19–20.

Freehof, Solomon B. 1967. "Recollections of Abba Hillel Silver." In Weiner, *Therefore Choose Life*, 4.

Frisch, Daniel. 1949. "The ZOA at the Crossroad." *The New Palestine*, January 13.

Gal, Allon. 1986. "The Mission Motif in American Zionism (1898–1948)." *American Jewish History* 75, no. 4: 363–85.

———. 1989. "Universal Mission and Jewish Survivalism in American Zionist Ideology." In *From Ancient Israel to Modern Judaism: Essays in Honor of Marvin Fox*, edited by Jacob Neusner, Ernest S. Frerichs, and Nahum M. Sarna, vol. 4, *The Modern Age: Theology, Literature, History*, 61–83. Atlanta: Scholars Press.

———. 1991. *David Ben-Gurion and the American Alignment for a Jewish State*. Bloomington: Indiana University Press.

———. 1999. "The Jewish Return to History in American Zionist Thought (1897–1967)." In Eisenstadt and Lissak, *Zionism and the Return to History*, 361–89.

———. 2000. "The United States in Abba Hillel Silver's World View." *Michael* 15: 20–25.

Gal, Allon, and Ofer Shiff. 1999. "Abba Hillel Silver: Judaism and Zionism." *Iyunim Bitkumat Israel* 8: 687–98.

Galambos, Louis, ed. 1989. *The Papers of Dwight David Eisenhower*. vol. 13. Baltimore: Johns Hopkins University Press.

Ganin, Zvi. 1984. "Activists versus Moderates: The Wise–Silver Controversy in the 1940s." *Zionism* 9: 317–58.

———. 2005. *An Uneasy Relationship: American Jewish Leadership and Israel, 1948–1957.* Syracuse: Syracuse University Press.

Gelblum, E. 1951. "Silver's Visit in Israel and Its Goals." *Ha'aretz*, April 25.

Goldmann, Nahum. 1969. *The Autobiography of Nahum Goldmann: Sixty Years of Jewish Life.* Translated by Helen Sebba. New York: Holt, Rinehart and Winston.

Goodman, Paul. 1953. *History of the Jews.* New York: Dutton.

Goren, Arthur A. 1997. "Between Ideal and Reality: Abba Hillel Silver's Zionist Vision." In Raider, Sarna, and Zweig, *Abba Hillel Silver and American Zionism*, 71–86.

Gorni, Yosef. 1976. *Partnership and Conflict: Chaim Weizmann and the Jewish Labor Movement in Palestine.* Tel Aviv: Kibbutz Ha'meuchad Publishing House.

———. 1999. "Negation of the Exile and the Return to History." In Eisenstadt and Lissak, *Zionism and the Return to History*, 361–89.

———. 2004. "Negation of the Exile and Its Centrality in Israel: Between Nachum Goldmann and Ben-Gurion." *Gesher* 148: 19–34.

———. 2006. *Converging Alternatives: The Bund and the Zionist Labor Movement, 1897–1985.* New York: State University of New York Press.

Gorny, Yosef. 2009. *A Cry in the Wilderness.* Tel Aviv: Hakibbutz Hameuchad.

Gottlieb, Moshe R. 1982. *American Anti-Nazi Resistance, 1933–1941: An Historical Analysis.* New York: Ktav.

Ha'aretz. 1951a. [Public receptions for Silver in his 1951 visit to Israel.] April 25.

———. 1951c. "Meyom Leyom" [the daily report]. May 6.

HaBoker. 1951a. [Public receptions for Silver in his 1951 visit to Israel.] April 25.

———. 1951c. [Huge crowd in a public lecture of Dr. Silver.] April 29.

———. 1956. [Silver's press conference in his 1956 visit to Israel.] April 5.

———. 1957. "The State and the Diaspora Must Not Be Divided." October 4.

Halperin, Samuel. 1961. *The Political World of American Zionism.* Detroit: Wayne State University Press.

Halpern, Ben. 1956. *The American Jew: A Zionist Analysis.* New York: Theodor Herzl Foundation. Reprinted as "America is Different," in *The Jews: Social Patterns of an American Group*, edited by Marshall Sklare, 29–39. Glencoe, IL: Free Press, 1958.

———. 1979. "The Americanization of Zionism, 1880–1930." *American Jewish History* 69, no. 1: 15–33.

Hazophe. 1951a. [Public reception for Silver in his 1951 visit to Israel.] April 25.

———. 1951b. "I Was Banished from the Leadership of the American Zionist Movement." April 29.

———. 1956. [Silver's press conference in his 1956 visit to Israel.] April 5.

Heine, Heinrich. 1837. "On the French Stage: Confidential Letters to August Lewald." 9th Letter.

———. 1976. *Sämtliche Schriften.* Vol. 5. Edited by Klaus Briegleb. Translated by C. G. Leland. Munich: Ullstein.

Herberg, Will. 1955. *Protestant, Catholic, Jew: An Essay in American Religious Sociology.* Garden City, NY: Doubleday.

Kallen, Horace M. [1924] 1998. *Culture and Democracy in the United States.* With a new introduction by Stephen J. Whitfield. New Brunswick, NJ: Transaction Publishers.

———. 1954. "The Tercentenary: Yomtov or Yahrzeit?" *Congress Weekly,* November 22, 9–11.

Kaplan, Mordecai M. 1934. *Judaism as a Civilization: Toward a Reconstruction of American-Jewish Life.* New York: Macmillan.

———. 1955. *A New Zionism.* New York: Theodor Herzl Foundation.

Kedar, Nir. 2009. *Mamlakhtiyut: David Ben-Gurion's Civil Thought.* Jerusalem: Ben-Zvi Institute and Ben-Gurion University.

Kenen, I. L. 1981. *Israel's Defense Line: Her Friends and Foes in Washington.* Buffalo, NY: Prometheus Books.

Kulber, Mina Neiger. 1993. *Silver Threads.* Cleveland, American Jewish Archives, sc-14334.

Laron, Guy. 2009. "'Logic Dictates That They May Attack When They Feel They Can Win': The 1955 Czech-Egyptian Arms Deal, the Egyptian Army, and Israeli Intelligence." *Middle East Journal* 63, no. 1: 69–84.

Lévi-Strauss, Claude. 1952. *Race and History.* Paris: UNESCO.

Livneh, Eliezer. 1952. "Israel and American Jewry, a New Approach—A Research of Independency." Report to the Israeli Foreign Office, Ben-Gurion Archives.

Ma'ariv. 1951. David Efrat, "A Greeting Card," April 26.

McDonald, James. 1954. "To the President and the Secretary of State—A Memorandum from James G. McDonald on Realism and the United States' National Interests in the Middle East," March 28. McDonald Papers, Dulles, John Foster, 1938–1954, 1949–1960, General Correspondence (D3-02-X364), The Herbert H. Lehman Papers of the School of International Affairs, Columbia University.

Medoff, Rafael. 1997. *Zionism and the Arabs: An American Jewish Dilemma, 1898–1948.* Westport, CT: Praeger.

Meyer, Michael A. 1997. "Abba Hillel Silver as Zionist within the Camp of Reform Judaism." In Raider, Sarna, and Zweig, *Abba Hillel Silver and American Zionism*, 9–32.

Morgenstern, Julian. 1934. "Judaism Accepts the Challenge." The Opening Exercise of the Hebrew Union College Chapel, October, American Jewish Archives, MS Co. 30, 14/2.

Neumann, Emanuel. 1976. *In the Arena: An Autobiographical Memoir.* New York: Herzl Press.

Orian, Noah (Herzog). 1982. "The Leadership of Rabbi Abba Hillel Silver on the American Jewish Scene, 1938–1949." PhD diss., Tel Aviv University.

Pfaff, William. 2007. "Manifest Destiny: A New Direction for America." *The New York Review of Books* 54, no. 2: 54–58

Raider, Mark A., Jonathan D. Sarna, and Ronald W. Zweig, eds. 1997. *Abba Hillel Silver and American Zionism*. London: Frank Cass.

Raphael, Marc Lee. 1989. *Abba Hillel Silver: A Profile in American Judaism*. New York: Holmes & Meier.

Russell, Bertrand. 1922. "Hopes and Fears as Regards America." *New Republic* 30, March 15, 70.

———. 1941. *Living Philosophy*. New York: Viking.

———. 1950. "Philosophy for Laymen." In *Unpopular Essays*, 21–33. New York: Simon and Schuster.

Sarna, Jonathan D. 2000. "The Question of Shlilat Ha-Galut in American Zionism." In *Beyond Survival and Philanthropy: American Jewry and Israel*, edited by Allon Gal and Alfred Gottschalk, 59–63. Cincinnati: Hebrew Union College Press.

Schindler, Alexander M. 1997. "Zionism and Judaism: The Path of Rabbi Abba Hillel Silver." In Raider, Sarna, and Zweig, *Abba Hillel Silver and American Zionism*, 1–8.

Segev, Zohar. 1991. "American Zionists in Israel during the 1950s: Political Opposition and a Liberal Alternative." *'Iyunim bi-Teḳumat Yiśra'el* 12: 493–519.

———. 1999. "The American Zionist Leadership, 1938–1948: Its Activity in the American, Zionist, and Palestinian Arenas." PhD diss., University of Haifa.

———. 2004. "The Jewish State in Abba Hillel Silver's Overall World View." *American Jewish Archives Journal* 56, nos. 1 and 2 (2004): 95–127.

———. 2007. *From Ethnic Politicians to National Leaders: American Zionist Leadership, the Holocaust, and the Establishment of Israel*. Sde Boqer: Ben-Gurion Institute.

Sentential. 1936. "Rabbi Silver and James G. McDonald to Participate in Sinai's Birthday Celebration." October 15.

Shacham, David. 1991. *Israel: Forty Years.* Tel Aviv: Am Oved.

Shafir, Shlomo. 1994. "Abba Hillel Silver and His Attitude towards Germany." *Yalkut Morsehet* 76: 35–62.

Shapira, Anita. 1997. "Silver and Ben-Gurion: Two Types of Leadership." In Raider, Sarna, and Zweig, *Abba Hillel Silver and American Zionism,* 33–44.

Sheffer, Gabriel. 1996. *Moshe Sharett: Biography of a Political Moderate.* Oxford: Clarendon.

Shiff, Ofer. 1994. "The Integrative Function of Early American Zionism." *The Journal of Israeli History* 15, no. 1: 1–16.

———. 2005. *Survival through Integration: American Reform, Jewish Universalism, and the Holocaust.* Leiden: Brill.

———. 2006. "The Challenge of Secularism to Jewish Survival in Abba Hillel Silver's Thinking." In *Jewry between Tradition and Secularism: Europe and Israel Compared,* edited by Eliezer Ben-Rafael, Thomas Gergely, and Yosef Gorny, 173–85. Leiden: Brill.

———. 2009. "American Jewish Response to Antisemitism after the Holocaust: A Coping Pattern or an Escape Mechanism." *Moreshet: Journal of Holocaust and Antisemitism* 7: 207–26.

Shimoni, Gideon. 1999. "The Ideological Debate in World Zionism since the Establishment of Israel." In *The Challenge of Independence, Ideological and Cultural Aspects of Israel's First Decade,* edited by Mordechai Bar-On, 104–32. Jerusalem: Ben-Zvi Institute.

Shpiro, David H. 1994. *From Philanthropy to Activism: The Political Transformation of American Zionism in the Holocaust Years, 1933–1945.* Oxford: Pergamon.

Silver, Abba Hillel. 1917. "Assimilation." November 25. AHSP IV 145.

———. 1918. "The American Jew of Tomorrow." December. AHSP IV 36.

———. 1919a. "The Immigrant vs. the Foreigner." December 13. AHSP V 49.

———. 1919b. "Isaac Mayer Wise: A Century of Reform Judaism." March 30. AHSP V 145.

———. 1920. "Zionism." *The Jewish Criterion,* April 30, 3–5.

———. 1927. *A History of Messianic Speculation in Israel from the First through the Seventeenth Centuries.* New York: Macmillan.

———. 1930. "The One and the Many." November 9. AHSP V 258.

———. 1932a. "Hitler a Haman." March 20. AHSP IV 421.

———. 1932b. "Why Cleveland Is Not Taking Care of Its Own?" April 13. AHSP IV 423.
———. 1932-1933. Diary. AHSP V, 304.
———. 1934a. "A Great Lonely Soul." January 10. AHSP V 321.
———. 1934b. "A People Acts." January 17. AHSP IV 346.
———. 1934c. "Relief Is Not Enough." February 7. AHSP V 321.
———. 1935. "The Cauldron of Europe, the First of Two Lectures on Rabbi Silver's Visit to Europe." November 3. AHSP IV 485.
———. 1936a. "Address Delivered on the Occasion of the 75th Anniversary Celebration of Chicago Sinai Congregation." Palmer House, Chicago, October 25. Ms. Col. 56, 6/7, American Jewish Archives.
———. 1936b. "We Should Not Attempt to Move Jews from Germany." *The Jewish Advocate*, March 10. AHSP V 346.
———. 1937. "B'nai B'rith Convention." May. AHSP V 424.
———. 1938a. "Austria and the Jews of Austria." March 20. AHSP IV 555.
———. 1938b. "Five Years of Hitler." February 6. AHSP IV 550.
———. 1939. "The Morals of Aid to Refugees." March 11. AHSP V 511.
———. 1940. "Beyond the Jewish State." AHSP V 180.
———. 1941a. "Only the Brave Shall Be Free, A Maccabean Message to a Nation at War." December 21. AHSP IV 647.
———. 1941b. *The World Crisis and Jewish Survival: A Group of Essays*. New York: R. R. Smith.
———. 1941–1942. "World Crisis and Jewish Survival." Sinai Temple Forum 1941–1942 Program. Stenographic reprints, Ms. Col. 56, American Jewish Archives.
———. 1942. "Too Little, Too Careless, Too Timid, Too Late!" February 22. AHSP IV 655.
———. 1943a. "Advance on All Fronts." May 1–2. AHSP V 620 (National Conference for Palestine).
———. 1943b. "American Jewish Conference." August 30. V 630.
———. 1944. "A Year's Advance." October 15. AHSP V 664.
———. 1945a. "Address at 48th Annual Convention of the ZOA." November 18. AHSP V 678.
———. 1945b. Speech at AZEC Executive Committee, March 20.
———. 1946. "Our Battle for Jewish Statehood." October 25. AHSP V 708.
———. 1949. *Vision and Victory: A Collection of Addresses by Dr. Abba Hillel Silver, 1942–1948*. New York: Zionist Organization of America.
———. 1949a. "Before the World Tribunal." In *Vision and Victory*, 123–33.

———. 1949b. "The Jewish State Is Born." In *Vision and Victory,* 192–95.

———. 1949c. "Nothing to Lose but Illusion." In *Vision and Victory,* 72–84.

———. 1949d. "The Test of the UN's Authority." In *Vision and Victory,* 160–74.

———. 1949e. "Trusteeship or Independence?" In *Vision and Victory,* 182–91.

———. 1949f. "We Will Make This Sacrifice." In *Vision and Victory,* 134–49.

———. 1949g. "Year's Advance." *In Vision and Victory,* 47–71.

———. 1950a. "Founder's Day Address." March 12. AHSP V 183.

———. 1950b. "Hebrew Union College." March 12. AHSP V 750.

———. 1950c. "A Letter to Mr. Truman." December 17. AHSP V 3.

———. 1951. "Israel Re-Visited." May 20. AHSP IV 773.

———. 1952a. "The Importance of Hebrew to Our Survival as a People." January 16. AHSP V 847.

———. 1952b. "Introduction to the History of the Jews." March 26. AHSP V 846.

———. 1952c. "Invocation: Republican National Convention." July. AHSP V 845.

———. 1952d. "National Conference of Christians and Jews." October 17. AHSP V 849.

———. 1953a. "Attaining Man's Hopes in the Atomic Age." April 11–June 13. AHSP V 860.

———. 1953b. "On the Threshold of the Fourth Century." April 21, New York City. AHSP V 852.

———. 1953c. "Stalin and After." March 15. AHSP IV 895.

———. 1954a. "American Policy in the Middle East." June 24. AHSP V 880.

———. 1954b. "The Berlin Conference—Its Success and Failure." February 28. AHSP IV 922.

———. 1954c. "Ethics—By God or Man?" November 11. AHSP V 884.

———. 1954d. "The Jewish Pilgrims to America." April 2. AHSP V 895.

———. 1954e. "Statement of S692, Civil Rights and FEPC." AHSP V 879.

———. 1954f. "Tercentenary Address." October 17. AHSP V 883.

———. 1954g. "Where Is Our Foreign Policy Taking Us?" November 7. AHSP IV 932.

———. 1955a. "Address Delivered before the World Brotherhood in Brussels, Belgium." July 14. AHSP V 898.

———. 1955b. "Address Delivered on the Occasion of the Silver Anniversary of Oglebay Institute." June 1, Wheeling, West Virginia. AHSP V 908.

———. 1955c. "Bridges and Walls." October 13. AHSPV 912.

———. 1955d. "Changes on the International Scene." February 20. AHSP IV 944.

———. 1955e. "Church of the Air." October 30. AHSP V 911.

———. 1955f. "The Crisis of Our Age." June 11. AHSP V 916.

———. 1955g. "Taking Stock of 1954." January 2. AHSP IV 939.

———. 1955h. "Tensions in the Middle East." March 13. AHSP IV 947.

———. 1955i. "What Brotherhood Means to Me." Address, Dinner in Honor of Benjamin F. Fairless, National Conference of Christians and Jews, Waldorf-Astoria, April 4. AHSP V 898.

———. 1955j. "The One and the Many." World Brotherhood, 2nd World Brotherhood Meeting, Brussels, 11–15 July 1955. AHSP V 910.

———. 1955k. "Zionism and American Jewry." February 21. AHSP V 902.

———. 1955–1956. "The Surest Guarantee." Excerpts from Address to Board of Governors. *BIG News* 5, no. 1: 1–3. AHSP I.

———. 1956. *Where Judaism Differed: An Inquiry into the Distinctiveness of Judaism.* New York: Macmillan.

———. 1957a. "150th Anniversary Luncheon Meeting of the Medical Society of the State of New York." February 18 and May 1. AHSP V 948.

———. 1957b. "1957 Jewish Welfare Fund Appeal." April 11, Cleveland, Ohio. AHSP V 954.

———. 1957c. "Goals and Outlook for Jewish Life in America." November 14–17. AHSP V 944.

———. 1957d. "How Judaism Differed." Teaneck Forum Address, February 13. AHSP V 932.

———. 1957e. "The Parting of the Ways." Symposium on the Occasion of the 50th Anniversary Celebration of Dropsie College, April 29. AHSP V 943.

———. 1957f. "Statement on Broadcast of President Eisenhower on the Middle East Situation." February 20. AHSP V 953.

———. 1957g. "With Our Eyes toward the Future." May 1. AHSP V 945.

———. 1957h. "ZOA Convention Address." September 14. AHSP V 949.

———. 1958a. "The Place of Sephardim in Jewish History." March 7. AHSP V 961.

———. 1958b. "The Problem Which Lies Ahead." June 26. AHSP V 962.

———. 1958c. "The Return from a Pilgrimage." May 4. AHSP IV 1014.

———. 1958d. "What Is a Jew? The Answer of the Maccabees." December 7. AHSP IV 1018.

———. 1960a. "Ancient Egypt—Modern South Africa." April 17. AHSP IV 1035.

———. 1960b. "As the Political Campaign Draws to a Close." November 6. AHSP IV 1039.

———. 1960c. "My Trip to Italy and Israel." March 20. AHSP IV 1033.

———. 1960d. "Shadows over the Summit." May 15. AHSP IV 1037.

———. 1960e. "Tumult and Shouting at the United Nations." October 23. AHSP IV 1038.

———. 1961a. "Building Walls and Shelter." November 19. AHSP IV 1052.

———. 1961b. *Moses and the Original Torah*. New York: Macmillan.

———. 1961c. "Mr. Abraham Lincoln Looks over the Scene." February 12. AHSP IV 1044.

———. 1961d. "My New Book, 'Moses and the Original Torah.'" November 5. AHSP IV 1051.

———. 1961e. "My Visit to the Soviet Union, Part I." October 15. AHSP IV 1049.

———. 1961f. "My Visit to the Soviet Union, Part II." October 22. AHSP IV 1050.

———. 1961g. "Once Upon a Time There Was a . . . ," March 5. AHSP IV 1045.

———. 1961h. "The Originality of the Prophets." January 8. AHSP IV 1042.

———. 1961i. "Taking Stock of 1961." December 31. AHSP IV 1054.

———. 1962. "Our Task Is Not Over." Sermon on the UJA 25th Anniversary, on the Occasion of a Sabbath Eve Service Marking the Anniversary at the UJA Annual National Conference, December 7, New York. AHSP V 1029.

———. 1963a. *Autobiography/Memoirs*. AHSP VII.

———. 1963b. "Brandeis Award." April–May. AHSP V 1042.

———. 1963c. "ZOA Convention, Israel." July–September. AHSP V 1049.

———. 1967a. "But Mordecai Bowed Not Down." March 8, 1936. In Weiner, *Therefore Choose Life*, 113–14.

———. 1967b. "The Democratic Impulse of Jewish History." November 4, 1928. In Weiner, *Therefore Choose Life*, 109–12.

———. 1967c. "Four Great Choices Which Moses Made." April 22, 1962. In Weiner, *Therefore Choose Life*, 105–8.

———. 1967d. "Seeing Our Problem against the Larger Background." UPA Radio Address, March 18, 1939. In Weiner, *Therefore Choose Life*, 114–16.

———. 1972. *A Word in Its Season*. Vols. 1 and 2. New York: World Publishing Company.

———. 1972a. "Arnold Toynbee and the Story of Purim." March 1955. In *A Word in Its Season*, vol. 2, 94–102.

———. 1972b. "A Day of Remembrance." Rosh Hashana, 1956. In *A Word in Its Season*, vol. 1, 23–26.

———. 1972c. "John F. Kennedy." In *A Word in Its Season*, vol. 2, 416–22.

———. 1972d. "Thoughts on Freedom." Yom Kippur, 1944. In *A Word in Its Season*, vol. 1, 46–51.

———. 1972e. "The Weak in the Hands of the Strong." Chanukah, 1939. In *A Word in Its Season*, vol. 2, 77–82.

———. 1972f. "When the Odds Are against You." December 16, 1962. In *A Word in Its Season*, vol. 2, 83–88.

———. 1972g. "Why Do Men Really Hate." Purim, 1963. In *A Word in Its Season*, vol. 2, 103–7.

———. n.d. [1963] "Zionism." AHSP V 160.

Silver, Abba Hillel, Papers (AHSP). Ben-Gurion Research Institute, Ben-Gurion University of the Negev, Sde Boqer Campus.

St. John, Robert. 1972. *Eban*. Garden City, NY: Doubleday.

Stauber, Roni. 2000. *Lesson for This Generation: Holocaust and Heroism in Israeli Public Discourse in 1950s*. Jerusalem: Ben-Zvi Institute and Ben-Gurion University.

———. 2001. "The Dispute during the 1950s between Religious Zionism and the Zionist Left regarding the Date of Holocaust Remembrance Day." In *State in the Making: Israeli Society in the First Decades*, edited by Anita Shapira, 189–204. Jerusalem: Ben-Zvi Institute.

Tevet, Shabtai. 2004. *Kin'at David: The Life of David Ben-Gurion*. vol. 4. Jerusalem: Schocken.

Time. 1953. "Old Flaw, New Crisis." November 9.

Udelson, Joseph H. 1990. *Dreamer of the Ghetto: The Life and Works of Israel Zangwill*. Tuscaloosa: University of Alabama Press.

Urofsky, Melvin I. 1978. *We Are One! American Jewry and Israel*. Garden City, NY: Anchor.

Weiner, Herbert, ed. 1967. *Therefore Choose Life: Selected Sermons, Addresses, and Writings of Abba Hillel Silver*. Cleveland: World Publishing Company.

Weisgal, Meyer W., ed. 1929. *Theodor Herzl: A Memorial*. New York: The New Palestine, 254–57.

Wyman, David S., and Rafael Medoff. 2002. *A Race against Death: Peter Bergson, America, and the Holocaust*. New York: New Press.

Yedihot Achronot. 1951a. [Silver's 1951 visit to Israel.] April 25.

———. 1951b. "Silver's Great Disappointment." August 28.

———. 1951c. "A Word to Ben-Gurion and Silver." May 24.

Yiddish News Digest. 1951. [Joseph Serlin heading the General Zionist delegation's visit to the United States.] No. 620, March 16.

Zangwill, Israel. 1892. *Children of the Ghetto*. London: W. Heinemann.

Index